JEAN ILLSLEY CLARKE, PH.D.,
CONNIE DAWSON, PH.D., AND DAVID BREDEHOFT, PH.D.

FOREWORD BY DAVID WALSH, PH.D.

How Much Is Enough?

**Everything You Need to Know to
Steer Clear of Overindulgence and Raise
Likeable, Responsible, and Respectful Children**

MARLOWE & COMPANY
NEW YORK

How Much Is Enough?: *Everything You Need to Know to Steer Clear of Overindulgence and Raise Likeable, Responsible, and Respectful Children*

Copyright © 2004 by Jean Illsley Clarke, Connie Dawson,
and David Bredehoft
Foreword copyright © 2004 by David Walsh

Published by
Marlowe & Company
An Imprint of Avalon Publishing Group Incorporated
245 West 17th Street • 11th Floor
New York, NY 10011

Library of Congress Cataloging-in-Publication Data is available.

ISBN 1-56924-437-5

9   8   7   6   5   4

Designed by Pauline Neuwirth, Neuwirth and Associates, Inc.

Printed in the United States of America
Distributed by Publishers Group West

PRAISE FOR
How Much Is Enough?

"This is a marvelously helpful book for those of us who want the very best for our children, but end up loving them in ways that are harmful to their growth and development. You'll find how to discover if you are overindulging your children and positive ways to resist harming by giving them too much too soon, too much power, too many things, with too few rules."

—REVEREND DICK LUNDY

❖

"*How Much Is Enough?* is a timely book for all Americans to read and reflect on. In many ways we are the most overindulgent culture in the world, and this book provides a well-researched, groundbreaking approach to understanding the impact of overindulgence on our children, on our communities, and on our planet. The authors have provided a no-guilt/no-blame strategy for raising our children in a more balanced and loving way. Highly recommended!"

—RICK INGRASCI, M.D., M.P.H.,
Director of Community Development, BigMindMedia

❖

"By applying what you will learn from *How Much Is Enough?*, you will give your child the skills to be successful in life, free your child from the burdens that unintentional overindulgence adds to their already challenging growing-up years, and answer many of the questions you've had about your own bouts with unhappiness."

—JOAN K. COMEAU, PH.D., C.F.C.S., C.F.L.E.,
Founder and Director, Family Information Services

❖

"What a wonderful and straightforward gift the authors have given our family with this book. Over the past few months, by applying the simple and thought-provoking tools outlined throughout the text, our family has progressed from our two little girls (ages three and five) running things to them being an important part of a well-centered family and understanding choices and consequences. They are much happier and so are we."

—KELLY H. DONALDSON, corporate executive and
recovering overindulgent father, Lake Independence, Minnesota

JEAN ILLSLEY CLARKE, PH.D., is an internationally known parent educator whose books include *Self-Esteem: A Family Affair* and *Growing Up Again: Parenting Ourselves, Parenting Our Children*. Clarke is the president of JI Consultants and the director of the Self-Esteem Center in Minneapolis, Minnesota, where she lives. CONNIE DAWSON, PH.D., is a family therapist, the co-author of *Growing Up Again*, and the author of many articles in parenting and adoption publications. She lives in Washington state. DAVID BREDEHOFT, PH.D., is the chair of the Department of Social and Behavioral Sciences at Concordia University in St. Paul, Minnesota, and has over twenty-seven years of experience as a researcher, marriage and family therapist, and university professor. He lives in Minnesota.

To Athalie Terry,
who dwells in the Land of Above and Beyond

❖

CONTENTS

FOREWORD

by DAVID WALSH, PH.D.

OUR culture is awash in excess. Although most of us meet all of our basic needs and then some, we are told over and over every day that we need more. Companies with stuff to sell barrage us with their powerful and clever media voices. They stay in business by convincing us our lives would be better if only we bought one more product, one more service, one more experience. Sometimes it seems like "Collect them all" isn't just an advertising slogan but our national motto.

We all know that giving in to the urge to have more can be hard on the pocketbook. Too often we don't pay attention to how constantly acquiring things can affect us, our lives, and our relationships. In the early '90s, T. Boone Pickens, the former CEO of Allied Stores, told stockholders, "Our job is to make people unhappy with what they have." That may be a great way to think about maintaining the company's bottom line, but it's a terrible way to protect your customers' health. All of that enforced unhappiness is bound to spill over into peoples' lives outside the store. And yet, the constant drumbeat of messages exhorting us to get more continues.

As parents, we are not immune to those messages. And many of the messages that target us try to get to our wallets through our love for our children. Visa tells us, "Maybe you can't give her everything she wants, but for everything else there's Visa Gold." Caring, if you take advertisers' word for it, is synonymous with giving and spending.

So many of us parents are lured into thinking that one of the best ways to show love is to give things, money, opportunity, and entertainment. But if you take parenting tips from the advertisers, you'll never be good enough. There is always something else to give your children. Get your son a new bike—he needs a car. Take your daughter to an amusement park—what she really deserves is a cruise. At every turn, our media-drenched culture promotes overindulgence.

The problem with overindulgence is that it undercuts one of the important assets that our kids need: self-discipline. If our kids always get what they want, how will they learn to deal with disappointment? How can they be expected to put another person's needs ahead of their own? How will they know how to delay gratification? Why would we figure they'll ever be satisfied with what they have? Overindulgence doesn't just drain your bank account; it can cripple your children's chances of becoming healthy, happy adults.

In tackling the problem of overindulgence head-on, this book exposes all the ways that we can rob our children of the opportunity to develop the critical skill of self-discipline. By recounting touching testimony and explaining rigorous research, Jean Illsley Clarke, Connie Dawson, and David Bredehoft give a full sense of the serious nature of the problem. Most importantly, *How Much Is Enough?* goes beyond describing the problem—it provides parents the answers they need to help their children, and, in the process, enjoy them more.

DAVID WALSH, PH.D., is the President and Founder of the National Institute on Media and the Family and the author of *Selling Out America's Children.*

A Letter to Readers

DEAR Readers:

This is what we have learned about overindulgence.

- ❖ It's not exactly the same as spoiling.
- ❖ It's all around us.
- ❖ It comes from a good heart.
- ❖ It causes much more pain than we ever imagined.
- ❖ Overindulgence is not just about money. It can happen at any income level.
- ❖ It's not just about "dysfunctional" families. It can happen in any family.
- ❖ It's not just about being an only child or the youngest child. It can happen to any child.
- ❖ It's not just about too much stuff or too many privileges. It's also about too much attention and wobbly rules.
- ❖ It's not just the grandparents who are major overindulgers. Parents are, too.
- ❖ Overindulgence isn't harmless. It sets children up for discomfort and failures in their adult lives and can make parenting their own children a very bumpy road.
- ❖ Overindulgence is unintentional. No parent gets up in the morning and says, "I think I'll harm my children by overindulging them today."
- ❖ Overindulgence can be identified and changed.
- ❖ Children and adults who have been overindulged can recover.

How do we know these things? We did three separate research studies on overindulgence, and this book is about what we learned. If you like, you can read about the studies in Appendix D (page 296) and at our Web site, www.overindulgence.info.

Now our job is to examine this new information in reference to our own families. We can celebrate what we are doing well, and change any practices that need to be improved. We can screw up our courage to resist the many outside pressures that encourage us to overindulge our children and ourselves.

Join us on this exciting journey.

Jean, Connie, and David

INTRODUCTION

WHAT IS OVERINDULGENCE, ANYWAY?

■

WHEN THERE IS TOO MUCH,
EVERYTHING BECOMES LIKE NOTHING.
—Susan Clarke

WE ALL WANT THE BEST FOR OUR CHILDREN

GABE startled at the wonder of his first child. As he strapped his newborn into the required infant car seat, he turned to the nurse: "The car seat has an owner's manual, but where is the manual for this baby?" The nurse smiled. His wife Ada smiled and shook her head.

Like all parents, Gabe and Ada want the best for their baby girl. They want to give her the best of everything that they can, but when Gabe looks at the gift stacks of tiny, tiny garments, he wonders how soon his little girl will outgrow them. He wonders how soon she, like her cousins, will be begging for trendy footwear, expensive clothes, the latest computer stuff, and a trip during spring break. Or, like the neighbor's boy, will she expect a new car for her sixteenth birthday? He looks at Ada and wonders, *Will we know when to say yes and when to say no?*

Parents, whether young or old, single, married, or partnered, have the same goals: to do the best possible for their child. They wonder, *Will I understand this child's needs and personality? Will I know how to comfort and support him? Will I be able to tolerate her discomfort when she needs to learn from her mistakes? Will I know how to set limits? How will I know when I have given enough in this more-is-better world?*

MORE IS NOT ALWAYS BETTER

As parents, we would like to provide our children with life-enhancing abundance without going overboard and risking the negative effects of overindulgence. To do this, we need to understand what overindulgence is, how it affects children when they are children as well as when they become adults, and how to avoid it.

The key questions are:

What is overindulgence?
How does overindulging children cause pain in their adult lives?
How do I avoid overindulging my children, my young adults, my grandchildren, and other people's children? What do I do instead?
If I was overindulged, how do I avoid passing on these habits to my own kids, and how do I overcome it in myself?

This book is based on three research studies on overindulgence[1] involving 1,195 participants. The studies told us what overindulgence is, what its effects are, who does it, and why. Furthermore, the studies reveal strong links between overindulgence during childhood and lack of important life-skills and unhelpful attitudes and beliefs in later life.

Adults who had been overindulged as children gave us the following descriptions of overindulgence.

WHAT IS OVERINDULGENCE?

*O*verindulging children is giving them too much of what looks good, too soon, and for too long. It is giving them things or experiences that are not appropriate for their age or their interests and talents. It is the process of giving things to children to meet the adult's needs, not the child's.

Overindulgence is giving a disproportionate amount of family resources to one or more children in a way that appears to be meeting the children's needs but does not, so children experience scarcity in the midst of plenty. Overindulgence is doing or having so much of something that it does active harm, or at least prevents a person from developing and deprives that person of achieving his or her full potential.

Overindulgence is a form of child neglect. It hinders children from performing their needed developmental tasks, and from learning necessary life lessons.

THE THREE WAYS OF OVERINDULGING

All three research studies revealed that there are three different types of overindulgence. One, of course, is *"too much"* and not understanding the concept of *"enough."* The second is over-nurturing. Parents over-nurture by overdoing, spoiling, giving too much attention, doing things for children that they should be learning to do for themselves, and allowing children to think only about themselves, not about others. The third is *soft structure*, which is when parents do not have rules, or don't insist that rules be followed; or when parents shield children from the consequences of their behaviors and choices, and don't insist that they learn life skills; or when parents fail to insist that children consider the impact of their actions on the family, the group, and society.

Overindulgence can also occur in two or all three of these ways simultaneously.

OVERINDULGING CHILDREN
CAN CAUSE THEM PAIN IN THEIR ADULT LIVES

However it happens, we now know that overindulgence can cause great pain in adult life, and is often hidden as a secret that elicits ridicule if spoken of. The pain often revolves around the embarrassment of not knowing how to do things that everyone seems able to do, the uneasy feeling that others resent you, expecting to stay the center of attention and have others be responsible for you, and the stresses from not knowing what is enough—enough food, clothing, money, work, play, and so on.

ADULTS WHO WERE OVERINDULGED AS CHILDREN CAN
ALSO CAUSE PAIN TO OTHERS

The attitudes, expectations, and lack of skills in adults who were overindulged can cause distress and irritation for others.

Listen to a conversation between Jean and a college athletic coach.

COACH: *What are you doing these days?*

JEAN: *I'm doing research on overindulgence.*

COACH: *Oh? What is that?*

JEAN: *Overindulgence is giving children so much of anything that it keeps them from learning their developmental tasks, and it has a negative effect on their adult lives.*

COACH: *Really? Like too many toys?*

JEAN: *Adults we surveyed who had been overindulged as children identified three ways they had been overindulged. Yes, by too many things, but also by what we call over-nurture and soft structure.*

COACH: *What are those?*

JEAN: *Well, if the athletes you work with were overindulged it will show in their attitudes and behaviors. The one who had too many things is apt to be careless about equipment. If something gets damaged or lost or misplaced, it doesn't matter because "they," meaning you, will provide more.*

COACH: *Sounds familiar.*

JEAN: *If the overindulgence was over-nurture, the athlete will expect to be taken care of. What he or she "needs" you should provide. Extra stipends, tutoring, even having a tutor write papers will seem okay. Over-nurture often shows in a lack of differentiation between wants and needs.*

COACH: *Also familiar.*

JEAN: *Athletes who were overindulged with soft structure may be cavalier about rules and regulations. They may know a rule but not really believe it applies to them, so they are free to circumvent or ignore it, even if it leads to bad publicity for the team and the institution.*

COACH: *I see. We get all three kinds. Many of the freshmen come in expecting to be lionized, to be athletes first and students second. They don't even know they've been overindulged. They just "know" that our athletic department is unreasonable because we want them to be students first and athletes second. It's a constant struggle. It saps precious time and energy from the foremost tasks of teaching students and training athletes. It holds the students back. It holds us all back. Sometimes it gets us all in trouble.*

THE MANY FACES OF OVERINDULGENCE

All of the stories in this book were told to us as true. Sometimes we changed details to protect the privacy of the people, but the circumstances of the overindulgence were preserved. If any story sounds contrived or bizarre, be assured, contrived it is not. Bizarre as the story may seem, some child, somewhere, has lived through that bizarre experience.

However, overindulgence doesn't necessarily look bizarre or even out-of-the-ordinary. Since overindulgence comes from good intentions, it can creep into any family. In fact, even the wisest of parents may overindulge their children once in a while. Occasional overindulgence is unlikely to be harmful; it's when indulgence becomes chronic, or an automatic pattern, that the harm occurs.

We've written this book for all parents—not just for "problem families." The examples we use are from a wide range of families, not case studies of families with psychological disorders.

This book will teach you to avoid overindulgence, how to spot it, and how to correct it. If you find that you are overindulging your child, it will help you turn your good intent toward a better outcome. No time here for guilt; just get on with today. More important still, we provide you with a wide range of skills, strategies, and guidelines to help your children grow up nurtured, supported, self-disciplined, and cared for—but not overindulged.

This book will help you deal effectively with the pressures to overindulge that you steadily receive from friends and relatives, from the media, and (of course) from your own children. And if you were overindulged yourself as a child, this book will help you to recover from the potentially painful effects of your own experience.

We designed this book to help you be the best parent you can be, whatever your family circumstances are. Most of all, this book is meant to help you love and enjoy your children as much as possible.

Turn the page and let's begin.

WE CAN ALL SING AND DANCE AND BE SILLY
WHEN THINGS ARE GOING WELL. BUT WHEN IT'S DIFFICULT
NO ONE KNOWS WHAT TO DO, SO WE OVERINDULGE.
—Pam Guiney

ONE
SECTION

*Recognizing
Overindulgence*

THE TRUTH ABOUT "WAY TOO NICE"

Does Overindulgence Really Make a Difference?

THE KEY WORD IN OVERINDULGENCE IS OVER.
—A. V. A.

OVERINDULGENCE AND GOOD INTENTIONS

*O*CCASIONAL indulgences add color, pleasure, and joy to life. When those same indulgences become a pattern, however, the result is very different. This pattern is called overindulgence.

Many of us, with good intentions, have provided abundance for someone only to discover that we have overindulged them. We can tell we have overindulged them, because instead of appreciation and joy, we get whines or demands for more. This happens when the positive intent of our indulgence has created the negative impact of overindulgence.

The almost 1,200 people we questioned have taught us that:

❖ Overindulgence is more than spoiling.
❖ Overindulgence occurs in three different ways: giving too much, over-nurturing, and structure that is too soft.

- Children may like being overindulged at times, but overindulgence can be painful to them—and to the people around them.
- Overindulged children often become demanding and unappreciative.
- Children who are overindulged with lessons (in music, sports, dance, etc.) may have admirable performance skills, but may lack everyday life skills.
- People who were overindulged as children suffer later in life when they run into situations where their overblown sense of entitlement is resented, and when they lack skills other people take for granted.
- Overindulgence is not necessarily confined to childhood. Sometimes adults chronically overindulge other adults or themselves.

OVERINDULGENCE IS MORE THAN JUST SPOILING

The words "spoiling" and "overindulgence" are not interchangeable. "Spoiled" is a word usually used to describe a child whose behaviors are annoying to adults. *He demands what he wants right now. She interrupts. He gets away with things.* However, a child can be overindulged and not act demanding, ungracious, and self-centered, especially if the parental message is *I'll do this for you if you make me look like a good parent.* Those children can be charming and well-mannered. Also, by reason of personality types, neurology, or early history, a child who is acting "spoiled" may have parents who are not overindulging but are doing everything they can to correct those irritating behaviors.

Furthermore, overindulgence involves much more than spoiling. Spoiled children act as if they expect everyone to love and adore them; but more than half of the adults in our study who were overindulged as children reported not feeling loved.

Overindulging children is giving them too much of anything that looks good, but hinders them from doing their developmental tasks, and from learning necessary life lessons. Overindulging adults is giving them too much of anything that looks good, but supports their excessive sense of entitlement or lack of competence, responsibility, or initiative.

THE SEVEN HAZARDS OF OVERINDULGENCE

Children who are overindulged can have difficulties in many areas of life, both when they are young and when they become adults. They may have:

- ❖ trouble learning how to delay gratification
- ❖ trouble giving up status as the constant center of attention
- ❖ trouble becoming competent in
  - ✦ everyday skills
  - ✦ self-care skills
  - ✦ skills for relating with others
- ❖ trouble taking personal responsibility
- ❖ trouble developing a sense of personal identity
- ❖ trouble knowing what is enough
- ❖ trouble knowing what is normal for other people

Look at the mixture of childhood feelings reported by participants in our first study.

Childhood Feelings Resulting from Overindulgence[1]

PERCENTAGE	FEELINGS
48%	I felt loved.
44%	I felt confused because it didn't feel right, but I couldn't complain because how can I fault someone who does so much for me?
40%	I felt embarrassed because at times I was expected to know some skills that I'd never had to learn.
31%	I felt guilty, bad, sad.
29%	I felt good at the time, but later I felt ashamed.
28%	I felt good because I got everything I wanted.
27%	I felt embarrassed because I knew it wasn't right.
23%	I felt bad because other kids didn't get what I did.
19%	No matter how much I got, I never got enough, so I felt sad.
15%	I felt good because I got to decide about everything.
15%	I felt bad because the other kids made fun of me.
14%	I felt embarrassed because other kids didn't have stuff.

continued

PERCENTAGE	FEELINGS
13%	I felt ignored.
13%	I felt confused.
11%	I felt embarrassed because other kids teased me.
11%	No matter how much I got, I never got enough, so I felt mad.

Subjects could select more than one response.

Notice that 48 percent said they felt loved. And the others? How did they feel? And 40 percent spoke of missing skills.

LACK OF SKILLS

Listen to Hannah speak about her own overindulged childhood:

I never learned to take care of my clothes. My mom always wanted me to be well-dressed. I had lots of clothes. I grew up with household staff, and if I dropped my clothes on a chair, the maid hung them up when she made my bed. My clean clothes always appeared in the drawers and the closet. If there was a hole or a rip in the garment, I tossed it. When I went to college my roommates were irritated with me a lot, and they ridiculed me unmercifully. When I asked which machine was the washer and which was the dryer, they thought I was kidding. They wouldn't tell me. You can't guess how many embarrassing mistakes I made. I got so sick of hearing "Everybody knows that!" I finally stopped asking for help. To this day I'm not ever sure I'm doing things right. Fortunately, I found a husband who is willing to do things for me, so I get along.

These complaints from Hannah are not about too many clothes; they are about a lack of life-skills. In fact, overindulgence may have nothing to do with things that cost money.

Michael, who grew up in a below-the-poverty-line family, described his inability to assume personal responsibility.

My mom figured that, since we had so few material comforts, I should be free to find my pleasure whenever I could. As a kid,

I was allowed to roam. I had no chores. I am independent now. I seldom see my folks and I feel no responsibility for my family, or about other things, I guess. Anyway, some of my friends tell me that is why I can't keep a job.

HOW WERE THEY OVERINDULGED?

Here are the top fifteen ways (from most to least common) in which people said that they were overindulged as children.[2]

Indicators of Overindulgence [3]

WHEN I WAS GROWING UP,

✓ My parents did things for me that I could or should have done for myself.

✓ My parents did not expect me to do chores.

✓ I was allowed to have any clothes I wanted.

✓ I was allowed lots of privileges.

✓ My parents gave me lots of toys.

✓ My parents gave me too much freedom.

✓ My parents allowed me to take the lead or dominate the family.

✓ I was not expected to learn the same skills that other children learned.

✓ My parents were over-loving and gave me too much attention.

✓ My parents had rules that I was not expected to follow.

✓ My parents did not enforce their rules.

✓ My parents scheduled me for activities, lessons, sports, and camps.

✓ My parents made sure I was entertained.

✓ I spent too much time on my own, and too little time with my parents.

✓ My drug use was tolerated or encouraged.

THREE TYPES OF OVERINDULGENCE

These fifteen ways of overindulging can be clustered into three types of overindulgence: *giving too much, over-nurturing,* and *too little structure.* Let's look at these one at a time.[4]

Too Much

"I'm having a hard time teaching Charlie to take care of his toys," his mom lamented. "He has so many that if something gets lost or broken, he doesn't care; he just plays with something else."

Too Much

Giving too much or too many things includes not only toys and clothing, but anything that costs money: sports equipment, lessons, entertainment, vacations, junk food, tobacco, alcohol, or illegal drugs. In addition to giving too much or too many things that cost money, too much can also mean allocating a disproportionate amount of family resources to one or more children. Often the "too much" form of overindulgence can appear to meet a child's needs, but does not. As a result, the child experiences scarcity in the midst of plenty.

With a constant barrage of too many and too much, children often experience a sense of scarcity because they fail to learn the vital skill of ascertaining what is enough. An issue that came through most vividly in our research was people's angst at not knowing how much is enough work, play, money, clothes, food, sex, alcohol, entertainment, excitement, or sleep. "Enough" is an elusive concept taught slowly over many years by adults who say, You've had enough, whether it's candy, presents, excitement, recreation, stimulation, and so on.

> **O**ften the "too much" form of overindulgence can appear to meet a child's needs, but does not. As a result, the child experiences scarcity in the midst of plenty.

The pain of "too much" can also be visited on the indulger. Consider the newspaper report[5] of the mother who, when told her son had robbed a bank, said with pain in her voice, "I can't understand why he did that. I always gave him everything he wanted."

Over-Nurturing

Three-year-old Sophie was carried whenever she demanded to be carried: in and out of childcare, the store, or the house of worship. At four, Mom was still dressing and undressing her. Sophie could not zip her own jacket. Mom loved doing it and hadn't noticed that the other children were managing their own clothing. At six, Mom was still using smother-love. "Sorry to cancel our luncheon," Sophie's mom apologized to her friend. "Sophie had a restless night and a bad dream, so I'm going to keep her home and just be with her this morning."

All children need nurturing in order to survive. *Over-nurturing* is doing things for children that they could or should be doing for themselves or keeping them from learning to handle situations they should be mastering. It is smothering children with too much care and attention. The result can be a child whose role in life is to be cute or helpless or manipulative.

Over-nurturing is not about giving too much love. There is no such thing as too much love. Loving your children allows them to grow. But true love does not hover or intrude or deprive a child of the opportunity to reach out, to learn new skills, to feel the thrill of achievement, or to experience consequences. Love does not continue to do things for a child that are no longer appropriate for his or her age.

Over-nurturing is providing too much care—care that may look loving, but that keeps a child from achieving his or her full potential.

Soft Structure

"My dad was rigid," Eric explained. "We had too many rules. That's not going to happen in my house. There will be no rules and no 'shoulds' for my children."

Soft Structure

Eric will most likely have one huge roller coaster ride during his children's adolescence, and his children will grow up emotionally stunted, because all children need firm structure in order to feel safe and become socially responsible. Firm structure includes establishing and enforcing rules, creating firm boundaries, monitoring children's safety, teaching children skills for living, and insisting that they do chores.

Soft structure is giving children too much freedom and license. It can mean giving children choices and experiences that are not appropriate for their age, interests, or talents. It can also be not insisting that they learn important life-skills.

There is no such thing as too much love.

Soft structure can include forgetting that adults are supposed to run the family, and giving that job to the children, either directly or by default. Letting children make decisions that should fall to adults gives children a false sense of power or an overblown sense of responsibility.

Not requiring children to do chores deprives them of the opportunity to contribute to the family's success and well-being. Not being given chores was the area of overindulgence that the adults we interviewed resented the most. Think about this the next time your children complain about their chores.

COMPOUNDING THE PROBLEM

An overindulgence problem is compounded when more than one area is involved.

Too Much and Over-Nurturing

Problem: *Emily misses the school bus regularly. Complaining and nagging by her parents have not resulted in on-time behavior.*

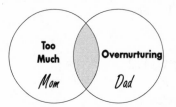

Dad, trying to be helpful, over-nurtures eleven-year-old Emily by driving her to school when she misses the school bus. He can stop himself from over-nurturing by leaving for work before bus time. Mom, wanting Emily to like her clothes, is providing too many outfits and contributing to the lateness by allowing Emily to take all the time she wants deciding what to wear. Mom can insist that Emily donate clothing that might not be worn during the coming year to a charity. Mom can also insist that Emily choose next day's outfit before she goes to bed. Emily's parents might do well to encourage independence, but either parent could provide her with better care simply by replacing overindulgence with clear parenting.

Too Much and Soft Structure

Problem: *Four-year-old Jacob's toys are always scattered across the floor. Parental pleading and scolding have not resulted in his picking up his toys.*

Grandpa enjoys buying toys and always returns from his weekly business trip with a new one for Jacob. Mom complains that there are too many toys and that they are too costly. Grandpa can stop providing too many toys by bringing one toy every second or third trip, and he can set a price limit on the gifts. He also might buy a toy for himself now and then to satisfy his need for the enjoyment of buying toys.

Mom says the toys must be picked up before the evening meal. To firm up her soft structure, she can make sure there is adequate storage space for the toys, box them temporarily, give some away, or sell them. She can signal Jacob by singing the same song each time toys are to be picked up. She can also help sometimes.

At age four Jacob can be expected to pick up his toys with reminding and help. Too many toys and lax rules about caring for them are a set-up for irresponsibility.

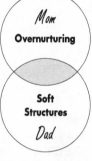

Over-Nurturing and Soft Structure

Problem: *In an effort to let Matthew use the car when he wants it, his parents made a rule that the family sorts out weekend use of the family car on Thursday evening. Matthew, once again, spent Saturday morning alternately lobbying for the use of the car and sulking.*

Mom over-nurtured Matthew by empathizing and feeling sorry for him, telling him how much she wishes they could afford another car, and wondering how she can help Matthew get where he wants to go. She could, instead, simply ignore the sulking and say, "This was Thursday night business. Today is Saturday." Dad's soft structure shows when he argues with Matthew, then gives in and changes his own plans so Matthew can have the car. Dad could say, "Matthew, if the Thursday night rule isn't working for you, you can propose a plan to adjust it. Until then, Thursday plans hold. Right now your sulking is not encouraging me to want to help you. That's my final word. Let me know what other transportation plans you make for tonight."

If both parents take this firm stance and hold to it, Matthew may escalate his negative behavior for a time, especially if his parents have been overindulging for a long time. But since all children, especially teenagers, need the security and safety of living with clear, loving structure, this behavior is apt to improve, especially if the parents are consistent.

Soft structure is giving children too much freedom and license. It can mean giving children choices and experiences that are not appropriate for their age, interests, or talents. It can also be not insisting that they learn important life-skills.

All Three: Too Much, Over-Nurturing, Soft Structure

Problem: *Madison's parents know that two-year-olds are apt to have tantrums, but her mom finds the frequent outbursts wearing, and is getting more and more impatient with them.*

Madison did her tantrum thing when another big box of toys arrived from her grandparents. The toys were too advanced for her skills, and Madison couldn't make them work. She threw them about and screamed. Yesterday Mom lost her temper and shouted at Madison to stop her caterwauling. Dad picked Madison up, rocked her and whispered, "Did mean Mommy yell at you? I'm sorry. Come on, little princess, you and Daddy will go for a walk."

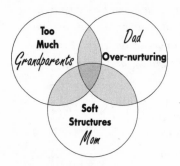

This is a family with good intentions, but Madison was getting a triple dose of overindulgence. Grandpa and Grandma may not have realized that the toys were too advanced for Madison and their need to be good grandparents, even from afar, resulted in too many toys. Perhaps they could satisfy their need to be involved grandparents by sending only one toy with a picture of them holding it, putting the balance of the money in a college or future fund, and asking for a picture of Madison holding the toy in return.

Madison's father had every good intention of being a loving, supportive daddy. But he was not with Madison as much as Mom, and didn't understand how wearing her tantrums could be. He also didn't understand that angrily overpowering a tantrum isn't helpful. Quietly holding the child until she settles may work, but simply giving in to her is over-nurturing. This allows the two-year-old to stay firmly in the center of the family's universe, when one of her developmental tasks should be to learn compromise.

Not being given chores was the area of overindulgence that the adults we interviewed resented the most.

The soft structure on Mom's part also comes from good intentions. She, too, wants to be loving and supportive. Since she doesn't know what to do about Madison's tantrums, she gives in until her frustration level gets so high that she lashes out. Then she feels ashamed for shouting and mad at Madison's dad for blaming her.

No one has helped mom step back and look at the situation. Box the toys until Madison is old enough for them, and treat the tantrum with a calm "You are okay and you will get through this" attitude. Parents can't remove all of the frustrations in a child's life, and that's a good thing because children need to learn how to handle frustrations in small doses and at every age. But too many, too advanced toys had created too much frustration for Madison. It is not surprising, when you think about it, that a two-year-old is extra frustrated by "too much" from grandparents, over-nurturing from Dad, and soft structure from Mom.

This example of overindulgence comes from good intentions, but causes pain for both the indulgers and the indulged.

ONE AT A TIME

In each of the stories above, the child is being overindulged by two or more adults, each in a different area. If one person indulges in two or three ways, it's a good idea to identify each problem separately and begin with the one that is easiest to change, rather than trying to change in all areas at once. When the change feels satisfactory, choose a second area. Often the improvement in one area will spill over and the other two will be less daunting. In the previous story, when Dad stopped giving in to Madison's tantrums and blaming Mom, Mom found it easier to handle the tantrums in a calm way. If, however, one area proves to be too sticky, try taking a careful look: *Is there some support I need and how will I get that? Is this an attempt to meet some need of my own that I have not recognized?* If the latter is true, remember that children do better with parents whose needs are met. The parents' task is to get needs met directly at a peer level, not through the child.

THE TEST OF FOUR: CLUES TO OVERINDULGENCE

There are four common clues to overindulgence:

1. Does the situation hinder the child from learning the tasks that support his or her development and learning at this age?
2. Does the situation give a disproportionate amount of family resources to one or more of

the children? (Resources can include money, space, time, energy, attention, and psychic input.)

3. Does this situation exist to benefit the adult more than the child?

4. Does the child's behavior potentially harm others, society, or the planet in some way?

If any one of these four clues is clearly present, there is an overindulgence problem.

We'll be returning often to the Test of Four throughout this book. As you use it in your own life, you'll discover that it is a simple, practical, and easy-to-use way to help you make the right decision. This first clue is especially important because, from birth on, children try to make sense of themselves and the world. Information on the developmental tasks of children, stage by stage, is in Appendix A (page 275). Children make observations, and from those observations come their decisions, decisions that can have major impact on their adult lives.

ONE CLUE IS ENOUGH

When using the Test of Four, usually it is helpful to assess all four clues. Nevertheless, a clear yes to any one of the four does indicate an overindulgence problem. Consider the story of Joe who cares only for his own needs and wants, and who is unconcerned with clue four, possibly harming others or the environment.

Frail Joseph's mother wanted the very best for him, so she provided him with the best of everything, and protected him from stressful experiences, especially from other children. Joseph decided that he was the center of the universe and that the world existed to meet his needs.

Now, no longer frail, Joe, as an adult, vigorously travels the world, but always in comfort. To make travel easy, he throws his suits in his suitcase. In his hotel, no matter what the clean water situation in that country, he hangs the rumpled suits in the bathroom, turns the hot water on full force, closes the bathroom door and goes out on the town. When he returns to his room hours later, his suits are wrinkle free. When a friend, appalled at this wastefulness, asked Joe if he felt it was okay to use clean water in this way, Joe shrugged. "Sure. It works for me."

Over-nurtured as a child, Joe overindulged himself as an adult. In this case, the answer to the question "Does it cause harm?" is all that is needed to identify overindulgence. An extreme example? Yes, but be prepared. The research results were full of astounding stories, stories you may want to reject or discount because they seem farfetched—but they most certainly are not. The result of overindulgence has many faces—some benign and some not benign at all.

THE RESULTS OF OVERINDULGENCE

Is overindulgence really as potentially damaging as these stories suggest? Judge for yourself. Listen to what some of our study participants had to say about the impact of overindulgence in their own lives. All of these comments, which are direct quotes, were echoed many times over.

In Their Own Voices

THE IMPACT OF OVERINDULGENCE ON ADULT LIFE

What is the result of overindulgence in your life?

✓ I feel sad and angry when I don't get my way or don't get what I want.

✓ I felt confused because they said they loved me, but I didn't, couldn't feel it, or didn't know it.

✓ I often feel disappointed in others. I feel let down by them. Again, the more I give, the more I expect back.

✓ Not growing up. Being unrealistic about realities of life.

✓ I'm so far in debt I can't see the light of day. I'm overweight and hate that I am too tired.

✓ Two failed marriages.

✓ I don't know what reality is—it's hard to think.

✓ I'm discontented, overweight, enjoy cocktails, overcook, and overfeed children and guests or don't feed them enough. Don't set enough reasonable limits. Have trouble budgeting time and money.

✓ It has affected my siblings more. It has been devastating for them. They don't follow rules, don't have coping skills. They are unhappy.

✓ Fat, and still feel empty.

These quotes *In Their Own Voices* tell about feelings, thinking, and behaviors resulting from overindulgence. Also, since children must and do strive to make sense of their lives, they make decisions or form beliefs about themselves, others, and life. Some of those early decisions or beliefs can have profound influences over their adult lives. Take a look at the chart on pages 17–18 to see examples of decisions children may make during each developmental stage.

WHO, ME?

If you recognize that you have been guilty of some overindulging, stay away from shame and remember that you acted with good intent. If you are not sure, use the Parental Overindulgence Assessment Tool in Appendix B (page 293). Use your good intent to help you stop one way you have been overindulging. Do it today. Do not expect your child to thank you. Expect resistance at first, but hold firm.

If you were overindulged, IT IS NOT YOUR FAULT! You can use this book to help yourself recover.

Also, avoid seeing overindulgence under every bush. Sometimes, when we are thinking about something in a new way, we tend to see it everywhere. Chapter Two reminds us that some common situations that look like overindulgence at first may not be.

OVERINDULGING IS NOT ABOUT WANTING TO HARM A CHILD.
IT IS A MECHANISM TO GET THROUGH THE DAY.
—Laurie Kanyer

Decisions Children May Make at Each Developmental Stage

JOB OF CHILD AT DEVELOPMENTAL STAGE	EXAMPLES OF HELPFUL PARENTING	HEALTHY DECISIONS A CHILD MAY MAKE	EXAMPLES OF OVERINDULGING	DECISIONS AN OVERINDULGED CHILD MAY MAKE
Birth to 6 Months To decide to be, to live, to bond with caretakers, to call out to have needs met.	Mom waits until baby Zach calls her or rustles loudly or otherwise communicates. Then she checks to see if he needs dry clothes, soothing, stimulation, loving, or food.	I can know what I need and ask for it.	Mom offers the breast or bottle to baby Zach every time he squeals, or just when he "looks hungry," or when she thinks he should be hungry.	I don't know when I am hungry. I don't need to ask for what I need, the world will supply it.
6 to 18 Months To reach out and explore her world and learn to trust her senses. To attach to her caretakers.	Parents provide a safe area with safe objects for Stephanie to explore in her own way. Parents let child play with pots and pans and provide a few toys at a time.	It is safe for me to learn about my world. I can trust my senses.	Every time little Stephanie reaches for a toy, a parent hands it to her or plays with the toy for her. Her parents surround her with toys too mature for her.	I don't need to reach out for what I want. I don't know how to explore my world.
18 Months to 3 Years To start cause-and-effect thinking, to give up the belief that he is the center of the universe. To learn to follow simple commands: come, stop, go, wait, sit.	Sometimes Charlie gets what he wants and sometimes he doesn't. Adults carry this out in a matter-of-fact way, with no criticism. Adults expect Charlie to follow simple commands: come, stop, go, wait, sit.	I have to take others' needs into account. I can say no and be angry and still be loved. I can learn to follow directions.	Every time Charlie says no, the adults give in. Charlie gets what he wants and more. A tantrum or a demanding attitude will get him anything.	I am the center of the universe. I can have whatever I want. I don't have to consider other people.

THE TRUTH ABOUT "WAY TOO NICE"

JOB OF CHILD AT DEVELOPMENTAL STAGE	EXAMPLES OF HELPFUL PARENTING	HEALTHY DECISIONS A CHILD MAY MAKE	EXAMPLES OF OVERINDULGING	DECISIONS AN OVERINDULGED CHILD MAY MAKE
3 to 6 Years To assert an identity separate from others. To learn ways of exerting power. To learn that behaviors have consequences.	Julie is told before entering the grocery story whether she may or may not have candy. That directive is followed without criticism or apology. Julie does simple chores.	I can ask for what I want and expect parents and their rules to be dependable. I can become capable.	Julie whines for a candy bar in the checkout line at the grocery store. Dad says no three times and then buys two bars for her.	Only my wants count. I dont have to take other peoples needs, wishes, or feelings into account. I can have whatever I want.
School Age To learn what is one's own responsibility and what are others' responsibilities, rules, and structures.	Father asks Jerrod if he needs ideas for getting himself ready for the school bus, no excuses to the school if he is tardy. More complex chores.	I need to learn to be responsible for myself and to others. I am capable.	Jerrod is often late for the school bus, so his dad packs Jerrod's lunch and waits for him and takes him to school.	I am not competent. I don't need to learn how to take care of myself. I don't need to care for others.
Teen To emerge gradually as a separate, independent person, responsive to others and responsible for her own needs, feelings, and behavior.	Parents negotiate with Rosa about what chores she can reasonably be expected to do and when and how she can get where she needs or wants to go.	I am responsible for myself and to others. I am a contributing family member. I am capable.	Rosa has many school activities, so her parents do her household chores for her. Her parents change their schedules to drive Rosa whenever she wants a ride.	I don't need to be competent. I am not competent enough or valued enough to be a contributing member of my primary group.

YIKES! LOOK AT THAT SPOILED CHILD

When the Situation Looks Like Overindulgence but Turns Out Not to Be

APPEARANCES OFTEN ARE DECEIVING.
—Aesop, 550 B.C.

I F we decide a situation is overindulgence only by the way it looks at first glance, we may sometimes be mistaken. Consider each of the following three stories.

TOO MUCH

Mom and five-year-old Elizabeth went to the department store to buy a birthday present for Elizabeth's friend. They walked up and down the aisles of the toy department, scanning for something they hoped Alexis might like. Elizabeth was quite taken with a dress-up doll she liked, but Mom reminded her that Alexis's mother didn't buy that kind of doll for Alexis. Elizabeth remembered that Alexis liked to invent play stories set in a castle, so they looked until they found a bejeweled crown. *I hope Alexis really likes this,* Elizabeth mused as they paid at the counter. *She can play princess of the castle.*

On their way out of the store they passed through the clothing department, where Elizabeth spied a blue-and-white play outfit. Pulling her mother's hand to go a little closer, Elizabeth looked up at her mother. "Could I please have that?" she asked.

Her mother examined it. "It's on the expensive side, but, yes, you can have it. You need another outfit anyway." Mother smiled as she handed the outfit to her very pleased little girl and proceeded to the counter.

If you are the observer of this scene, could you tell whether, in buying the outfit, Elizabeth's mother is overindulging her? Let's apply the *Test of Four.*

TEST OF FOUR

1. Did buying the play outfit keep Elizabeth from learning her **developmental tasks**?

2. Did the purchase require spending a disproportionate amount of the family's **resources**?

3. Did Mom agree to the purchase to please Elizabeth, or was it to satisfy her own **need** to look like a good mom?

4. Was there any **harm** done to others, the environment, or society?

Here is the information we have: Elizabeth did not fuss or whine when her mother reminded her that she herself might have liked the doll, but it wasn't an appropriate gift for Alexis. Elizabeth then found a gift that was both age-appropriate and sure to please her friend. And when Alexis asked Mother to buy the play outfit, she asked clearly and without whining or intimidation.

Furthermore, Elizabeth needed a new play outfit, and, though her mother wasn't wild about the price, the family could afford the outfit. Purchasing it did not mean going without something else.

HOW MUCH IS ENOUGH?

A casual observer might be concerned about overindulgence, because all Elizabeth had to do was ask for the outfit, and her mother bought it willingly. In fact, if such purchases were common, then Elizabeth's mother might indeed be overindulging her. But if her mom made these impulse purchases rarely, or only when her daughter genuinely needed something, then she clearly was not overindulging Elizabeth.

But does her mom overindulge herself?

Elizabeth does not have too many clothes, but her mom has stacks of shoeboxes carefully labeled and stored. Most of them are dress shoes she has worn. One is a new, never-worn duplicate of the comfortable pair she currently wears several days a week.

Let's apply the Test of Four once again.

1. Is there an impact on either her or Elizabeth's **development**?
2. Do her mother's shoe purchases use an undue amount of the family's **resources**?
3. Is it clear whose **need** is met by having so many shoes? Is it a healthy need?
4. Is any **harm** being done? Do Mom's shoe purchases model adult overindulgence for Elizabeth?

The whole story is not clear to an observer who glances in the closet. Yes, Elizabeth's mother has many pairs of shoes. But consider the following: Some of the shoes are many years old, and Mom has kept her shoe purchases within her (reasonable) clothing budget for over a decade. Her feet are extremely hard to fit, so she has learned through the years to buy a second pair when she finds shoes that fit well, especially if they are on sale. Her care has paid off, as her feet have no corns or bunions. She takes excellent care of her shoes, and when shoe styles change, she checks her reserve boxes of dress shoes to find shoes that look current enough for her to feel well-dressed in them. Elizabeth and her mother have discussed why she keeps her old shoes and how important it is to wear properly fitting shoes. Mother has also taught Elizabeth how to polish her own shoes, and insists that her daughter take good care of them.

So what can look like overindulgence to the casual observer would, in this case, be a prudent use of family resources and an example of good purchasing and parenting.

OVER-NURTURING

Over-nurturing

If an adult does something for a child that the child is capable of doing for himself or herself, how do you tell if it's a case of over-nurturing? Let's take Christopher's school problems with a bully as an example.

Christopher's mother went to his school, determined to get a problem stopped. She strode into the office with firm steps and spoke very clearly to the principal. "This problem has been going on too long. I want you to do something about it. My son is having to spend too much of his energy trying to fend off this girl in his class."

At least five times, Christopher, a fourth grader, told Mom that Sarah, a girl in his class, yelled swear words and nasty names at him during recess. She had also slid past him in the hallway a number of times, saying in a breathy, loud whisper that she'd like to have sex with him. When she grabbed at his crotch, he told his mom he'd had enough.

At the end of her conversation with the principal, his mother added, "And if the school district administration needs to be involved to help you solve the problem, I hope you will get their help. You have a responsibility to my son and the other kids. I want to know what you do and I'm willing to help in any way I can."

Here's some additional information. Christopher had asked his mother three weeks ago for ideas on how to get Sarah to stop bullying him. She suggested that he ignore the girl, which he tried, with no success. He'd reported Sarah's behavior to the playground aide and to his teacher, and asked them to stop Sarah, but nothing had happened and Sarah's bullying had escalated.

Christopher's mother had spoken with the principal before and was told that he knew Sarah's behavior was a problem. The principal said, "We have talked with this mother in the past and we don't get any cooperation. Teachers in this school still remember Sarah's mother and her behavior when she was a student here. This is just more of the same. We've done all we can do." The principal did not explain why no action had been taken by teachers or the playground aide.

An observer of only the mother's second visit to the principal might conclude that she is meddling, over-protective, and overindulging her child by doing something for him he could do for himself. However, early on, she had encouraged her son to solve the problem on his own and helped him identify some coping behaviors. She continued to monitor the situation by asking Christopher how he was managing. It was only when Christopher became almost as mad at the teacher and principal as he was at Sarah that Mom took action to get the bullying stopped.

Let's ask the Test of Four questions once more:

1. Did Christopher's mother's actions keep Christopher from learning any **developmental tasks?**
2. Did her action consume an inordinate amount of her **time or energy?**
3. Did she do what Christopher could do for himself? Was she meeting her **needs** or Christopher's?
4. Was anyone else **harmed** by her actions?

In all likelihood, this was not overindulgence. But let's look more closely at question 3. It is quite possible that Christopher's mother went to the school in part to meet her own need to feel that she was a good parent. However, so long as she was also meeting her son's legitimate need, her actions were not overindulgence. In fact, *not* intervening would have been harmful to both her son and Sarah. After all, it is the responsibility of adults to keep children safe from both physical *and* emotional harm. When children have done their best to accept responsibility for themselves and it still isn't enough, parents should intervene.

SOFT STRUCTURE

According to our studies,[1] one of the indicators of childhood overindulgence is a lack of regular chores, or of negative consequences if chores were left undone.

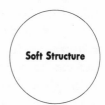

Life went on. *See, it wasn't important that I put out the garbage.*

Doing chores teaches a child the importance and value of contributing to the success of the family. Chores also teach reciprocity. Someone cooks dinner. Someone chauffeurs. Someone buys the food.

Someone takes out the garbage. Life is bumpy with resentment and blaming when some members contribute and some don't. When all members work together, however, the family unit is strengthened.

Listen to Lauren's story:

> Lauren was visiting her brother's family in Dallas for a week. As each day passed, she noticed something quite remarkable. In this well-run home, her sister-in-law, Jessica, took out the garbage. *What's going on here?* Lauren thought. *Nephew Nicholas is shooting hoops or talking with his friends or on the computer and not taking out the garbage. My brother and his wife must be slipping.*
>
> On the fourth day, as Jessica returned from putting the garbage curbside, Lauren could not hold back the question: "What happened to Nicholas's doing that?" Jessica chuckled. "Oh, I forgot to pick Nicholas up from soccer practice last week and he waited for fifty minutes before I got there. I apologized and offered to do garbage detail for a week in restitution for the time I caused him to lose. He was very happy to accept my offer! And the week is up tomorrow."

Once again, let's use the Test of Four:

1. Did Jessica's doing Nicholas's chore keep him from learning important **developmental tasks?** Was Nicolas given too much power?
2. Did Jessica's chore use a disproportionate share of her personal or **family resources?**
3. Whose **needs** were being fulfilled? Jessica's or Nicholas's?
4. Was **harm** done?

Jessica places a high value on living up to agreements—and on making amends to others when an error has been made. In part, her offer to make up for the inconvenience she caused Nicholas was a deliberate attempt to model amends-making behavior for him. She has also made it clear to Nicholas that if he fails to live up to his agreements, he is also expected to make amends to the person he inconvenienced. What's the result of agreements like this? Mutual respect and responsibility. The family and the trust relationships within it are all strengthened, and this was not soft structure and not overindulgence.

An important feature of any successful family structure is the ability to set and enforce limits that are age-appropriate and that take into account the responsibility level of the child. This includes making clear with all family members:

- ❖ who does what jobs
- ❖ what happens if they are not done
- ❖ the certainty that something *will* happen if they are not done

GETTING THE WHOLE PICTURE

When you have only part of the picture, what looks like overindulgence might or might not be. But when you do have the full picture in front of you (and if you don't, try to get it), simply apply the Test of Four. It will tell you whether something you are thinking of doing will be in the best interests of your child—and your family.

If Elizabeth's mother had bought her the play outfit to make Mom feel good about *her* ability to give Elizabeth anything she wanted, it would have been overindulgence. If Christopher's mother had gone to see the principal to satisfy *her* needs for power and control, or to rescue her son and do what he could have done for himself, it would have been overindulgence. If Jessica had done Nicholas's chore so her son could tell his friends what a great mom *she* was, it would be overindulgence.

If what appears at first to be overindulgence sometimes isn't, is it possible that what *doesn't* look like overindulgence really is? It certainly is, and that is the subject of the next chapter.

■

OCCASIONAL INDULGENCES ADD COLOR AND PLEASURE
TO LIFE. ONLY IF THOSE SAME ACTS BECOME A PATTERN,
BECOME CHRONIC, DO THEY BECOME OVERINDULGENCE.
—Indira Newell

WHAT'S WRONG WITH THAT?

When the Situation Looks Normal but Actually Is Overindulgence

THE IMPACT DOES NOT ALWAYS MATCH THE INTENT.
—Valerie Batts

WE just examined situations that looked like overindulgence but were not. However, it is also true that there are situations where the overindulgence isn't obvious at first glance. By examining three situations where assistance initially looks helpful but turns out not to be, we can become more discriminating between truly supportive help and help that actually disempowers, patronizes, or carries a price tag.

TOO MANY RESOURCES

Too Much

Taylor is fifteen, very bright, a good student, and a terrific ice skater. Taylor's mother drives her to the rink five days a week, a journey of about ninety miles each way, usually in congested traffic, for her two-hour practice. Taylor does her homework during the drive. She regrets not having time to hang out with friends and do after-school activities. She'd like to go to her church's youth group, but, because of her skating, doesn't have the time. Next summer, Mom and Taylor will take up residence in a distant city for eight weeks so Taylor can work with a nationally known coach.

Let's use the Test of Four to see if this qualifies as overindulgence.

1. Are Taylor's parents keeping her from learning her **developmental tasks**?
2. Do Taylor's parents devote a disproportionate amount of family **resources** on her?
3. Whose **needs** are being met?
4. Is any **harm** done?

Providing opportunities for youngsters to learn and develop skills is part of a parent's job. In this case, Taylor's mother seems to be dedicated to helping Taylor develop her skating skills. However, this mom also appears to be disregarding some of Taylor's need for opportunities to engage in the developmental tasks of adolescence (See page 285). Adolescence is a time of associating more and more with peers. Taylor does not have the time or opportunity to do this. Taylor should be figuring out who she is, what she believes and values, and how she is like and unlike significant others in her life. How well is Taylor able to do this with her time devoted to only one activity with only one group?

Also, consider this further information. Taylor's mom grew up with a disinterested mother, one who neglected to pay attention to her daughter's giftedness and ignored her passionate requests for skating lessons. From the day Taylor was born, her mother swore that Taylor would not be denied the opportunity that had been denied to her.

Adrienne, Taylor's younger sister, takes riding lessons at a stable within walking distance from home. Her instructor believes she is a gifted horsewoman and has recommended she get further training in jumping at a stable in the next town. This is not possible because it would interfere with the demands of Taylor's training.

According to all four Test of Four questions, Taylor is being overindulged. Yes, Taylor's opportunity to accomplish developmental tasks is restricted. Yes, Taylor's mom's needs are a big factor in the encouragement of her daughter. Yes, Taylor's training appears to consume a disproportionate amount of family resources (Mother's time). And yes, Taylor's younger sister is being slighted.

The issue of whose needs are being met is extremely important in determining whether someone is being overindulged. The question can be posed this way by the parent: *Is what I am about to do more for my child or is it more for me? Was that behavior, that choice, that event, that object, more for me or more for my child?* An honest answer to these questions will help us keep from inflicting the pain resulting from overindulgence on those we love and care for.

If Taylor's energy were the driving force behind this situation, if her sister were to be totally supportive of Taylor's goals to compete and excel, if the intent of the whole family was to help a child get to the Olympics, or some goal important to her, and the impact of that effort was positive for each family member, it might not be overindulgence. Some children actually seem to exist for a particular sport.

FOR THE WELFARE OF THE CHILD

For most children, the sport should exist for the child. Annie, age five, was about to participate in a dance recital. On rehearsal day Annie mounted the stage to dance with her group, and then rejoined her mom in the audience to watch the rest of the show. On recital day Annie was to wait in a classroom until her group danced, then return to the classroom until the recital was over. She balked: "I want to be with you, Mommy."

"No, Annie, you are to stay here."

"Then I want you to stay with me!"

"Annie, I can't do that today. Yesterday at rehearsal you sat with me and watched all the dancing." Mom put her arm around Annie and looked into her eyes. "Today we have different jobs. You are a performer. It's your job to stay here, go to the platform and dance, and come back here to the classroom. It's my job to be in the audience. I have to go now and do my job. I'll come and get you when the recital is over. Grandpa and Grandma came to see you dance, and we'll all have dinner together."

Back in the auditorium, Mom told Grandma, "I think this is good for Annie. It teaches her how to be part of the group. It gives her a chance to be on the platform without being the center of attention. I like this dance studio. It's not expensive. It's so close to our house we can walk to lessons and the children are a hoot to watch. The teacher makes sure all of the children succeed."

This mom understood how a sport could help her daughter learn some important developmental tasks of the five-year-old. When Mom insisted that both she and her daughter do their jobs and play their appropriate roles, she helped Annie with the important five-year-old identity tasks of Who am I?, Who are they?, and What does that mean?

This passes the Test of Four.

1. The activity supported Annie's **development** and gave her a chance to practice socially appropriate behavior, to discover her effect on others, and find her place in groups. (See page 280 for further information.)
2. The cost in time, energy and money fit within the family's **resources**.
3. Her parents were not ego-invested in her performance, did not put their **needs** ahead of their child's.
4. No **harm** was done.

OVER-NURTURING

Nate, a curly-haired, active two-year-old, takes delight in playing with his father, Bryce. They have good fun together rolling on the floor amidst a little tickling, Dad "flubbering" on his son's tummy, playing peek-a-boo, and making animal sounds.

It's Bryce who puts Nate to bed at night. They go through a regular routine of bath, cuddle, story, then stuffed animal and blanket. Dad kisses Nate good night, and, three minutes later, Nate is bellowing for Dad. Dad carries the boy out to the living room, saying, "Okay, Buddy. I see you need some more time with your ol' dad."
Bryce looks like a loving dad who enjoys caring for his son.

Test of Four questions to ask:

1. Is Dad helping Nate learn his **developmental** tasks? Tasks include learning to follow simple safety commands like stop,

come here, go there, stay there, and starting to give up beliefs about being the center of the universe. (See page 278 for more information.)

2. Is Nate receiving a disproportionate measure of Dad's **emotional resources**?
3. Whose **needs** are being met, Nate's or Dad's?
4. Is **harm** being done?

Sounds like some good Dad time for Nate, but could Dad be overindulging? We don't have enough information to be sure. Perhaps the keys to the answer lie in what happens next.

> When Nate gets to the living room, Bryce pulls his boy up onto the couch, cuddles him, and resumes reading the newspaper. Nate wiggles and wiggles. Bryce says, "No, Nate," but Nate begins hitting the newspaper and pushing at his dad's glasses and roughing up his hair. By now, Bryce is irritated with Nate and for the moment it appears that Nate is clearly in charge of his father and the situation.

This should be Bryce's cue. If Bryce wants Nate in bed, he should claim his position as the one who knows what is healthy for his son and for himself and act accordingly. If he is bothered by Nate's annoying behavior, he should not give in to it but get Nate to stop the annoying behavior. Nate should not be learning that he is the center of the universe and that any behavior is acceptable. He should be learning that he can trust and rely on competent adults who love him and who know when to stand in the way of his demands. A two-year-old who is allowed to dominate adults learns to be annoying and obnoxious and eats up the emotional resources of the parents.

Now it is clear Nate is being overindulged. Here are some things Bryce can do instead. He can enjoy his snuggly fun and bedtime rituals and then end their time together by saying something like, "Okay, that's enough for tonight." Then, without hesitation, but with reassuring warmth, give Nate a good-night kiss or hug.

If Nate comes out of his room, Dad can let Nate know by the look on his face that he is not pleased. He can calmly ask Nate if he wants to return to his bed by himself or if he wants Dad to walk with him. Or he could scoop Nate up in his arms and carry him there. If Nate whines or cries, Bryce can say, "Love you, Nate. See you in the morning," and leave the room.

But this isn't just about the relationship between father and son. Let's look at the family system.

Mom comes home from shopping, sees Nate in the living room and exclaims, "Nate, you should be in bed by now!" Nate scoots off the couch and makes a beeline for Mom, pounding on her upper leg. In one motion, she picks Nate up, restrains his arms and says, "No hitting!" Dad reacts by reprimanding his wife. "Don't yell at him! You shouldn't squelch him." Mother puts Nate down and leaves the room.

If Dad and Mom continue to give in, what might Nate's behavior look like when he goes to school? When he's a teen? An adult? As for the determination of whose needs are being met, more information is needed. Do Dad and Mom agree on basic parenting practices? Are the parents acting out unaddressed difficulties in their relationship? Is either parent parenting to please a grandparent? A peer group?

SOFT STRUCTURE

Damian's parents were conferring with his fifth grade-teacher about Damian's schoolwork. Satisfied with his progress in reading and math, they moved to expressing concern about Damian's poor spelling test scores. "When we help him study the night  before the test, he does so much better," Dad ventured. "And he feels better about himself when he does well on the test! But he doesn't remember to bring the words home," added Mom. "Can you help us?"

Test of Four questions to ask:

1. Are Mom and Dad helping Damian learn his **developmental tasks** or are they discouraging him from doing so? Tasks include learning skills, learning from mistakes, deciding to be adequate, and developing the capacity to cooperate. (See page 282 for more information.)
2. Are Mom and Dad expending an inordinate amount of their **energy** on solving Damian's problem?

3. Whose **needs** are at stake?

4. Is **harm** being done?

Is this a case of overindulgence? Mom and Dad appear eager to help Damian. Do you have enough information to know? Here's more.

> After the teacher applauded the parents' interest in their child's work, Mom asked, "Will you see to it that Damian has the spelling list with him when he leaves school on Tuesdays?" When the teacher politely declined to do so, saying that was Damian's responsibility, Dad perked up and cast a knowing glance toward his wife. "He doesn't get his chores done if we don't remind him. And remind him. And remind him. And even then, we mostly have to ask his big brother to mow the lawn because Damian doesn't."

Now the picture is clear. Remember that in this chapter, we are examining situations that do not appear to be overindulgence. The truth is in the details. Damian is not learning the many skills that school-age children learn while doing chores. Damian's parents don't hold him accountable when he doesn't follow through, but there are negative consequences for the parents and his brother. It is not their intention to be resentful of Damian, but they do resent it when he doesn't pull his weight in the family. This soft-structure overindulgence spills over to the classroom as well—Damien is clearly not pulling his weight there, either. He is not a lazy kid or a bad kid.[1] He is a kid who has learned that life goes on without any problem for him when he doesn't contribute. As long as he tunes out nagging, he is able to avoid his chores without experiencing discomforting consequences. Consequences that cause Damian more serious discomfort are needed.

Mom and Dad had a talk and agreed on a plan of action. Here's what they said to Damian: "We want to apologize for doing more than you do to learn to spell. From now on, it's all your job. If you want our help, ask us. And by the way, remember what we said about missing your little League Practice or game if you hadn't finished mowing the lawn? Well, we fell down there too. Sorry. From now on, no mow, no go."

Looks can be deceiving if we don't have full information about a situation, and it can be easy to mistake overindulgence for healthy parenting behavior. But with the Test of Four, we can tell when we're being wise and loving parents—and when what we're about to do (or what we're already doing) is a form of overindulgence. If you haven't used the Parental Overindulgence Assessment Tool in Appendix B, you may want to do that now.

WHEN PARENTS ARE OVER-FUNCTIONING,
CHILDREN RESPOND BY UNDER-FUNCTIONING.
—Mark Henningsen

TWO

Too Much

HAVE SOME MORE

The Many Ways of Giving Too Much

■

IF YOU WATER A PLANT TOO MUCH, IT DIES.
EVEN IF YOU ARE WATERING IT TOO MUCH OUT OF LOVE,
IT STILL DIES.
—Ada Alden

Mʏ ANY of us have watered a plant too much, and who among us, wanting our child to experience abundance, has not sometimes given a bit too much? It is often difficult or impossible to know how much is exactly the right amount. And so we do the best we can. Sometimes too much, sometimes just right, sometimes too little. This section is about too much and too many, too often and too long.

TOO MANY AND TOO MUCH

Too Much

Too much means providing many resources or too much of something that is purchased. Ask for a sweater and get three. Shop for clothes with your mother and get two pairs of jeans because you can't decide between them. Get a pair of in-line skates, use them once, and ask for a skateboard. Ask for a different skateboard because it's better and more expensive. Lose it and your parents buy another. Too many inordinately expensive sports clothes. Too many expensive toys in the toy box. Toys in the garage so there's no room for the cars. No stopping, no pausing when you're opening presents. Going from one to the next and finishing the frenzy of opening with a feeling of disappointment. Too many lessons and no practice. Too many sports events. Too many movies. Too much TV. Too many trips: *Been there, done that.* Compact discs, DVDs, laptops, Palm Pilots, programs, accessories, computer games, video games, stuff.

STUFF

A class of college students[1] wrote a group poem telling what happens when children have too much stuff.

Stuff—too much	Child handles the *Stuff* by:
	Disregarding it
	Destroying it
	Displaying it
	Boasting about it
	Instead of:
	Appreciating it
	Using the *Stuff* to enhance life
	Child may decide:
	Stuff needs no investment on my part.
	I am confused about what price I may have to pay for *Stuff.*
	I need *Stuff* right when I want it.
	I have the power to manipulate the adults to get my *Stuff.*
	I don't have to work and plan for getting the *Stuff* I need.

A BOX OF PRUNES

A woman told us this story about growing up with too much stuff:

I had everything. They gave me everything whether I asked for it or not. I didn't ever say I liked something because somebody would run out and get it. At Christmastime they said, "What do you want?" I didn't want anything. I had everything. I had more than I wanted. But they insisted that I tell them, so I said, "I want a box of prunes." I don't know why I wanted a box of prunes. I just thought a box of prunes would be nice. So I asked for it. They were disgusted with me.

On Christmas day I got boxes and boxes of presents. Toys, clothes, books, music, theater tickets, everything I already had, but no prunes.

At night I dreamed about being surrounded with shelves, shelves loaded with boxes. Boxes and boxes. The boxes kept falling off the shelves onto my head. They didn't hurt but they kept falling. I couldn't stop them.

One day a teacher asked me, "Do you help around the house?" I said, "Yes, I sweep." I had never swept. I had never held a broom. I had never helped clean in any way. In college I got part-time jobs cleaning houses. I loved it. I finally got to learn how to clean.

This woman was able to recognize that she got too much and to move beyond it. Not so for everyone.

WHAT HAPPENS WHEN WE OVERINDULGE WITH TOO MUCH

Our research indicates that children who experienced a constant stream of overindulging with too much usually:

- ❖ do not know what is enough
- ❖ disrespect others and property
- ❖ believe and act as if they are the center of the universe

VOICES OF PAIN

Some of the overindulged adults reported that they had confused *getting* with *being*. "I am if I get," one said. "I have to get in order to be sure I'm alive."

Listen to the voices of some of the adults we spoke with as they describe their feelings.

In Their Own Voices

When your parents overindulged you, what feelings resulted?
✓ I felt angry when people gave me gifts that were meant for them.
✓ I felt bad because other kids didn't get what I did.
✓ I felt embarrassed because other kids didn't have stuff.
✓ I felt embarrassed because I knew somehow it wasn't right.
✓ I felt hurt because frequently my needs/preferences were not considered in my parents' gift giving.

Which messages do you think parents send to children when the parents overindulge the children?
✓ Don't ask for what you need.
✓ Ignore guilt about receiving gifts. Learn not to listen to your conscience. You must receive the gifts whether you want them or not, even if it's at another's expense or bad fortune. I think the pressure of being forced against your self-regulating conscience is a very difficult internal struggle and very abusive.

As a child did you ever try to stop the overindulgence?
✓ As a teenager I started returning unwanted and expensive Christmas presents.
✓ Yes. After receiving a new car (unwanted) from my father when I was sixteen, I vowed and refused to accept any consequential gift from him again—other than to be overpaid while working for his company summers. Only with her death when I was forty did my mother stop her contribution of time and money. I was unable to cope with her obsession. She insisted on keeping books for the family business, duplicating the work of my hired accounting firm for years.

TOO MUCH OF WHAT?

The overindulged participants in our research studies identified five areas in which they received too much.

- ❖ When I was growing up, my parents gave me lots of toys.[2]
- ❖ When I was growing up, I was allowed to have any clothes I wanted.
- ❖ When I was growing up, my parents scheduled me for activities, lessons, sports, camps.
- ❖ When I was growing up, I was allowed lots of privileges.
- ❖ When I was growing up, my parents made sure I was entertained.

We will discuss the impact of all of this "too much" in future chapters as we consider how to give enough but not too much in each of the five areas.

REMEMBER THAT NOT GETTING WHAT YOU WANT IS SOME-
TIMES A WONDERFUL STROKE OF LUCK.
—Dalai Lama

I WANT SOMETHING TO PLAY WITH

When I Was Growing Up, My Parents Gave Me Lots of Toys

HE WHO HAS THE MOST TOYS LOSES.
—j.i.

CHILDREN'S PLAY IS CHILDREN'S WORK

DOLLS of bone, leather, straw, fabric, or wood—through the ages little girls have loved dolls made from whatever natural materials were available. For eons our little female ancestors watched their mothers and cared for their dolls. Play, yes, but children's play is children's work in which they are learning life-skills that prepare them to become productive in their society.

Traditionally, around the world, toys have played a crucial role in the games and experiences that prepare children for adult roles in their cultures. In hunting cultures boys used sticks as spears in their play. In warrior cultures the stick was a sword. But getting a new stick did not involve a trip to the toy store, and the sticks were probably not piled up in the boys' bedrooms or left to accumulate on the family room floor.

In the mechanized Western world, children still play with sticks, but they also have toy trucks and cars and play in small kitchens with toy dishwashers, washing machines, and dryers. They even have little computers. And dolls made of plastic. Many dolls made of plastic. As in earlier cultures, toys reflect the activities of adult life. However, with batteries and the sophistication of the chip and the skill of marketers, many of the toys demand nothing more of the child than the push of a button. Very different from the toys of old that depended upon imagination and activity. So now, as we survey the toy field, we need to ask not only are there too many, but are there too many of only one kind. Are the toys merely preparing children to become consumers?

Ashley is three. She has many toys, all battery powered, many of them very expensive. One doll walks, another talks, another dances. Play-boards sing songs and make animal noises. These toys are scattered throughout the house. When a battery dies, Ashley throws the toy aside or noisily demands a new battery—right now. When Papa comes home from a trip, Ashley's first words are, "What did you bring me?"

If children's play is truly children's work, what is Ashley learning from her play/work? Is the plethora of toys helping her or interfering? Is she being overindulged? Remember the Test of Four.

TEST OF FOUR

Developmental Tasks?

Possible Harm?

Family Resources?

Whose Needs?

1. This array of toys does not support Ashley in learning her **developmental tasks.** If she gets the new battery right now, she isn't learning to delay gratification. If she is not taught to care for and store her toys, she is not learning responsible life-skills. If the toys do not allow her to construct and manipulate and design, her creativity is not enhanced.
2. We don't know if the toys cost an inordinate amount of the family **income.**
3. We can guess whom the toys are really for. These expensive technological toys must serve some **need of the parents.**

4. All these toys may not be **doing harm** to others. They do increase the profits of the toy companies.

Ashley is clearly overindulged. The first clue gives enough evidence. Her parents, who provided the toys out of love and good intent, could shift their intent from what they want to give to giving what Ashley needs. They could pack some of these mechanical toys away, get some plain blocks and some flexible dolls without batteries, and, at least half of the time, Papa could give her the gift of his time instead of a toy. Her parents could read the book *The Play's the Thing* to get a grasp on how unstructured play stimulates brain growth and creativity and teaches social skills.

The Menzas also choose mechanical toys. The children are teenagers and the garage is spilling over with scooters, jet skis, powerboats, snowmobiles, and motorcycles. Inside the house are three computers, seventeen computer games, and loads of software.

Is this overindulgence?

1. Do these toys support the accomplishment of **developmental tasks?** Are the teens doing well in school? Behaving responsibly? Are they responsive to adults and pleasant to be around? Are they learning to care for all these toys? Learning social skills? Learning to be aware of and empathic toward others?
2. Do these toys claim a disproportionate amount of the family's **resources?**
3. **Who** are all these toys for? Are these toys that fit the interests and the talents of the children or are these things the parents want or wanted as youths and didn't have?
4. Are these toys doing **harm** to other people? To the community? To the larger society?

If there are too many toys or computer games in a family with firm structure, children will be okay because they won't have too much time to play with those toys.

—*Kaara Ettesvold*

We need more information about this family in order to use the Test of Four, but if the situation doesn't meet all four criteria, then overindulgence is occurring.

TOO MANY TOYS AFFECT COMPETENCE

Adults who grew up with lots of toys also have problems with competence issues in adult life. Participants[1] who agreed with the statement *When I was growing up, my parents gave me lots of toys* also agreed with the following:

❖ One of my problems is that I cannot get down to work when I should.

❖ I give up on things before completing them.

❖ If I meet someone interesting who is very hard to make friends with, I'll soon stop trying to make friends with that person.

Note: The above bulleted items are reproduced with permission of authors and publisher from: Sherer, M., Maddux, J. E., Mercandante, B., Prentice-Dunn, S., Jacobs, B., & Rogers, R. W. "The Self-efficacy scale: Construction and validation." *Psychological Reports*, 1982, 51, 663-671. © Psychological Reports 1982.

This implies that too many toys interfere with the development of the important life-skills of focus and perseverance. Of course the experience of being overindulged is individual and so is each child's response, the beliefs the child chooses, and the decisions he makes, but it is challenging to guess why these particular lacks in competence relate to having had too many toys. You can add your own observations about the possible effects of having too many toys.

The "Wecked" Teddy Bear

Two-year-old Amantha was playing at Grandma's house. "Need new teddy bear," she announced. Grandma dug out Amantha's daddy's old, beloved Poo Bear, one eye missing, one ear torn. In her mind's eye, Gram saw a sturdy three-year-old boy lugging Poo everywhere. "This was your daddy's bear. He loved it dearly. You can play with it." Amantha's insulted "No" echoed through the house as the little girl hurled the bear down the stairs. "It wecked! Mine wecked! Need new bear!" Gram lovingly retrieved the bear and put it away. Time for the *Velveteen Rabbit*, she thought.

What has Amantha already learned about caring for her toys?

WHEN GRANDPARENTS AND OTHERS
GIVE TOO MUCH TO CHILDREN

Parents who are thoughtful and firm about how much they give sometimes can't stop others from giving "too many." See how Joshua's parents used that "too much" to build strengths in the child and the family.

Birthday Toys

Joshua's extended family visited as often as they could. Joshua was the first grandchild on both sides and a great favorite of his aunts and uncles. The week before Joshua's seventh birthday, packages poured in from loving relatives in many states. Dad insisted that Joshua wait for his birthday to open them. On that big day the boy's in-town relatives arrived with more gifts. Joshua tore through the whole pile, throwing the wrappings aside, barely glancing at each gift before dropping it, ignoring anything that was said to him, and grabbing for the next gift. When the pile of presents was gone, he looked startled and demanded, "Is that all?"

Was this overindulgence?

Clearly. Joshua's behavior is common in two-year-olds, but it is definitely not appropriate for a seven-year-old. He showed no appreciation for the gifts and no consideration of the gifters. His parents were embarrassed. They even lost track of what gift came from whom. Did the surfeit of presents interfere with Joshua's learning his developmental tasks? He is demonstrating his inability to consider the difference between wants and needs. He's not behaving as though he has regard for anyone but himself.

What to do? It was futile to ask the relatives to stop the flow of gifts. Joshua's parents devised a plan. Before the next event they asked the relatives to send a picture of themselves with only one gift. Days before his eighth birthday, the parents helped Joshua clear his toy shelves and give some outgrown toys away. Joshua resisted but his parents held firm. Joshua got to open the first gift the afternoon before the big day. He was told he could not open another gift for two hours. He whined and manipulated, but his parents were unyielding. His parents examined each gift with him and talked about how he would use it and how he would care for it. Together they looked at the picture of the givers, remembered the last time they had seen those folks, and imagined what they had said when they chose the gift. The remainder of the two hours was time for Joshua to play with the gift and to choose to write a thank-you, draw a thank-you picture, or make a thank-you phone call. Only after the thank-you was finished could Joshua open the next gift.

The next afternoon, when the in-town relatives arrived, Joshua's parents insisted that he show each of the pictures with the gifts from the out-of-town relatives before he opened any more presents. This changed the day from one of tearing open packages to a time of appreciating extended family.

Joshua was still the center of attention on his birthday, but he learned about including others, something about delayed gratification, and he was moved beyond the excessive sense of entitlement he had first displayed.

This "too much," which had been such an appalling experience the year before, became a cherished family ritual.

LIMITING GIFTS

Parents use many strategies to limit excessive gifting by others. Here are some examples:

- ❖ Melinda asked Grandpa to cut the gifts by two-thirds and put the extra money into a college fund.
- ❖ Mark tried to limit the amount of candy brought by relatives by being very specific about how much of what kind was welcome. "One bag of red licorice or two boxes of Milk Duds only!"
- ❖ Tony told his parents that he was angry about their preference for their grandson over their granddaughter and that he expected equal treatment and gifts for his children.
- ❖ Georgia asked Grandma to sing a new song as her gift on every other visit.

LIMITING TV

One dad told his parents how damaging too much TV watching is to young brains and that his children may not have a TV set in their room. He suggested his parents might like the new set for themselves or offered to return it to the store and put the money in a savings account.

Wise dad. He knows that enormous brain development occurs after birth, and that the child's experiences and activities profoundly affect the quality of that development. A child is born with billions of brain cells, but only 18 percent of them are wired together. That connecting occurs over the days, weeks, months, years, and beyond. That is why the American Academy of Pediatrics recommends that children younger than four spend no time in front of a screen. There are so many activities they need to be doing that they can't do while watching a screen. David Walsh reminds us that neuroscientists are fond of saying "neurons that fire together wire together" so what the child experiences on the screen tends to stay in the brain.[2]

Being in charge of how much time your children sit in front of a screen is one way you can protect your children.

WHEN ADULTS GIVE TOO MUCH TO THEMSELVES

Managing their money and finding some balance between spending on needs and wants is a challenge for many people, especially during early adult years. Intervening with a young adult who is overindulging himself is not as easy. Listen to what one ingenious mom did:

> Rosie thought carefully about how to get into the head of her twenty-year-old son, who was working only part-time, but thought he needed twelve subscriptions to twelve magazines to be paid for over twenty-four months. He accused Rosie of being critical if she made any comment about the magazines, so she posted this poem on his door.

Fuel

"They're giving me a 'bargain,' Mom,"
was my middle son's reply.
"They're treating me REAL SPECIAL,
cause I'm the COOLEST GUY."

"The payments aren't expensive."
(They are if you are broke!)
Don't want to wake you from your dream,
but . . . it's time . . .that you awoke!

Yes, you might save a little,
on ALL your "special books,"
but, you'll be paying for two years,
I think that you got took!

I hope you learned a lesson,
Cause you're NOBODY'S FOOL!
If ever we get desperate,
We'll use those "books" for FUEL![3]

Did it work? Rosie said, "Not right away, but he didn't get defensive."

HOW MANY ARE ENOUGH?

Toys are important for children's play/work, but too many toys stifle learning. As you consider how many toys and what kinds are appropriate for your child in your setting, you can:

- ❖ Apply the Test of Four.
- ❖ Consider how the number of toys affects other members of your household.
- ❖ Consider how much space you want to give to the toys.
- ❖ Consider how the number influences the interpersonal relationships in the family.

SOMETIMES HAVING MORE THAN ENOUGH IS GOOD, BUT
ALWAYS HAVING TOO MUCH IS BAD, BAD, BAD.
—An overindulged adult

6

I'VE GOT NOTHING TO WEAR

When I Was Growing Up, I Was Allowed to Have Any Clothes I Wanted

PERHAPS TOO MUCH OF EVERYTHING
IS AS BAD AS TOO LITTLE.
—Edna Ferber

NOTHING TO WEAR?

DINO: *Mom, I have nothing to wear!*

MOM: *Your closet is full!*

DINO: *But I've nothing to wear tonight. Mom, this is special.*

MOM: *Well, wear your new blue shirt.*

DINO: *It's in the laundry.*

MOM: *Wear the brown.*

DINO: *It's ripped.*

MOM: *You should learn to take care of your clothes.*

DINO: *Yeah, yeah, next week. Mom, I need something for tonight.*

MOM: *Okay, Dino. Get what you need. You can use my credit card.*

Anything going wrong here for Dino? Yes, indeed.

Children's clothes do much more than just cover the outside of their bodies.

Clothes project an image of who we are and what we want people to think we are. They can be a great source of pleasure and an expression of creativity. On the other hand, the peripheral damage done to children's internal attitudes and thinking by having too many clothes can be amazingly far-reaching.

Was Dino overindulged?

Check out the clues:

- ❖ *I have nothing to wear!* No clue there. That's a familiar comment from a sixteen-year-old.
- ❖ *Your closet is full!* Might be a clue there, but not necessarily.
- ❖ *The blue one is in the laundry.* Overindulgence clue. Any reason Dino isn't doing his own laundry at age sixteen?
- ❖ *The brown one is ripped.* Overindulgence clue. Any reason Dino has not mended the rip or asked someone else to do it?
- ❖ *You should learn to take care of your clothes.* Overindulgence clue. Learning to care for belongings is an important life-skill task for adolescents. Who has been caring for his clothes for sixteen years? Who has not been teaching him how? Over-nurturing here?
- ❖ *Yeah, yeah, next week.* Overindulgence clue. Sounds as if Dino feels free to avoid learning how to care for his clothing. Soft structure here?
- ❖ *I need something for tonight.* Does Dino have an over-blown sense of entitlement?
- ❖ *Get what you need.* Overindulgence clue. Sounds as if Mom is not teaching clear differentiation of wants and needs.
- ❖ *Use my credit card.* Overindulgence clue. No price limit? Why Mom's card? Doesn't a sixteen-year-old have a clothing budget? His own money? His own bank account? Does he ever have to pay for part or all of anything?

Has Dino been overindulged? Yes, definitely. What is Dino learning about caring for clothing and managing money? Probably, *I don't need to learn wardrobe-planning skills,* or *If you want it, she will provide,* or worse, *If I want it, I deserve it now.* If these attitudes become the way he decides to conduct his life now, he is looking at lots of pain in the future.

CHILDHOOD DECISIONS THAT CAN HAUNT ADULT LIVES

If you haven't thought about possible decisions your children may be making, the following exercise can help you guess. Remember that your guesses are only guesses and that you need to watch for clues about your children's decisions and applaud them if they are healthy and counter them if they are not.

Some people, who, like Dino, got all the clothes they wanted when they were young, made unhelpful conclusions or decisions as adults. Think about the decisions each of the children in these examples could be making or have made because they were allowed to get by with the following:

> Tyler, three, has many clothes. He is allowed to wear whatever he likes. Parental good intention: We want him to be comfortable and to make up his own mind about what he wants. The outfit he puts together for the preschool parents' program is both unattractive and inappropriate. Other parents comment, and Tyler's parents are embarrassed. When they ask him not to wear that outfit again, he says, "I'm going to because I like it."

Tyler's decision: _____

> Four-year-old Ryan loses his shoes in the park. Auntie asks him to find them but he refuses to look. "I have lots more shoes at home; I don't need those."

Ryan's decision: _____

> Samantha, seven, is told to pick up her clothes that are on the floor. "I don't need to," she replies, "because I don't like those clothes." The clothes stay on the floor.

Samantha's decision: _____

Jeff, thirteen, leaves clothes in a heap under a wet swimsuit. "It's okay," he explains, "they're not new."

Jeff's decision: _____

Brianna, fifteen, is asked to wear something more suitable to a formal wedding. "I have to wear this," she insists, "because it's what's 'in.'"

Brianna's decision: _____

Hiroshi, sixteen, is told he is to have his own clothing money and to present a budget. He refuses because he knows he can get more clothes by asking for things as he wants them. His parents back off.

Hiroshi's decision: _____

For the following scenarios, think about the decisions each of these adults may have made as children.

Olivia, twenty-two, "can't" wear the clothes she bought last year because they are no longer in fashion.

Olivia's childhood decision: _____

Anthony, thirty-five, can't find what he wants to wear because his closet is too crammed with clothes, so he buys more. He gets them at discount store closeouts at fabulous prices. His credit card? Maxed.

Anthony's childhood decision: _____

Anna, forty-seven, only feels wonderful in a garment the first time she wears it. After that she feels less special. "This is old," she says, "I've already worn it." Every closet in the house is bulging with her clothes.

Anna's childhood decision: _____

If you were right about the decisions these people made as children, how might that play out ten years from now? Twenty-five? Listen to the voices of three overindulged people.

Do you overindulge yourself?

Sometimes. I'm thinking of clothes. I know I have so many more than I need and I hardly ever wear anything out. My reasons? It's fun and doesn't cause a financial strain. But, as I think about it, I lose the specialness that comes from having a new outfit. Sometimes I'm not satisfied. It can seem that I "never" have the perfect thing to wear. And I realize that this was probably the area of my childhood (as a teen) that I was overindulged by my parents.

Do you overindulge yourself?

Sometimes. My weakness is running up my charge cards then paying them off and starting again. I use everything I buy but I really do not need so much stuff.

What is the result of that overindulgence in your life?

I pay my own bills but it would be nice if I didn't have the bills that completely drain my paycheck so that I have a hard time saving.

Do you overindulge yourself?

Often. Overindulging myself is part of my modus operandi. I do it with clothes, food, everything. Not that I like it very much—the overindulging wreaks havoc by making me feel that I can't control my life.

THREE PARENTS WRESTLE WITH THE TOO-MANY-CLOTHES MONSTER

Consider the following parenting strategies.

Thirty-two little dresses

Little Alyssa is the first granddaughter on both sides of the family. Finally, a chance to buy those dear little dresses. Aunt Emma, visiting from out of town and planning to send a dress after her visit, peered in Alyssa's closet to see what was needed. There they were, thirty-two little dresses, each on its own tiny hanger, clean and neatly arranged. Lace, rosebuds, smocking, ruffles, pleats, a sailor collar. Aunt Emma approached Alyssa's mom, "Jennifer, tell me about Alyssa's dresses."

Jennifer giggled, "Aren't they darling? They are all gifts!"

"That's great, but I notice Alyssa is in comfortable, practical play clothes."

"Well, I keep track of who sent the dresses and make sure Alyssa wears that one when she is going to see the person who sent it. I thank the giver and encourage Alyssa to do the same."

"What a good idea. I was going to send a dress, but I guess I'll look for a book."

Jennifer giggled again, "Thanks, big time!"

If Jennifer consistently uses firm structure about care of clothing, what kind of decisions is Alyssa likely to make about caring for her own clothing? And about her appreciation of gifts?

Gussy up

Belinda keeps one dressy outfit for each of her three children ages four, six, and nine. Belinda chooses the outfit. When the child outgrows the outfit, it is replaced. When the occasion calls for it, Belinda makes an announcement: "Today we go to Grandma and Grandpa's anniversary party. This is a day to gussy up so wear your dressy clothes, the ones in the zipper bags. Since we will stop at a park on the way home, put play clothes in your backpack so you can change in the car."

If Belinda is consistent about this way of teaching appropriate dress, what skills are the children likely to develop?

Wardrobe planning

Abigail has been helping choose her own clothes for three years. Interested in colors and color combinations, she also loves organizing things. Now, at age twelve, she is sure she is able to choose her wardrobe on her own and requests the money to do so. After consideration, her parents decide to give her money at the beginning of each season to cover underwear, socks, skirts, slacks, and tops. They find a bank that provides accounts with parents as co-signers so she will learn about writing checks and balancing a checkbook. Each season Abigail is to present her plan for approval, and one parent shops with and guides her. Her parents hold back the money for shoes, boots, coats and one dress-up outfit, which they choose with her help.

What lessons will Abigail probably learn? What will she learn about "enough?" What decisions might she make?

THE GOOD MOTHER'S SACRIFICE

What about spending a disproportionate amount of family income on kids' clothing? Children need adequate clothing, but parental sacrifices to clothe children better than the adults are clothed can make a child anxious, as Christina's British mother learned.

Christina, seven, announced to her mum that she was never going to grow up. Her single-parent mother, who struggled to provide for her three children and to help them grow up well, was taken aback. "Christy! Not grow up? Why ever not? Why do you say that?" Christina looked away. "You never have a new coat, Mum. We all get new coats. You never get one. I don't want to grow up." That day Mother made a Mum's New Coat label for an empty jar, set it above the sink, and started dropping money into it. "I thought I was being a good mum," she told a friend. "I had no idea about the message I was sending."

For this mother, who had not been overindulged as a child, it was easy to claim her good intentions and turn them in a more productive direction.

A GIFT FROM THE HEART

Mother was choosing needed undershirts for Mariah when the five-year-old noticed a Powder Puff Girl wallet. She wanted it. She "needed" it! She asked quietly and then demanded loudly.

Her mother did a quick mental survey. Could they afford it? Yes. Did Mariah need it? Five-year-olds don't need wallets. Anyway, Mariah already has the one her aunt had given her. Mom said, "No." Mariah wailed. Mom spoke softly but firmly. "You are acting spoiled. Stop it. We are going home." Mariah pouted.

That evening Momma and Poppa had a short consultation before Poppa told Mariah to get her wallet and they would go for a walk. As they moved in the direction of the neighborhood gift shop, his voice was matter-of-fact. "Mariah, I'm disappointed in you for giving your mom a hard time this afternoon about the wallet. You know you are supposed to be a helping family member, not a whiner." He reminded his daughter that tomorrow was her mother's birthday. He explained about gifts from the heart, and that he would help Mariah find a gift that her heart wanted to give her mom, and that it had to come from

Mariah's own money. She had $3.19, so they looked and looked. Finally Mariah found a beautiful eraser that she thought her artist momma would like and would use. It cost almost all of her money, and Mariah hesitated. Poppa asked her what her heart said, and she bought the eraser. On the way home her father didn't mention the whining, but told her that he was pleased with her decision. They played an animated game of stepping on sidewalk cracks.

At home, Mariah ran to her mom and apologized. Then she announced that she had a project to do and retreated to her room to custom-color her wrapping paper and create a birthday card.

What did Poppa teach? Think of the seven hazards of overindulgence:

❖ trouble learning how to delay gratification
❖ trouble giving up being the constant center of attention
❖ trouble becoming competent in
    everyday skills
    self-care skills
    skills for relating with others
❖ trouble taking personal responsibility
❖ trouble developing a sense of personal identity
❖ trouble knowing what is enough
❖ trouble knowing what is normal for other people

This poppa and momma offered a lot of learning in one day. Mariah made no further mention of the desired wallet, so she had caught her mother's displeasure and learned something about delayed gratification. The focus of attention was shifted from Mariah to someone else. Mariah got a beginner's lesson on shopping competently. Spending within her means was being responsible. And Mariah got reinforcement of her personal identity as one who is a contributing family member rather than a demanding, whiny consumer. Mariah could have had two wallets instead of all these important learnings. Lucky Mariah. Putting a child's needs ahead of her wants is the greatest gift parents can give.

THE UNINTENDED IMPACT

Some parents who were greatly overindulged as children do not have reliable bone-knowledge of how to be strong parents. For them, it is not so easy to change. They may have to look hard at some assumptions about who needs to be in charge of what in the family. In our research, the parents who were *highly* overindulged during childhood by being allowed to have any clothes they wanted also told us:

❖ The children make the decisions in our family.[1]
❖ Rules change in our family.
❖ I certainly feel useless at times.

Think about the implications of their childhood decisions on how these adults rear their own children. How can "getting any clothes I wanted" as a child contribute to a parental practice of letting children make the decisions in a family? Having rules be too lax? How could "getting any clothes I wanted" lead to feeling useless at times? Surely this is not what their well-intentioned parents wanted for them.

Putting a child's needs ahead of her wants is the greatest gift parents can give.

Those of us who have been providing lots of clothes, on the assumption that it will make our children happy and perhaps raise their self-esteem, may think again as we consider a possible undesirable, unintended legacy we may be creating for our children and their children.

HAPPINESS IS A WAY STATION
BETWEEN TOO MUCH AND TOO LITTLE.
—Channing Pollok

SO MUCH TO DO, SO LITTLE TIME

When I Was Growing Up, My Parents Over-Scheduled My Time

I CAN'T TALK NOW. I HAVE TO GO.
—A fifteen-year-old

𝒫ARENTS, recognizing that idle hands are the tools of the devil, and wishing to provide quality learning for their children, sometimes over-schedule them.

At Jack's house his dad and two other parents were bemoaning how little family time they share, how busy and tired they are, how seldom the family eats a meal together, and how heavily scheduled their children are. Jack's dad pondered, My son is in soccer, orchestra, chess club, debate, Boy Scouts, and he has a church group that meets every Wednesday night. If we were to limit our children's after-school activities, what's a good number? How about three? Yes, three activities would be an improvement. I want my son to have more free time.

At this point twelve-year-old Jack walked in. He paused behind his father, put his hand forcefully on his dad's shoulder and announced in a determined voice, "You can't limit me to three after-school activities. That's not nearly enough. Just forget it!"

Jack's heavy hand and demanding voice clanged a wake-up bell in his father's head. Dad decided to reassert his leadership, get back in charge of his family, and reschedule Jack so the family could eat meals together and so Jack could do his homework and his chores. Did Jack complain? Yes. Did Dad hold firm? Yes. Jack got to be in charge of some things, but Dad held the responsible adult power.

Is Jack a self-centered, spoiled child, or is he just reflecting local norms? In many schools and communities there is a plethora of activities for children of all ages. In some of those communities it is customary for parents to expose their children to as many activities as possible and for the parents to be involved. Some parents, if they can, not only attend every game, but also every practice. Some coaches schedule practices and games without regard for other school activities or for family needs. One coach we know scheduled soccer practice for Thanksgiving afternoon and several parents shifted Thanksgiving dinner from Thursday to Sunday!

In his books *The Intentional Family* and *Take Back Our Kids*, William Doherty warns that many families are over-scheduled outside of the family and under-scheduled inside the family.

The over-scheduling is not limited to grade or middle school. High school senior Alexandra regularly leaves the house at 5:45 A.M. for before-school dance line practice. After evening games or rehearsals or parties she gets home between 10:00 and 11:00 P.M. Then it is study time. No time for Alexandra to just hang out or to do chores at home. Remember, missing skills from not having to do chores was the most frequent complaint of adults who had been overindulged as children.[1]

Even though being with peers fits with the developmental tasks of adolescence, if Alexandra dropped one activity to let her get more sleep and to give her some unstructured time with family and friends and the opportunity to contribute to her family by doing chores, her life would be in better balance.

OVER-SCHEDULING AND PARENTAL PUSHING CAN START EARLY

Charra's mother scribbled on her clipboard as the teacher of the ballet class led the three-year-old children through a series of steps.

Mom made note of everything her little girl did not do perfectly and vowed to make Charra practice every move during the week so she would be "better than the other children" at the next lesson.

Zachary, age seven, had gone from school to a club meeting to swim team practice before his violin lesson at 6:30. Scolded by his violin teacher for not having practiced and for not trying, Zachary burst into tears. His mother decided that the teacher was out of line and vowed to find a teacher who was more "kid friendly."

Over-scheduling and over-emphasis on excellent performance can be harmful to children. Brad Steinfield in *Shedding Light on Mental Illness in Children*,[2] found that trying to excel at many activities instead of enjoying one or two may contribute to a child's mental illness.

Overindulgence? For each of these two examples, check the Test of Four.

1. Does too many activities or too much focus on perfection keep these children from learning **age-appropriate lessons?**
2. Do the activities consume an unbalanced amount of family **resources?** Time? Physical energy? Emotional energy? Money?
3. **Who** is the activity really for?
4. Does doing too many activities **harm** others?

Remember good intent. Charra's and Zachary's moms each wanted the best for her child. You can bet they did not get up in the morning and say, "Today I will push my little girl to an unreasonable level of perfection," or, "Today I will overload my son with so many activities that I risk pushing him toward mental illness." No, this is not what parents intend.

Zachary's mom needs to rethink her priorities and turn her good intentions toward freeing up his schedule. Give the kid a break! He's only seven. Charra's mom, with good intent, is out of sync with the needs of a three-year-old. Maybe Mom needs to be the one who is dancing. Mom's needs are important, too.

In his books *The Intentional Family* and *Take Back Our Kids*, William Doherty warns that many families are over-scheduled outside of the family and under-scheduled inside the family.

If the activities become more important than family relationships, children miss out. Rachael, fourteen, observed, "The best part of summers for me is the two weeks I spend on my grandparents' farm. At home, every day is filled with lessons or camps. At grandma's, we don't do anything special, just everyday stuff, and we talk a lot—about everything."

MY PARENTS OVER-SCHEDULED MY TIME

The study participants who complained about being over-scheduled listed activities such as lessons, camps, sports, clubs, church, and other organizations. Sometimes the activity was something they didn't want to do or were not interested in, but mostly the resentment was not about the activities themselves but about the number of them, the pressure of being too busy, and about not having any time for themselves.

Before we explore the issue of time, let's consider how seductive the offerings are. Look thoughtfully at your school calendar, your local community recreational calendar, your newspaper entertainment section. List all of the offerings that you think might be helpful or interesting for your kids. Ask your children to add to the list.

Here are the February activities the Schraders, a Minnesota family, listed as attractive to one or more of their children:

❖ downhill ski lessons
❖ cross-country ski lessons
❖ skating
❖ snowboarding
❖ skateboarding
❖ swim lessons
❖ swim team
❖ acrobatics
❖ ballet
❖ jazz dance
❖ tap dance

❖ babysitting lessons
❖ art classes
❖ musical instrument lessons
❖ musical group practices
❖ vocal lessons
❖ choir
❖ Boy Scouts
❖ Girl Scouts
❖ Campfire Girls
❖ children's theater

Add to the list the things their family already does regularly:

❖ nature walks
❖ trips to the zoo
❖ trips to the library

❖ regular attendance at temple
❖ temple youth group

- ❖ weekly visits with grand-parents
- ❖ shopping

Add the sometimes activities:

- ❖ ball games
- ❖ birthday parties
- ❖ holiday parties
- ❖ recitals
- ❖ movies
- ❖ weddings

Add the trips to the:

- ❖ dentist
- ❖ doctor
- ❖ eye clinic
- ❖ speech therapist

All of these things look good or useful or enjoyable. It's no wonder it's easy to slip into the overindulgence of over-scheduling. Add to this picture the fact that some parents grew up in situations where the schedules were light and there were no such things as "play dates." Some parents, when they were young, just went out after school and played. Every day. Those parents have no built-in experience with today's schedules. Their schedule was "Be home in time for dinner." Now, many of their children live in areas where it is not safe to say, "Yes, you can go out. Just be home in time for dinner." No wonder it is tempting to schedule children full-time just to assure their safety.

FREE TIME

"But," one parent asserted, "the time is there so why not fill it?"

Little Cynthia, when asked why she didn't want to do something, always replied with the insistence only a two-year-old (or the parent of a two-year-old) could muster: "Because I said. Because!"

That's why study participants needed free time. *Because they said:*

- ❖ I need time when I can decide what I want to do.
- ❖ I need time when I don't have to do anything.
- ❖ I need time to just hang out.

And those adults who grew up with that free time could add time to muse. Time to wonder. Time to notice. Time to see pictures in the clouds or the bare tree branches. Time to wonder if other people see colors the same way they do. Time to wonder about God. Time to dream. Time to think.

Time to Think

Enis was discussing a philosophical question with her husband. She remarked, "I've wondered about that ever since I can remember."

"You've said things like that before. You must have been a very intelligent child."

"I don't know about that. I grew up on a farm without playmates, and I had lots of time to think."

We're not suggesting you consider eliminating playmates; just consider putting balance in your family schedule.

LOOKING FOR BALANCE

The Schraders decided to try a backward approach. Instead of starting with the activity list, they started with the time available. They wanted to figure out how to schedule every day so there would be time for each child to:

- ❖ do chores
- ❖ do homework
- ❖ read
- ❖ chat
- ❖ hang out
- ❖ think

They realized they had become so habituated to being fully scheduled that whenever they had some free moments, they turned on the TV. What to do about that? How many activities to add?

Did they get it right the first time? Admittedly not, but they have learned a lot about listening to each other and about negotiating. The parents set as their goal that at least three times a week each child would have enough free time to ask him or herself, "What shall I do now?" And they cut way back on TV time.

A wise choice. David Walsh of National Institute on Media and the Family reports that the average American school-age child spends thirty-five hours a week in front of a TV screen. That is the equivalent of a full-time job. The only activity to which more time is devoted is sleeping.[3]

CHILDREN TAKE ADVANTAGE

When parents overindulge, do children take advantage of them to get what they want? The people in our studies said, "Yes, often." Jack, in the opening story, pushed hard for what he wanted. After all, children work with what the family system offers. Did children feel good about getting so much? Some did. Were there sometimes price tags for getting so much? Yes. Some children had to act in certain ways or keep secrets—sometimes very difficult, guilt-producing secrets. Many felt embarrassed or confused or ashamed. Listen to the following voices of overindulged people.

In Their Own Voices

Did your parents overindulge you because you knew how to manipulate them by being agreeable and appreciative?

Often.

Were there price tags or expectations in return for the overindulgence?

Yes. The overindulgence was a payoff for cooperation and it was to ensure I wouldn't leave the family. I was supposed to stay in the family.

Along with overindulgence, were there areas in which you didn't have enough?

Love. Time with parents.

When your parents overindulged you, what feelings resulted?

✓ I felt bad because the other kids made fun of me.

✓ I felt confused because it didn't feel right, but I couldn't complain because how can you fault someone who does so much for you?

✓ I felt angry when people gave me gifts that were meant for them.

✓ I felt bad because other kids didn't get what I did.

✓ I felt embarrassed because other kids didn't have stuff.

✓ I felt embarrassed because I knew somehow it wasn't right.

✓ I felt hurt because frequently my needs/preferences were not considered in my parents' gift-giving.

continued

Which messages do you think parents send to children when the parents overindulge the children?

✓ Don't grow up.

✓ Don't be who you are; don't be capable.

✓ The adult's needs are more important than child's needs. Child's needs are more important than adult's needs (depending on the type of indulgence).

✓ We can't both get our needs met at the same time.

✓ Love is conditional upon accepting the indulgence.

✓ Don't think for yourself.

✓ It is not okay to say "no."

✓ Don't expect clear boundaries.

✓ Don't ask for what you need.

Surely the mesages these people heard as children were not what their parents intended. As parents, we need to hang onto our good intent and make sure the impact of our behaviors is equally positive.

◼

GIVING CHILDREN WHAT THEY NEED IS IMPORTANT.
GIVING CHILDREN EVERYTHING THEY WANT IS DANGEROUS.
—Bernie Saunders

HOW MUCH IS ENOUGH?

I Don't Know What Enough Means

TO KNOW WHEN YOU HAVE ENOUGH
IS TO BE RICH BEYOND MEASURE.
—Lao Tzu

ENOUGH! *Go outside and play right now!* The noise level had risen steadily despite Mother's polite requests to turn it down. This mother was clear about when she had reached enough, but *what is* enough?

Enough does not stand alone. It is always used in reference to an amount of something, to this much or to less or more.

I DON'T KNOW WHAT IS ENOUGH

"I don't know what is enough" is a frequent complaint of adults who have been overindulged.[1] Their combined list is long. Enough money? Enough clothes? Enough toys? Enough electronic games? Enough food? Enough liquor? Enough speed? Enough cars? Enough work? Enough recreation? Enough sleep? Enough drugs? Enough friends?

Enough does not stand alone. It is always used in reference to an amount of something, to this much or to less or more.

Enough sex? Enough power? Enough control? Enough excitement? Enough practical jokes? The list goes on and on. Some people had one bothersome area, some two or three. Other folks carried the pain of an overriding sense of not knowing what was enough of anything. They could settle for too little or want too much, but they never felt sure that they had a healthy balance, the satisfying feeling of enough. One person said, "I am terrified of being empty." Another mourned, "I'm afraid I'll go to my grave without having lived half a day when I knew what was enough."

In Their Own Voices

In your adult life, do you have difficulty knowing what is enough or what is normal?

✓ Yes. Especially in relationships, I want so much from my partner.

✓ Yes. I buy more clothes than I wear, more books than I read, have a compulsion to have a decorator-perfect home for approval of others. I am a workaholic. Sometimes I think I don't deserve to play or rest because I haven't finished all the work.

✓ Yes. I especially don't know what is enough sexually, and in cooking proportions and liquor consumption.

Parents not only face the challenge of figuring out how much is enough for a particular child, but also: enough of what? Think about the five ways children like to have love expressed:

❖ physical touch
❖ words of affirmation
❖ quality time
❖ gifts
❖ acts of service

Gary D. Chapman and Ross Campbell, the authors of *The Five Love Languages of Children*, suggest that each child has a preferred way. So, the child that prefers touch may feel overloaded by gifts. The one who likes acts of service may find too many hugs phony. The lover of touch can accept words or quality time as acts of love if accompanied by a hug, a pat, a tickle, or, for some children, by wrestling.

But we can't make those distinctions until we understand what enough means.

TOO LITTLE, ENOUGH, ABUNDANCE, TOO MUCH

Try thinking about "Enough" by putting it on a continuum ranging from too little to too much. "Too little" is insufficiency. "Enough" is sufficiency. Occasional indulgence is part of abundance. Too Much indicates *over*indulgence. Write your own description of each word, or make your own definition. Be as general or as concrete as you like.

TOO LITTLE _____

_____

ENOUGH _____

_____

ABUNDANCE _____

_____

TOO MUCH _____

_____

Todd and Eva arrived at these general definitions:

TOO LITTLE is not having adequate resources to maintain health, life, or safety.

ENOUGH is having what is needed so you don't have to worry.

ABUNDANCE is having some extras that make life more enjoyable or exciting or interesting. It is having extra to share or give away.

TOO MUCH is having abundance so often or all of the time that you no longer appreciate it or enjoy it.

Grace wrote her examples about food and eating.

TOO LITTLE is having so little food that you lose weight, strength, and health.

ENOUGH is having the amount of food that keeps you healthy and your weight steady.

ABUNDANCE is having an occasional feast.

TOO MUCH is eating more than your body needs, not knowing when you are satisfied, eating when you are not hungry, eating to try to comfort sadness or fear, or to please someone else.

Nathan wrote about control and power.

TOO LITTLE is not being able to be in charge of your own life, letting others run it for you.

ENOUGH is having the control that you need to be able to do what is right for you and others.

ABUNDANCE is being able to get some things that you want in addition to what you need.

TOO MUCH is running roughshod over others.

Carol wrote about excitement.

TOO LITTLE is living a gray life, every day the same.

ENOUGH is having enough variety or new experiences to feel alive, stimulated, and challenged.

ABUNDANCE is having some really memorable peak experiences.

TOO MUCH is so much excitement that if life is calm you think something is missing and you go stir something up, even if you intrude on or hurt others.

You can ask everyone in your family to write their definitions and then compare them.

HOW DO CHILDREN LEARN ABOUT ENOUGH?

Unfortunately, parents do not have a list of ten things to do to teach a child what is enough. We teach, step by step, money management skills, how to set the table, how to build a birdhouse, how to drive a car, but we have no checklist to tell us that we have taught enough about "enough." We teach about "enough" informally. A bit at a time. As the situation arises. We know the children are getting the lesson if they play it back to us.

> **T**o be overindulged is not only to have more than enough. It is to have more than abundance.

Enough for Now

Christian, thirteen, was in an awesome growth spurt—four inches in one year. His arms grew longer. His feet grew bigger, even his skull was expanding. He frequently needed a whole new wardrobe from shoes to cap. One day his mom called his attention to a sale on jeans. "Christian, look at this sale. Do you need a new pair of jeans?"

"No, don't get any," he responded, "I have three pairs that are okay. You know they won't fit in three months and I'll need everything new again."

Christian was letting his mom know that he understood what constituted enough clothes for his current situation.

Enough for Me

At every family meeting the Petra family talks about family values, and that includes sharing what they have. Before every shopping trip a parent announces the rule for the day. *Today we get only what's on the list.* Or, *Today we can get one treat.* Or, *Today each person gets to choose a treat.*

Noah, age twelve, has recently transferred to a new school where there are many children who are overindulged with things. At family meetings he talked about some of the attitudes and behaviors of the kids who have so much. He ended by saying, "Thank you for not buying me everything I asked for."

Noah was letting his parents know that, not only was he getting a grasp on what is enough, but also that he could identify some of the hazards of overindulgence.

Enough to Share

Eight-and-a-half-year-old Ksenia and her big brother are being taught to handle money. Both have savings accounts into which they are encouraged to deposit some of their allowances and gift money. The children's parents are also encouraging sharing and learning about empathy. Back from a tour abroad and living in the Washington, D.C., area, Ksenia had seen the Pentagon many times from her mom's office window. On September 12, 2001, the day after the terrorist plane struck that building, with some good mentoring by their moms, she and a friend set up a lemonade stand on their suburban street. They collected $62.20 for the victims of the September 11 attacks. Her parents let her know they were pleased about her charitable contribution but didn't make a huge deal of it. Imagine their surprise when, in December, they looked at her Christmas wish list. The first item was a *toy*, the second *clothing*, the third was to give $60.00 to *charity*.

MOM: *To charity? You've already given your lemonade proceeds.*

KSENIA: *Yes.*

MOM: *Are you saying you have $60.00 to give to charity?*

KSENIA: *No, Mom. I don't have $60.00.*

MOM: *Are you saying that you want us to give $60.00 instead of spending that on gifts for you?*

KSENIA: *Yes, Mom. I'll have enough. It's all right, isn't it?*

MOM: *Yes, of course. I think it's wonderful. Do you know which charity you want us to give to?*

KSENIA: *No.*

After some discussion, this little girl decided that it should go to the Children's Hospital.[2]

We can guess that this child is getting a pretty firm grasp on several lessons. She is not only experiencing enough, but also being taught that she lives with some abundance. She has enough to share. Although her grasp of the level of family resources may not be completely accurate, we can guess that she has been told enough about what this game or those shoes cost to name an amount she thinks her parents could afford.

In the various places Ksenia has lived, she has seen children with too little. She knows she has enough. She is being taught to appreciate abundance by parents who worry about overindulging her and about playmates who seem to have too much. When Ksenia's mom was asked by a friend, "How did you do this?" she responded, "If you start teaching kids this early on, they pick up on it and make it their own."

THE SLOW JOURNEY OF LEARNING ABOUT ENOUGH

Exactly how do children learn about enough? Probably no adult could report "I learned it at precisely this moment." It is taught informally by family members, by friends, and by schools. It is taught by the shopkeeper who looks at the child's coins and says, "You don't have enough money for that toy." It is taught slowly with hundreds or thousands of repetitions.

Mom puts infant Elly in her crib: "Time for a nap. You have been up long enough."

Dad scoops up toddler Justin: "You and I are going into a quiet room for a rock and a song. You have had enough excitement for now."

Mom picks up the cookie jar and turns to two-year-old Grace: "You've had enough cookies. I'm putting them away."

While two-year-old Brandon visits Grandpa, Dad shops for groceries. On the way home Brandon points to a bag of food. "I want some cookies."

DAD: *Well, let's see. Did you have cookies or crackers at Grandpa's?*

BRANDON: *Yes. Cookies.*

DAD: *How many?*

BRANDON: *A few.*

DAD: *You have probably had enough cookies or crackers for today. Are you sure you are hungry now?*

BRANDON: *Yes.*

DAD: *I think since you have already had cookies that I'll cut up an apple for you when we get home.*

BRANDON: *I don't want an apple. Cookies!*

DAD: *No more cookies, honey.*

Brandon wailed the rest of the way home and Dad did not comfort or sympathize with him.

Auntie kisses three-year-old Lysetta: "Time to go to sleep. You've had enough stories for one night."

Grandma, in a store with four-year-old Ashia, says "We aren't buying that doll outfit today. I know you like it, but you have enough doll clothes at home."

Carrie, age five, wants to wear her sweater instead of her jacket. Mom agrees, "Yes, I think your sweater will be warm enough."

Dad is shopping for groceries with his eight-year-old son: "John, count out ten oranges. We want to have enough for the weekend."

Uncle calls to nine-year-old B.J., "Come out and play catch with me. You've been watching TV long enough."

Ten-year-old Haley loves to receive tiny gifts. In front of a store display of little ceramics she begs, "Mom, look how sweet these are. Please will you get me one?" Mom replies, "They are sweet, Haley, but not today. When we get home, go to your curio cupboard and think about the people who gave you all those little gifts. Think about how loved you are. You have enough for today. In fact, you have an abundance. Spend some time enjoying the beautiful things that you have and then come and tell me what you remember."

Leah, age eleven, has presented her parents with a long Chanukah wish list. The next day her father hands back the list tucked in the book, *Just Enough Is Plenty*. He looks deep into her eyes and says, "Tonight we read this book together, as a family, and talk about it. Then you can revise your list."

James, age twelve, is begging for expensive sports shoes. Mom calls a halt by saying, "After we get your jacket and jeans we'll see if there is enough money left in your clothing budget for those shoes."

HOW MUCH IS ENOUGH?

Austin, fourteen, is lobbying for a very expensive camera. Dad says, "No, I don't see you as responsible enough yet to take care of that expensive a piece of equipment."

Nathan, sixteen, wants his own car. Dad asks, "If I give you one, how will you earn enough money to pay for the insurance, gas, and repairs?"

Auntie says, "Come for a walk with me. I haven't seen enough of you lately."

The Baxter family had been discussing what is enough since the children began attending a school with affluent classmates who have many things. Mom found a book called *The Table Where Rich People Sit* by Byrd Baylor with wonderful pictures by Peter Parnall. In this story, the young daughter calls a family meeting to ask her parents to earn more money. Through an accounting system that puts dollar values on the abundance their mountain setting offers, little daughter comes to appreciate the wooden table. The Baxters don't live in the mountains so the story didn't exactly work for them, but over a period of weeks they were able to list the things they have enough of, and the many special kinds of riches their family has. They could write their own book. So could you.

"ENOUGH IS A LOVELY WORD"

In a workshop exploring the meaning of "too little," "enough," "abundance," and "too much," people were instructed to work in pairs. One person in each pair was given an empty paper cup. It was mid-afternoon so people were neither very full nor very hungry. Bowls of raisins, nuts, potato chips, grapes, crackers, corn chips, jellybeans, and tiny cookies were available on a supply table. The people with cups were to think carefully about exactly how much of which foods they wanted and to mark their cups. Their partners were to listen carefully to what was wanted, to fill the cup exactly as directed and to present it in a cheerful way. While the person with the cup munched, the pair talked about what it was like:

❖ To be asked to think about exactly what was wanted.
❖ To receive exactly what had been asked for, no more, no less, no substitutes.
❖ To be told exactly what would satisfy the partner's wants.

The sounds in the room were quiet, even peaceful.

The people who did the giving said things like:

> ❖ It was great to know I was doing what someone really wanted.
> ❖ It relieved me of the stress of guessing.
> ❖ I felt free. I knew I could succeed.

The ones who had asked and received gave a wide variety of responses.

> ❖ It felt normal.
> ❖ I was surprised. I've never been asked before.
> ❖ I loved it. I'd like to be treated this way all of the time.
> ❖ It was hard. I'm not used to thinking about what I want.
> ❖ I felt respected.

In the second part of the activity the partners who gave were secretly told to take the cups, fill them to overflowing, and then get their partners to eat the food using any persuasive method they could think of. They could plead, command, accuse them of being ungrateful, make them feel guilty, say they knew better, say they wouldn't like the other person, anything.

There were some raised voices. Some givers were loudly insistent. Some receivers were loudly resistant. When they discussed their reactions, the givers gave varied reports.

> ❖ It felt natural! I realized I do this all of the time. I'm shocked!
> ❖ I indulge you so I can indulge myself! Wow!
> ❖ I felt uncomfortable urging so much, but I got her to eat some.
> ❖ My partner was tricky; she tried to get me to eat it.
> ❖ I was surprised at how many ways I knew to urge him to eat more.
> ❖ I don't want to urge someone ever again. I got the feeling of how disrespectful it is.

The receivers had a lot to say.

> ❖ I hated it.
> ❖ It felt natural. This is how I grew up.
> ❖ It felt like I wasn't supposed to know what I know.
> ❖ It was hard to say no.

- ❖ This is what my whole family does.
- ❖ At first I resisted. Then I gave up. It was easier to eat than to resist.
- ❖ No wonder I don't know when I've had enough to eat.
- ❖ I'll never do this to my children again.
- ❖ I felt trapped.
- ❖ This felt so normal, it's scary.

THIS FELT SO NORMAL, IT'S SCARY

The emotional responses of adults to this simple exercise reminds us about how strongly we resent it when we realize we have been cheated of an important life lesson. Instead of being taught to know what was enough, some of these people had been taught the opposite: Don't realize when you have enough. Ignore what your body is telling you. Let others decide for you.

Overindulged children too often don't have the chance to know and identify what they need. They don't learn to trust that they know what or how much they need. Since they don't know what "enough" is, they can't experience abundance.

Overindulged children too often don't have the chance to know and identify what they need. They don't learn to trust that they know what or how much they need. Since they don't know what "enough" is, they can't experience abundance.

"ENOUGH" IS THE STEPPING-STONE TO ABUNDANCE

Abundance, that glorious experience that warms the heart, sends waves of satisfaction through the body, and lets the soul sing, is cut off and unavailable to any who do not know what is enough. What irony! When parents who want to provide abundance give so much that the children fail to learn what is enough, they develop a mind-set of too little, of scarcity, in the midst of plenty. The stepping-stone from too little to abundance is missing. Unformed. A treacherous hole. Consequently, abundance, unrecognized and unappreciated, not only fails to be satisfying but often becomes too little, a source of dissatisfaction, even a painful addition to the empty hole of scarcity.

Abundance depends upon enough. Look again at the descriptions of abundance:

ABUNDANCE is having some extras that make life more enjoyable or exciting or interesting. It is having extra to share or give away. If you don't know what is enough, you can't know what is extra.

ABUNDANCE is sometimes having a feast. If there is always more than enough, the word feast becomes meaningless.

ABUNDANCE is being able to get some things that you want in addition to what you need. If you can't separate needs and wants, how can you know if you have more than you need?

ABUNDANCE is having some really memorable peak experiences. If every day is an exciting high, the highs get flat and are never high enough.

If enough is judged by comparisons and someone else's standards, there may never be enough. When an adult's enough is based on internal values, the stepping-stone of enough is firm and a visit to abundance is easy to recognize. Not knowing what is enough and not being able to differentiate between abundance and too much was greatly troubling to many of the overindulged people in our research project.

In Their Own Voices

What childhood decision did you make that affects your life now?

✓ I am not enough. I will never be enough.

✓ I'm not enough. I need to work hard. Appearances are everything. I will never have enough. I need to be perfect.

✓ My Prince will come. I need to be taken care of. I'm not really all that capable of making a lot of money, and besides I don't need to, 'cause of my Prince.

✓ Girls are supposed to be overindulgent. I fear not having enough. Fear that I can't make it on my own financially. I need a man to give me security. The fears are subsiding and I'm moving on, but they still surface.

continued

HOW MUCH IS ENOUGH?

In your adult life do you have difficulty knowing what is enough or what is normal?

✓ Yes. When is there enough money?

✓ Yes. I tend to overdo everything—work, spending, acquiring things, talking, eating.

✓ I am terrified of being insatiable.

Do you overindulge yourself?

✓ Sometimes. Spending too much when I feel insecure. Eating too much when I feel insecure. Reading too many books at once (insecure). Acquiring things to not feel feelings.

What is the result of that overindulgence in your life?

✓ I always feel as if I'm searching for that one more thing that will be the answer. I'm never satisfied or at peace in the moment. I have a hard time believing I'll have enough money.

MONEY ITSELF IS NOT THE CLUE TO OVERINDULGENCE

It is easy to assume that overindulgence occurs more often in affluent families than in poor ones, but that's not the case. The people involved on our first study varied in age from eighteen to eighty, making it practical to compare income levels, so we asked them to compare their childhood family financial situation with the families around them. "More money than" doesn't tell us the family was wealthy. It tells us the child's perception.

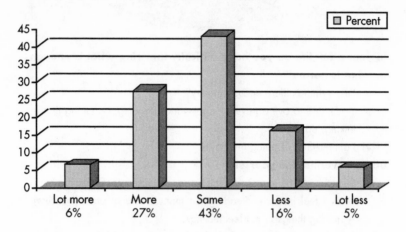

Money My Childhood Family Had Compared to Other Families[3]

| | Lot more 6% | More 27% | Same 43% | Less 16% | Lot less 5% |

We don't know if this distribution reflects the income distribution in the nation. It is interesting to notice that about the same percentage reported "a lot less" as reported "a lot more." But remember, overindulgence is not about money. It is not about old money or new money. It can occur in an affluent setting or in poverty. It is about "too much," over-nurturing, and soft structure. Enough can be taught in any family and overindulgence can happen in any family.

> **E**nough can be taught in any family and overindulgence can happen in any family.

THE CHALLENGES OF WEALTH

I Never Had Them

Katherine lamented: "I grew up with money. I had what they wanted me to have, but I never had them. I didn't like what I was given. One Christmas I wanted a $39.95 record player. I get seven other gifts I didn't want including a pair of pumps I couldn't wear. Now I mistrust anything that is given to me. It is time for me to get this solved."

Jealousy

Sydney confessed: "I was jealous of my wealthy cousin. I wanted a horse and she had a beauty. When I was visiting, her father brought home fifteen pairs of jodhpurs. He wanted her to wear a new pair at every competition. When I asked her if she liked competing, she just looked out the window. After that I didn't feel so jealous."

Entitlement

Dylan was overindulged by his wealthy grandfather who had promised him a Porsche for his sixteenth birthday. Grandpa died two weeks before the birthday and Dylan did not get his special car. He never forgave his grandfather for dying too soon. For him nothing was ever enough.

Having too much can mean nothing is ever enough.

You Can Afford It

When saying "We can't afford it" is out of the question, how do parents keep children from developing an overblown sense of entitlement? Giving children what they need, teaching money management, and instilling values of compassion, industriousness, and initiative can be especially challenging for parents who are wealthy. Acknowledging that wealth does not make parenting easier, advice about raising children of privilege often focuses on values. Advisors to wealthy parents say, "Create a family mission, vision, and values statement. Ask the hard questions: What am I worth as an individual? What are my social values? What is my accountability to the community I live in? How can I use the abundance I have in a responsible way for myself, others, the environment?"

Having too much can mean nothing is ever enough.

These questions all point to the issues of recognizing enough in the midst of plenty and of keeping a perspective of abundance without slipping into the entitlement of overindulgence.

Cynthia Iannarelli, owner of Business Cents Resources in Bridgeville, Pennsylvania, who works with families of privilege, says that well-adjusted wealthy children should know the following:

❖ marketing skills
❖ people skills
❖ leadership skills
❖ money skills
❖ self-starting skills

This is a good list of life-skills about handling personal and family resources for children of any income level, especially considering the persuasiveness of marketers. Children in the privileged class will need special lessons in each of these areas. For example, people skills need to include understanding and communicating with people of other social classes. Several books speak directly to helping parents handle children in the midst of wealth (See Recommended Reading on page 304).

THE DARK HOLE OF SCARCITY

When we hear stories about children of the rich and their exorbitant spending, or read a novel like *Twelve* (the story of young adults in Manhattan with way too much money) and its tale of scarcity in the midst of plenty, it is tempting to assume that overindulgence is the province of the rich, but if we fall into that trap, we risk confusing overindulgence with outright neglect.

Adults who grew up in any income setting and who missed developing the stepping-stone of "enough," who didn't learn enough about "enough" as children, can learn it now. Laurie Ashner and Mitch Meyerson's book, *When Is Enough, Enough?: What You Can Do If You Never Feel Satisfied*, is especially helpful for adults who want to capture Enough. They quote Rumer Godden:

> *There is an Indian belief that everyone is a house of four rooms: a physical, a mental, an emotional, and a spiritual room. Most of us tend to live in one room most of the time, but unless we go into every room every day, even if only to keep it aired, we are not complete.*

They suggest that spirituality is an important source of power for the never-enough thinker. One could have a solid sense of "enough" in the physical part of life, but be mentally bored, feel unloved, or be stumbling on the spiritual journey and wonder why the stepping-stone to the feeling of abundance isn't really there.

Each of us can ask the everyday questions: *Do I have enough or abundance in my physical life? In my mental life? In my emotional life? In my spiritual life? What shall I do to keep myself in balance?*

I WISH YOU ENOUGH

Enough of what? Enough of everything. The ability to know what is enough is one of the most important skills you can teach as parents. "Enough for now" is a crucial component in teaching children about delayed gratification, a skill many overindulged adults lack. Knowing what is enough supports good health; it protects other people and the environment, and it can be a bulwark against greed and unethical behavior. Listen to the folk wisdom in this old toast, and think about the abundance it attracts into a family that says it regularly.

"Enough for now" is a crucial component in teaching children about delayed gratification, a skill many overindulged adults lack.

I wish you enough sun to keep your attitude bright.
I wish you enough rain to appreciate the sun more.
I wish you enough happiness to keep your spirit alive.
I wish you enough pain so that the smallest joys in life appear much bigger.
I wish you enough gain to satisfy your wanting.
I wish you enough loss to appreciate all that you possess.
I wish enough Hellos to get you through the final Good-bye.[4]

ENOUGH IS AS GOOD AS A FEAST.
—P.L. Travers, *Mary Poppins*

THREE

SECTION

Over-Nurture

I WANT THE BEST FOR YOU

What Is Nurture?

NURTURE is the name of all the ways we care for others and ourselves. Children must be nurtured, or they do not survive. They must have food, clothing, protection, touch, recognition, and love. But too much nurture can smother a child's growth.

THE MOTHER-SAINT WHO SMOTHERED

Listen to what these two sisters had to say about being raised by a smothering mother:

> "People said our mother was a saint. I guess she was. She did everything for us. We kids always came first. She never thought about herself.

Today when you mentioned that you were studying overindulgence and asked if anyone in the group who had been overindulged during childhood was willing to be interviewed, we knew we had to come to you. But now it's so hard to talk about it."

"Yes," her sister agreed. We had a friend whose mother did everything but then she demanded that her daughter always look good, always make her mother look good, always tell her mother how wonderful she was. But our mother didn't do that. She did everything for us and we could do whatever we wanted. She was totally unselfish. She wanted us to have everything. How can you complain about somebody like that?

"Then what did you come to tell me?" the overindulgence researcher asked.

"Well, it doesn't work. You see, sometimes we wanted to do things for ourselves. Sis, do you remember the time you wanted to learn to make doll clothes and when we got up in the morning Mom had stayed up late and made a whole new outfit for your doll?"

"Yes," the other sister said. It isn't just about remembering the past and what we didn't get to do. It's about now, too. Sometimes I think I play too much bridge instead of taking care of my family. I don't want to do it the same way Momma did, but I don't know what to do instead. So sometimes I just stay away from home.

Sometimes when we get together we cry and we're not even sure what we are sad about. It's so hard to talk about. We made each other come to you."

The interview with the sisters lasted a long time. They poured out their story, asking again and again if they sounded silly or selfish. At the end they told the interviewer how relieved they felt to have finally talked about it, and how she was the first person who had ever listened.

IT'S TIME TO LISTEN

It's time to hear that what looks so good can often feel really bad. The sisters were the first of many volunteers who came forward to talk about this type of overindulgence. Almost every interview ended with the same message: *You are the first person who ever listened.*

Now the time has come for us, all of us, to learn to listen. That is the first step in healing. And it's time to learn more about overindulgence so you can learn how to listen with empathy and without judgment.

These sisters grew up with the burden of over-nurturing, of living with a mother who over-functioned so much that she inhibited their abilities to function for themselves. This is sometimes called over-loving, but what looks like too much love is really too much attention or doing too much for someone. It's nurture gone overboard.

TRUE NURTURE

Nurture is half of the parenting sandwich—the half without which we die. The other half is structure, which we discuss in chapters 15 through 22. But we start with nurture, the soft side of care. Nurture is all the ways we provide for the soft needs; love, touch, warmth, attention, support, stimulation, recognition, and response. True nurture is about one's being, one's right to exist and to have one's needs met. It does not need to be earned. It has no price tag. It does not have to be paid for by obsequiousness or obedience. True appreciation and responsiveness will naturally grow out of it, and obedience, made easier by the strong connection that true nurture fosters, is the province of structure. Nurture forms a bond with the nurturer that helps a child feel grounded and sure of him or herself. It is a loving gift from the caregiver. It enhances self-esteem.

> **N**urture is all the ways we provide for the soft needs; love, touch, warmth, attention, support, stimulation, recognition, and response.

LEARNED INCOMPETENCE

Think about the sisters and recall the Test of Four criteria for identifying overindulgence.

1. Did this situation keep the sisters from learning age-appropriate developmental tasks? Yes, indeed.
2. Did it use an inordinate amount of family resources? Yes, Mother's time and energy.
3. Who was it really for, the mother or the girls? It denied the girls' needs so it must have been for the mother. This is not to imply

that the mother intended to harm the girls. It is somehow as sad for her as for the girls.

4. Did it do harm to someone, society, or the environment? It may be harming these grown girls' families.

The sisters clearly identified that their stress as children and as adults was about not learning how to do things for themselves, about not mastering some of the developmental competencies. In their case it amounted to learned incompetence.

It is the nature of human beings to become competent. Listen to the young child say, *Can I do that? Can I help break the eggs, stir the batter, water the plants, open the box, put the toy together, pound the nail, make the doll clothes?* The sisters, instead of learning how to be competent, had to settle for learning how to be incompetent.

This learned incompetence is especially damaging to a child's self-esteem. The authors grieve the unintentional subversiveness of the self-esteem movement that started as a healthy push to encourage children to feel lovable and be capable and, lamentably, was turned into an overindulging, feel-good debacle. Actually, self-esteem is not just about feeling good. One's self-esteem may be highest when the situation is grubby, but the person feels worthwhile, strong, and able to cope. Self-esteem is important. It is related to both competence and a sense of self-worth. Over-nurturing, too much attention, and doing too much for children are sure ways to damage a child's self-esteem.

OVER-NURTURING EQUALS OVERINDULGENCE

In this section we explore how nurturing can become over-nurturing, how over-nuturing becomes overindulgence, and how, even though it may look good, it keeps children from becoming successful and self-confident. The impact on the child who receives this overprotective kind of care does not match the good intent of the one who supplies it.

Overindulging by over-nurturing is doing too much of a good thing. It is a smothering kind of care. It keeps the child from becoming competent and it also puts the child at risk of becoming self-centered and spoiled.

The four outcomes of over-nurturing we discovered are:

1. confusion about what is enough
2. trained helplessness
3. confusion of wants with needs
4. believing and acting as if one is the center of the universe

In our studies, over-nurturing was consistently noted as occurring in four ways:[1]

1. When growing up, my parents did things for me that I could or should do for myself.
2. When I was growing up, my parents were over-loving and gave me too much attention.
3. When I was growing up, I was allowed lots of privileges.
4. When I was growing up, my parents made sure that I was entertained.

Learned incompetence, whether slight or pervasive like that of the sisters, must be carefully taught by doing too much for a child. Let's explore that first.

YOU CAN'T PROTECT CHILDREN FROM LIFE BECAUSE, IF YOU
DO, THEY WON'T LEARN HOW TO LIVE IT.
—Delphine Bowers

I'LL DO IT FOR YOU

*When I Was Growing Up,
My Parents Did Things for Me
that I Should Have Done for Myself*

GOD GIVES FOOD TO EVERY BIRD,
BUT DOES NOT THROW IT INTO THE NEST.
—Montenegrin proverb

LESSONS FROM NATURE

Young Samuel watched, fascinated, by a butterfly's struggle to get out. With the intent of being helpful, the boy cut away the chrysalis. But, to his dismay, Samuel's butterfly, released from its struggle, couldn't fly!

Often, for good reason, we do things for children that they can do for themselves. We may be in a hurry, or maybe they are stressed, or today we want something done in a certain way. Helpful, loving reasons all. So we dress the child or make the bed or do the chore or make the phone call. But, if we do that too often or too long, we keep our children from flying.

WHEN WE DO TOO MUCH FOR CHILDREN

Overindulgence by over-nurturing occurs when a parent consistently does things for a child that the child is developmentally capable of doing for himself.

* Ask your dad for help with math homework and he completes the whole page of problems.
* Mom rushes to school when you tell her a teacher is being unfair.
* As a teenager, you forget your project on the kitchen table. It's due today, and your mom brings it to school without your asking.
* Dad complains of having to engage in extraordinary means to get you out of bed in the morning.
* You live at home at the age of thirty-one, have a good job, and pay no rent. Mom does your laundry, cleans your room, and prepares your meals. You take out the garbage only when asked.

Over-nurturing gives the child a message that she lacks the skills or abilities to solve problems and act wisely on her own behalf. When parents over-function for a child able to function for herself, the child tends to under-function. As the parent tries harder, the child's efforts fall back. Over-nurturing is a sure way to create trained helplessness and learned incompetence.

There are many ways that well-intentioned adults do things for children that they should do for themselves. Some instances of over-nurturing look benign, others extreme, but they all deprive children of chances to learn how to care for themselves and others.

Overindulgence by over-nurturing occurs when a parent consistently does things for a child that the child is developmentally capable of doing for himself.

Sometimes the Parent Enjoys Playing with the Child

Noah was the youngest child and his mother was enjoying prolonging his babyhood. She made a game out of dressing him and they both enjoyed the fun. One morning when they were going somewhere Mom asked her son to put on his shoes. Noah climbed on a chair and waited. Mom asked Dad to put the shoes on Noah. Dad paused and questioned, "Aren't most three-year-olds able to put on their own shoes?" Mom's turn to pause. "I guess so, but I like doing it." As Dad went out the door, he winked at Mom and asked, "Do you plan to go to kindergarten with him?"

Startled, Mom told the lad to put on his own shoes. Her good intentions turned quickly from enjoying her child to helping him become competent. Would you believe a contest ensued and Mom ended up putting on the shoes? Oh, yes. Mom's habit held her hostage. She realized that she would have to do something to keep herself from helping. Her solution was to stop using the dishwasher in the morning. With her hands in the suds she could manage the pleading.

"Noah, put your shoe on."

"I can't."

"You're fooling me. I know you can."

"Don't want to."

"I hear that you don't want to, but it's time."

"You do it."

"My hands are wet. I'm busy. As soon as you have your shoes on, you can get a book for us to read." She busied herself at the kitchen counter until the shoes were on.

Mom maintained her loving position while she reassigned Noah's job from being helpless to being competent and put that ahead of her own need to enjoy a familiar game. She could find other games to play, games that encouraged her son to learn helpful skills.

Sometimes the Parent Over-Cares from Love of Caring

Dalia loved nursing her infant. She offered the breast to the baby even when he had not fussed or rustled or cried.

Dalia was depriving her tiny boy of the opportunity to let himself know what he needed, to learn how to signal his mother, and to decide he can be competent to get care when he needs it. Of course, he isn't thinking in big words like "competent," but recent research on how children learn has revealed astounding information about how much and how fast learning occurs. In *The Scientist in the Crib*,[1] Alison Gopnik and co-authors describe the important life lessons children learn from normal interactions with their caregivers. The child, from the moment of birth and before, is a magnificent learning machine!

HOW MUCH IS ENOUGH?

Sometimes a Parent's Enjoyment of a Child's Cuteness Leads to Blindness

Ian's job was to be cute. As an infant, he was adorable. As a two-year-old he used the twinkle in his eyes to do as he pleased and get his mom to laugh at how cute he was. At three he ignored directions to stop, or come, in such an innocent and engaging way that both parents chuckled. They did everything for him. They picked up his toys, wiped up the milk he poured on the floor, vacuumed his trail of crumbs, and then complained of being tired. When he was told not to pick up a fragile object he did so with exaggerated care. Dad laughed and changed the directive to "Carry it gently then."

When the grandparents came to visit and were not entertained by Ian's constant string of misbehaviors, they consulted about what to do. Ian had not received enforced Nos from eighteen months on. His misbehaviors had not been blocked by adults who expected him to learn appropriate behaviors. The grandparents decided on a way to ask their children to change.

"We know you both love Ian. We do too. Very much. We notice that he has become very, very good at being cute, but we wonder what will happen when people outside of the family don't find him cute, just irritating. How will that be for him?" The parents were shocked. They hadn't noticed that their adult friends were beginning to see them only when Ian was not present.

Loving intent, unfortunate impact. Ian needs a new job. Being cute is not enough. If his parents can't figure out what that new job is, they can call for help. Raising a child is too complex a job to be done by two loving people who have become blinded by cuteness. We all need a village to help us raise our children.

Sometimes a Parent's Unchecked Anger Blocks a Child's Growth

Umpire Bryan was appalled when a dad jumped him after he called a strike on a seven-year-old Little Leaguer. It took three other dads to pull the angry parent off, while the frightened young batter peed on home plate.

A chance for a boy to learn in a natural and safe way how to handle the umpire's call was replaced by a fearful, unsafe, and very confusing episode.

Sometimes a Parent's Pride Leads to Interference

Aunt Berta was questioning Eduardo about his science project and all the awards he had won. Stepfather, a scientist himself and bursting with pride and love for this boy, answered every question.

Eduardo got to bask in the pride. He did not get to organize his thoughts, give coherent answers to the questions, and get direct strokes from his aunt for his responses. Eduardo learned to be passive. He missed the chance to think for himself and to strengthen his connection with his aunt.

Sometimes Parents Don't Notice a Growing Pattern of Over-nurturing

Helping a child in an emergency is supportive. Responding to repeated last-minute requests signals over-nurturing.

Family members were seated at the table eating dinner when Amber announced that she had to be at a special student council meeting at 7:30, and she was to bring two dozen cookies. Glancing at the clock, her mother hopped up from her unfinished meal, and started to measure flour for a batch of chocolate chip cookies.

"I hope we can get you there on time. I have asked you again and again to tell me the day before when you need to take something to school."

Amber, with an arrogant toss of the head, continued to eat.

A guest quietly asked, Couldn't she buy them?

Mother shot back, "They don't taste as good, and besides, that costs more."

This was not an isolated incident. It is regrettable but not surprising that when this over-functioning mother became aged and infirm her daughter continued to under-function and neglected to be aware of her mother's needs.

Sometimes parents do things for children out of a mistaken notion of what is good for children.

Rachael as a ten-year-old was interested in learning household skills. She taught herself to make her bed and did it regularly without reminding. This is a normal age for children to be expected to make their beds.[2] But Rachael's mom, intending to be the best mom possible, started saying, "Don't make your bed today. Go and have fun. You're only young once."

Rachael's family job assignment was to have fun. Eventually Rachael stopped trying to learn household skills and became very good at having fun. As an adult she lacked automatic housekeeping skills, which frustrated her and her family.

Patrick had a similar problem. When his bride objected to his habit of dropping his clothes on the floor, he acted surprised and said, "Well, you can pick them up. A few weeks into the marriage, Patrick's mother called and asked,
"Does Patrick hang up his clothes?"
"Sometimes."
"Well, when he was a boy I asked him twice, but he didn't so I picked them up for him. You'll have to do that too."
Shocked, the bride hung up the phone, silently thanked her mother-in-law for the information, and determined never to hang up her husband's clothes, and never to mention it again, no matter how long it took him to catch on.

This man's mom thought she was being helpful. Her intent was good. The impact wasn't. Patrick eventually learned to hang up his clothes. We can learn childhood skills at any age, but it is often harder than if we learned them at the appropriate age
The parents' habit of over-nurturing can follow a child into adulthood.

Dad was deeply concerned that his son do well in college. In order to be supportive, the father called regularly, asking his son if assignments were in, telling him what hours to study, urging him to get tutoring. When his son, a good student, couldn't stop the calls, and finally failed a class, Dad couldn't understand what had happened.

Wake up, Dad! No matter that we are motivated by love and caring. Healthy nineteen-year-olds need to be figuring out how to be competent and successful. With support? Yes. But not with parents trying to manage their lives.

CARRY ME!

Over-helpfulness Can Delay Skill Development and Independence

"When I realized that there were several three- and four-year-olds whose parents carried them into the child-care center, I decided to observe them throughout the day."

Maria, the center director, frowned as she continued: "Compared to the children who walked in, the children who were carried seemed to be less responsible about other things. I noticed that they had also developed good skills of getting teachers to carry them. How they wind up getting an adult to carry them was specific to each child, but I noticed the ones who walked in on their own were more independent and seemed more confident throughout the day."

She added: "The ones who were carried seemed to accept less responsibility during center activities and clean-up time, and they were more apt to need help taking their coats off and hanging them up. Don't you think that's interesting?"

When asked if she had any hunches about why parents carried such big kids, Maria hesitated. "I hate to say this but those parents seem to have an inability to let their children grow up. Yet some of them are the very ones who want us to have reading and math worksheets in preschool."

TEST OF FOUR

Developmental Tasks?

Possible Harm?

Family Resources?

Whose Needs?

Is this a case of overindulgence?

1. Does it hinder learning **developmental tasks?** Yes, the preschool child needs to be learning to stand on his own two feet literally as well as figuratively.
2. Is it an appropriate use of **resources?** For the teachers, maybe too much energy and possible back strain.
3. Whose **need** is being met? Not the child's. Wanting worksheets in preschool is an example of over-nurturing by pushing the child to do tasks too early. Worksheets in preschool sends a hurry and

grow up message. Carrying the child, even if it's just to enjoy a last hug, sends a don't grow up message. Hurry and grow up/don't grow up becomes a double-bind. The parents have good intent but double-bind messages confuse a child. Parents can refocus their good intent on learning about their child's developmental tasks.

Center director Maria made a new ruling that all children walk on their own as soon as they are inside the building door. She also scheduled a parent information night on the developmental tasks of preschoolers and the ways the center is encouraging the learning of pre-reading skills and why those need to precede worksheets.

Another child-care director noticed that a teacher was over-nurturing children.

Her need to be loved by the children is too great. The children sense that and have become very demanding of her. She is so responsive that children do not try to meet their own needs. She spends the entire day responding to them. This results in their not playing with others or taking part in sustained play, and the children in her group seem to get into one difficulty after another around the center. I need to go into action!

Lucky teacher! Her director will suggest ways she can get the help she needs. Lucky children! The over-nurturing will be replaced by supportive structures that guide the children in play activities that provide rich learnings. For more information about the value of sustained play and why letting children invent their own play scenarios is so important, read *The Play's the Thing*.

You may ask, "But don't the children invite this over-nurturing?" Of course. Children learn to use whatever environment they are in. They not only ask, they demand. One child-care director commented, "The three-year-olds turn on the attitude or the water works, and they get what they want."

UNINTENDED IMPACT

Children can experience identity confusion if too much is done for them. They develop faulty beliefs about their being and conclusions about who they are:[3]

❖ "I am" becomes "I am because they care for me."
❖ "I am capable" becomes "I don't have to do, they do it for me."
❖ "I didn't do that well enough, I'll do it over" becomes "If they don't like what I did, it's their fault."

When the child does do something, and the adult says, "I've done that for you a hundred times, why didn't you do it right?" the child experiences a very confusing double bind: "I'll do it for you" and "Why on earth don't you do this for yourself?"

Over-nurturing can impede a teenager's identity development. Adolescents need to be dissatisfied with life as it is in order to go on their own life-vision quest.[4] They need to find a new identity and become responsible in many different ways. That's hard to do if they haven't become responsible at all.

If adults over-function (that is, do for the child what he should be learning to do for himself) they deprive the child of valuable life lessons:[5]

❖ He does not learn the skills of coping.
❖ He may decide that he can have what he wants because he wants it.
❖ He does not learn to take the needs of others into account.
❖ He may decide that he does not need to learn how to function, do things for himself, or consider the needs of others because he can expect and manipulate or bully others into caring for him. He develops strategies to keep people in his service.

WHAT TO DO?

If you notice that you have been keeping your children from breaking out of their cocoons by over-nurturing, you can:

❖ Gird up your good intent and direct it toward your child's developmental needs.
❖ Spread your nurturing around, take on a volunteer project, or get a puppy.
❖ Lovingly assess your own needs to help and feel important, and get them met in other places. One overindulged teenager remarked, "I wish my parents would get a life other than mine."

- ❖ Continue to help your children, and expect them to help you in return.
- ❖ Get some mentoring or counseling if over-nurturing is a long-standing habit and difficult to change.

Children learn skills and earn a place in the group by helping adults. We help children, but we also insist that they help us. Then we say, "Thank you for helping me. I see you are learning how to. . . . That's what we do in our family. We help each other."

CHILDREN, IT SEEMS, WILL TAKE ANY FAMILY JOB THEY ARE ASSIGNED, EVEN IF THAT JOB IS OF BEING HELPLESS.
—Russell Osnes

SMOTHER LOVE

When I Was Growing Up, My Parents Gave Me Too Much Attention

▪

NO MATTER HOW WELL INTENTIONED A PARENT IS, TOO
MUCH OF A GOOD THING IS NOT A GOOD THING.
—Kaye Centers

GRANDMA SPOILS THE BABY

*Her arms want to hold, her mouth wants to kiss, her whole being
wants to be in the service of this new grandchild. Lucky baby Grace
living close to her grandma, Victoria. Lucky Victoria having this wonderful first grandbaby to love. Grandma can hardly wait for Gracie's
visits.*

This works well for the first few months. The visits are short enough.
Victoria gets tired but not exhausted. As Grace grows older, the entire
focus stays on Grace every minute of her visit. With no effort to fold
her into her Grandma's activities or interests, Victoria gets more tired
as she responds to the every demand of a two-year-old whose favorite
words are "I want" and "Gamma do!" Sometimes Grandma feels

impatient, but she doesn't complain. Gracie's mom, however, does. "After a grandma visit it takes me a day or two to get Grace back to normal. She is whiny and demanding. When I say, 'You can't do that,' Grace sulks or screams. Grandma spoils her."

Is this spoiling? Yes, as the word is usually used in the Western cultures. But, be careful with the word "spoiling." In some families and cultures the word implies: "they take good care of me." One mother from such a country was pleased to dress her little boy in a T-shirt with the word Spoiled across the front, meaning "they take good care of me." In this chapter we are using the Western meaning of spoiled, like a rotten tomato. Spoiling a child means not expecting her to perform at her age and ability level.

Now, back to the grandma who is spoiling. Is she overindulging? What do we learn from the Test of Four?

1. Is Grandma's over-loving and complete availability preventing Gracie from learning crucial **developmental tasks**? Well—possibly not. Gracie's not with her grandma all of the time and Mom insists that Gracie do for herself the things she can do. The folks in our first study listed grandmothers as only 4 percent of their overindulgers.[1]

2. Is Grandma spending a disproportionate amount of family **resources** on one child? Money? No. Grandma's energy? Possibly. Mom's energy? Yes, Mom would like to be doing something other than sorting out Gracie's behavior after each visit.

3. Whose **needs** are being met? Does this constant time and attention meet Gracie's needs or Grandma's? Clearly this is for Grandma.

4. Is this situation **harming** others? You decide.

Is Grandma overindulging? Yes. She needs to expect Gracie to do what Gracie is capable of doing for herself.

Should we condemn her? Certainly not. Grandma knows that children need attention, she just doesn't realize she is giving too much of it. Her intentions are sterling, but the impact is spoiling. What can Gracie's parents do? Often in response to reasoned requests, a grandma can be convinced to redirect her love into setting a few

> **S**poiling a child means not expecting her to perform at her age and ability level.

boundaries and helping a grandchild become competent. At first the child may escalate, may become more demanding or even blaming of Grandma, but if Grandma is consistent, the child will settle down and be more agreeable. Children thrive on clear structure and feel safe when adults are firmly in charge. Soon, Grandma will be less tired and will be enjoying the child more.

This is overindulgence, not a serious case, but it is overindulgence. It would be very serious, however, if the situation were reversed. If Gracie were receiving daily doses of overindulgence at home and had only occasional visits with a grandma who was not focused on the child every moment and who was expecting the little girl to be learning to do things for herself.

SO WHAT IS ENOUGH ATTENTION?

It's enough to feel secure in the care of someone else, to feel supported but not patronized. Enough to feel encouraged to reach out and try things for him or herself. Enough to feel recognized and to build connections.

Strong connections with others are a healthy and sustaining part of life. Jean Illsley Clarke's book, *Connections: The Threads That Strengthen Families*, explores the many ways you can build life-supporting connections.

What is too much attention? Attention that robs a child of initiative. Attention that allows the child to believe he or she is the center of the universe. Attention that eventually lets the child's wishes run the family.

YOU WANT HIM TO BE HAPPY

Good parents want their child to be happy. But if that is your sole purpose, if you are unable to tolerate your child's frustration when he is thwarted or expected to accommodate to other people, you are apt to raise an unhappy tyrant.

From the beginning Jared was a fussy eater. His loving parents responded by stocking the few foods he liked and putting only those on his plate no matter what other people were eating. He liked to eat small amounts and so he ate several times a day between meals. Whenever he was grumpy his folks assumed it was because he was hungry and offered him food. Every feeding had to include at least one sweet, which his parents provided because they wanted him to be happy. He seldom agreed to try a new food and, when he did, if it was not sweet, spit it out as soon as it touched his tongue. If he didn't get what he wanted, his squalls were unbearable. At a restaurant he had to have some food as soon as he was seated. At age five his diet had not evolved and expanded, and he needed dental repair.

Overindulgence? Let's apply the Test of Four.

TEST OF FOUR

Developmental Tasks?

Possible Harm?

Family Resources?

Whose Needs?

Adverse effect on Jared's development? The need for dental repair tells us yes. Jared's parents were loving but they simply did not know that it takes many children two weeks to accept a new food. One nutritionist suggests:

Once a day put the new food on the child's plate and insist that he take one bite. At the end of two weeks if he has not accepted the food, stop offering that food for a few months. Watch for signs of allergies. Of course this method will not work if the parents and the child are in a control battle. Then the parents need to pull back their emotional energy.

TOO MUCH ATTENTION, TOO LITTLE CONNECTION

The Grandmother's Laments

"I didn't get to know my grandchild or to connect with her parents." Julia sighed. "The whole week they were at my house, baby Sophia's mother hovered over her. This was my first chance to get to know my granddaughter and I couldn't get near. All conversation was about the baby. The only thing I found out about my son and his wife is that they have given their lives to their child. They say it's because they both work and they want to spend every minute they can with her."

"I know," her friend sighed in reply. "And it doesn't necessarily get better. I spent a week with my daughter and her teenage children. The parents' total focus was on 'teen life.' Their music, their clothes, their sports, their tattoos, their friends, their schedules, their need for the car—right now. I came with so many things to tell or ask them. Nothing. My grandchildren don't know me any better than before I came and I scarcely know them any better either. I believe my daughter is trying to do the very best for the children, but I worry. They don't seem to know there is any world beyond their own, except maybe an outside world that inconveniences them at times."

Overindulgence?

Yes, these are clear cases of over-nurturing. Baby Sophia was being smothered, which kept her from getting to know her grandmother and from learning to comfort herself when the adults are talking with each other. The teens were allowed to be totally generation-centered. They did not gain understanding of their place in a multigenerational family, or expand their sense of family history. Adolescence is a time for reaching into the world, a time for creating some image of self as a part of that larger world. This total preoccupation with self and peers is not good preparation for the adult world. Lucky are the teens who do volunteer work with people of another class or culture. Or whose parents insist that they contribute within their own community. Or who are not so over-scheduled they have no time to hang out, to think, to dream.

Sports Parents

Infants and teenagers are not the only ones that are over-attended. Even the independent grade-schooler can be blanketed by smothering.

Jack liked sports and his parents provided every opportunity they could find to let Jack engage in or observe a sport. They took him to high school, college, and professional games. They attended his games and every practice they could manage. They kept track of his batting average and shared it with their entire e-mail list. He got every piece of sports equipment he wanted and some he didn't want. He was not expected to study if it would interfere with a practice or a game. His parents worried about his health, watched his diet, monitored his growth, and his mother regularly inquired if he was constipated.

The extent of Jack's parents' over-involvement and even intrusiveness into his life tells us the attention is to meet their needs, not his. Jack's age group needs to be growing in independence and responsibility, not the star center of the parents' world.

Attending Builds Connection

One of our basic human needs is a need for connection. That need is so strong that children will connect, or attach, to their caregivers no matter what quality of care is offered. Loving parents understand this so they bond with the baby and stay present and available but not smothering with the toddler and the preschooler. As the child grows and learns to trust that the parent is reliable, he will be able to move away and come back in increasingly independent ways. If parents hang on too tightly, this natural separation is inhibited.

WHEN THE THREADS OF CONNECTION BECOME ROPES THAT BIND

When parents nurture in an overindulging way, they intend to care for the child and to encourage self-esteem and to build a strong bond with the child. But what they end up doing is building a too-strong connection. The bond becomes a chain, a tether. Many of the people we talked to told us how much they loved their overindulgers, how they knew it came from a good heart, and often how beholden they felt. But still, they report being crippled by their early experiences.

> Life in the war-torn countryside was not easy. Sara's mother did the best she could. With a husband away in the war, the young mother gathered her infant daughter close to her bosom and moved in with her parents. Grandma and mother doted on this lovely little girl. During an interview Sara had identified that she had been strongly overindulged by her mother and grandmother. Grandpa sometimes intervened, but the tug of the connection with the mom grew stronger and stronger as the years passed, a bond that became a restricting band.

Later Sara wrote:

> *You asked me what I consider the consequence to me as an adult of overindulgence. In one word, I said, Narcissism.[2] But of course it's a difficult word to define. Another notion that*

became important is how difficult it was for me to become autonomous. I was independent, all right, capable of earning my living, managing under difficult circumstances, etc., etc. But autonomy is something else: an inner freedom that took years to gain, and of which I am still not quite certain.

I believe I leaned over backwards in raising my children, perhaps overemphasizing independence and holding back manifestations of love. Nowadays I believe I overdid it.

By coincidence yesterday I picked up Fraud *by Anita Brookner (Random House, 1992). Although it's about a contemporary Englishwoman, Anna Durant, the style is reminiscent of Jane Austen, and Anna's life, as described, corresponds more to that of someone of my generation in Europe; it couldn't have been in the U.S! Here in America the characters described and their standards are totally anachronistic, but they are very reminiscent of all I was raised with. Though well-written, it is a boring book; hardly anything "happens" in it because it describes precisely the uneventful life of a fifty-year-old "spinster" who was overindulged and caught up in a symbiotic bond with her mother.*

A gray life? Certainly that was not what Sara's mother intended. Safe, yes. Boring, no. Clearly Sara's mother's motivations were noble. She loved her little girl and wanted her to be happy. But the price tag for Sara was a too-strong connection with her mother, and this resulted in Sara's having great difficulty claiming her place in life as "a person of worth."

INDIVIDUAL RESPONSES TO OVERINDULGENCE

Sara's story reminds us that children's responses to overindulgence are individual. They depend on the specific situation, the content of the overindulgence, and the temperament of the child. The conclusions and decisions the child makes will be specific to that child. Sara reported that she became very capable, but that's not always the case for children who have been overindulged.

Many parents who reported, "When I was growing up my parents were over-loving and gave me too much attention," also agreed with the following statements.[3]

❖ One of my problems is that I cannot get down to work when I should.

❖ If I can't do a job the first time, I do not keep trying until I can.

❖ When I set important goals for myself, I rarely achieve them.

❖ When I have something unpleasant to do, I don't stick with it until I finish it.

❖ I do not seem capable of dealing with most problems that come up in my life.

Note: The above bulleted items are reproduced with permission of authors and publisher from: Sherer, M., Maddux, J. E., Mercandante, B., Prentice-Dunn, S., Jacobs, B., & Rogers, R. W. "The Self-Efficacy Scale: Construction and Validation." *Psychological Reports*, 1982, 51, 663-671. © Psychological Reports 1982.

One person told us that having too much attention had given her a basic mistrust of people. Now, if someone starts to get close to her it echoes the old smothering, and she pushes them away. "It's like I can't breathe. So when I like someone I find some flaw and use that as an excuse not to get to know them better."

What a woeful set of self-observations. Surely the parents or grandparents of Grace, Jared, Sophia, the teenagers, Jack, and Sara did not intend to set their children up for such serious problems in their adult lives. But good intent is not enough. Loving parents must contain their wish to attend to children's every whim and must allow children to experience the normal frustrations that come with giving up their positions as the center of the universe.

As parents we must learn to tolerate children's discomfort at times so they can gain the important lessons about how to trust themselves and others, how to take their places in groups, and how to become capable.

FATHERING AND MOTHERING ARE GREAT FOR KIDS.
HOVERING IS NOT.
—Deane Gradous

THE LITTLE PRINCE AND PRINCESS

When I Was Growing Up, I Was Allowed Lots of Privileges

■

"I AM THE PRINCE"
THE SMALL BOY SAID
AND STAMPED HIS FOOT
AND SHOOK HIS HEAD
AND WOULD NOT, WOULD NOT GO TO BED.
—Anonymous

𝓟RIVILEGES are enigmatic. A privilege is the right to do something. If children grow up with too many privileges that they have not earned, or that carry no obligations, they can grow up to be a pain in the neck. Without invitation or permission some of them have been known to:

❖ walk in any door
❖ interrupt a meeting
❖ borrow anything
❖ change the channel
❖ ask a stranger a personal question
❖ break any appointment
❖ open someone else's mail
❖ barge into any conversation
❖ call a friend in the middle of the night

- sit down, uninvited, with a group of acquaintances at a restaurant table
- rearrange a cupboard or a drawer in someone else's home or office
- break something of a friend's and not report the breakage
- break into a conversation
- tell a stranger who is shopping what to buy
- break any interpersonal boundary

We're sure you can think of many more examples of unearned privileges, but first let's consider the positive value of earned privileges.

EARNED PRIVILEGES

An earned privilege is granted in recognition of demonstrated competence. It doesn't involve overindulgence.

- Now that you have your certificate, you are qualified to apply for these kinds of jobs.
- Since you have passed your test and acquired your driver's license, you can drive without a licensed adult in the car.
- Now that you have passed the test for beginning swimmers, you can take the intermediate class.

We honor children and encourage accomplishment and responsibility by celebrating these new privileges. An open house party for relatives and friends recognizes the graduate. A family dinner featuring a special cake with a toy car perched on top celebrates the newly licensed driver. A new set of swim fins honors the young swimmer's achievement.

UNEARNED PRIVILEGES

Some privileges are not earned. We honor children on their birthdays, signaling that we are glad they are alive and that they are entering new areas of competence. However, if the parent provides not one small favor but a bag of candy, toys, and games for each child who attends a birthday party, why do the guests get that privilege? How big does the birthday child's gift need to be for him to feel special?

When little sister wants to blow out the candles and they are re-lit so she can, what is the message to the birthday boy? When younger children are allowed to rip the wrappings from big brother's gift, what is the implication?

This is a kind of well-intentioned over-nurturing that teaches the small guests what? That they deserve a gift because someone else has a birthday? This is an unearned privilege. It not only discounts the one being celebrated, but it also deprives the guest children of the opportunity to learn that they can let someone else be the center of the universe for a little while. That is a first step for children in learning the vital lesson that the world does not revolve exclusively around them.

Overindulging with too many unearned privileges becomes an insidious form of over-nurturing.

WHEN YOU MAKE YOUR CHILD TOO SPECIAL

Children who have too many unearned privileges can develop an overblown sense of entitlement.

> Five-year-old Devin has been made to feel so special that he feels entitled to be the center of attention at all times and to interrupt whenever, whomever he pleases. The engaged couple, planning their wedding guest list, decided not to invite Devin or his cousins because they all expected to be at the center of attention and the adults let them. The couple explained, "We love these kids, but we want the adults to have a good time and to talk with each other. These adults let the kids dominate and we don't want that. We want this to be our wedding."

These children will miss the opportunity to be part of an important family ritual because they haven't learned to sit still, be quiet, and to stay on the periphery of someone else's limelight.

They are already missing skills in self-management and learning respect and empathy for others. They suffer from the lack of parental coaching necessary for children to learn self-regulation of their emotions as John Gottman describes in his helpful book, *Raising an Emotionally Intelligent Child*.

> Ten-year-old Denise "knows" that she "deserves" to have her own TV and computer in her room, and that she can come and go when she pleases. Denise gets lots of privileges because she is manipulative and

her parents are charmed by her cleverness. If they demur, she nags and they give in. Denise's parents buy what she wants, lament the money spent, and sigh that raising children is expensive these days.

Both Devin and Denise are in serious need of lessons on delayed gratification. Delaying gratification, not getting something as soon as you want it, is a mark of emotional maturity.

A recent research study found children reported nagging an average of nine times before their parents gave in.[1]

THE ABILITY TO DELAY GRATIFICATION

That ability to have a want or a wish and be able to wait to have it met is an internal strength that is taught slowly beginning in infancy.

- ❖ "I know you want your bottle, but you will be okay until your milk warms."
- ❖ "No, you can't play with the puppy while he is eating."
- ❖ "I see that you like that toy. Your birthday is coming soon. Maybe you will get one then."
- ❖ "You can ride your bike after your chores are done."
- ❖ "We'll talk about your having a car when you can pay half of the insurance."
- ❖ "It wouldn't be wise for me to help you buy that house. Think about what kind of monthly payments you can handle now. It looks like a starter castle."

Do these delays in gratification cause frustration? Probably, but children cannot learn to handle their feelings and act on them in appropriate ways if they have never felt frustrated. Without the ability to delay gratification they lack one of the skills needed for feeling in control of their lives and for functioning well in society. They are set up to manipulate or exploit or come unglued instead of planning, sharing and cooperating.

It may not be easy for a parent to stand the child's discomfort, but it is a parent's obligation to foster the child's ability to delay gratification. Think of it this way: It is every child's right to have some discomfort and learn to handle it.

A recent research study found children reported nagging an average of nine times before their parents gave in.

THE HAZARD OF BEING TOO SPECIAL, TOO PRIVILEGED

Grandma understood the dangers of being too special. When her granddaughter swore at her, Grandma's eyes flashed and her voice was sharp. "No one speaks that way in my house. If you continue to speak that way, you may not come here any more."

Kaitlyn's eyes flashed back. "I can, too. I am your granddaughter. I can always come here and I can say anything I want to."

When a child or anyone mis-behaves, keep the discomfort where it belongs—with them.

Grandma's eyes went steely. "No, you can't. Being my granddaughter does not give you the privilege of swearing at me. You follow the rules at my house when you are here. You are not welcome here until you make a genuine commitment to following my house rules."

Loving someone does not mean condoning self-defeating behavior. Lucky Kaitlyn. Her overblown sense of entitlement, if not checked, could get her in big trouble. Her overprivileged expectation was blatantly displayed. But sometimes, when a privilege has gone on too long, the signals are more subtle. David's grandma didn't catch it as soon.

Every birthday since he was two, David's grandma had made an elaborately decorated railroad-train birthday cake, one car for each year, each car a separate cake, carefully linked with licorice sticks. She loved doing it and Grandpa, proud of his wife's baking expertise, encouraged her. Little David was delighted with his special cake, a candle on each car.

By age six he seemed to be taking the gift for granted. He barely said thank you. At seven, David almost ignored the cake and no one said anything about his inappropriate behavior. Grandma was wondering if it was worth it. As the eighth birthday approached, Grandma was engrossed in her gardening and really didn't want to schedule her time around making the cakes. But Grandpa intervened: "It's a tradition. It's a ritual. And you do it so well. Surely you can find time."

Grandma felt resentful, but she acquiesced. She did, however, change the train to make it easier for her. She made the usual fancy engine but added only four cars with two candles on each. At the party, after balloons and presents, and games and more presents, Grandpa brought in the cake, candles glowing.

David exploded! "Four cars! You are making me into a baby. I'm

114

eight! I'm not going to eat any of your old cake!" He jabbed the serving knife into the elegantly iced engine, knocked it off the tray onto the table and stomped out of the room. The adults said nothing.

What happened? David felt inappropriately entitled to the cake. And when he didn't get what he expected, he felt entitled to be rude and violent.

Let's apply the Test of Four to David's situation:

1. **Developmental tasks?** David was not learning appropriate relationship skills, like the skills of showing appreciation and controlling his temper that can be expected by age eight. We can only guess that he was being overindulged in other areas by being allowed to remain the center of the universe, a position that should have been addressed firmly when he was two.
2. Over expenditure of family **resources?** Yes. Grandma resented the demands on her time.
3. Whose **needs** were being met? Grandpa's.
4. **Harm?** Grandma was stressed and family relationships were strained.

Grandma's part? She missed the six-year-old clue, when David failed to say "thank you," when he took her loving gift for granted. She missed the seventh birthday's clue, his lack of response, and she had wondered if all the work was worth it. She got the eight-year-old's clue, the destruction of the cake, when she felt resentful and hurt. She remained silent but determined to make her garden instead of the cake next year.

Is this a case of overindulgence?

Clearly. What should his parents do? David is a lucky boy if his parents recognize this behavior as a call for help, insist that David make amends, and teach him how to do that. He is lucky if they also look carefully at other areas where they need to provide clear nurture and clear, even stern, structure.

WANTS AND NEEDS

Too many privileges deprive children of experiences that help them to separate needs and wants. Each child needs to feel special at certain times, like at his birthday. But it is also important that each child learn that he can't always have what he wants. Needs are essential for safety, health, growth, and the accomplishment of goals. They change over time and reflect the culture in which the child lives. American children *need* a reliable way to get to school. They may want to be chauffeured every day. Wants are desires, but to the young child *I want* and *I need* feel the same. The child learns to separate them as the adults describe and define them and see to it that the child's needs are always met if at all possible, but that she gets what she wants only part of the time.

At this time in the U.S. many students are leaving colleges and universities with enormous college debts. One of the problems is that these students often don't differentiate needs from wants. For some of them, the desire for a new DVD player and many discs is deemed as important as paying tuition fees.[2] A student who grasps the implications of the huge debt for the first time after graduation is truly shocked and faces some restrictions on his next few years that he has not anticipated. Personal spending may be drastically restricted. He will be paying for the past instead of building financial resources for his future. This is a heavy price to pay for a lesson missed during childhood.

> **W**ants are desires, but to the young child *I want* and *I need* feel the same.

PRIVILEGES OF SOCIAL CLASS

Another definition of privilege is "a right, advantage, or prerogative belonging to a person or class."

Hunter grew up in a social class of privilege. His parents were wealthy, well respected, and well connected. The many privileges, the clothes, money, education, travel, that Hunter experienced were given and accepted as a matter of course and because his family could afford them. He was not "special" among his peers.

Hunter's family milieu with its special privileges also had many special demands. His privileges were surrounded with many obligations. He was expected to excel in several areas, bring pride to the family name, and make significant contributions to his community. In their book *Silver Spoon Kids*, Gallo and Gallo tell how wealthy parents raise responsible children without an obnoxious or disdaining sense of entitlement.

Was Hunter overindulged?

1. Did the privileges interfere with his learning skills and mastering his developmental tasks?
2. Did Hunter receive a disproportionate amount of the family's resources?
3. Were his privileges for his welfare or to make the parents feel good?
4. Did his privileges do harm to him, to others, to society?

Hunter would certainly have been overindulged if his family treated him with over-nurturing and soft structure. It is a cultural myth that all people of privilege are overindulged. Our research does not support that notion. The majority of adults who had been overindulged as children reported that their family had the same, less, or much less money than their neighbors. Affluence alone is not an indicator of overindulgence. In *Privileged One: The Well-Off and Rich in America*, Robert Coles describes not only the special privileges, but also the expectations, demands, and burdens that children of the wealthy, privileged class often experience. Children like Hunter.

GOOD INTENTIONS

There are other kinds of groups who get and need special privileges, but too many privileges are sometimes extended by well-meaning adults out of a real lack of understanding of just what is needed.

Ethan, who has a physical disability, is given more privileges than his brothers in order to try to reduce his stress level. His brothers have to speak respectfully to adults, but Ethan curses his parents, the doctor, and anyone within earshot when he feels frustrated.

It is a cultural myth that all people of privilege are overindulged. The majority of adults who had been overindulged as children reported that their family had the same, less, or much less money than their neighbors.

Too bad. One of the major skills Ethan needs to learn is self-control in social situations. Ethan's parents have good intentions. So does Caleb's teacher.

The teacher knows that Caleb comes from an especially tough home situation so she accepts late assignments carelessly done with no penalties.

Too bad. Caleb, perhaps more than any other member of the class, needs skills to become competent. Even if the teacher's intentions are the best, special privileges detract from the child's opportunity to accomplish desired developmental tasks, to learn the important skills that school teaches. The impact of the over-nurturing is profoundly negative.

Sometimes outsiders worry about the overindulgence they see being done by parents and others with good intent.

My friend's twelve-year-old grandchild is in her second round of cancer treatments. I am pained when I hear that when the child wants salmon to eat, it must be purchased at a special store. My friend, the girl's grandfather, contributes to her care. Her every wish is treated like a demand. The family is exhausted and broke. The diagnosis is grim, but the girl may survive. And I shudder to think how she'll handle her survival if she can no longer use her illness to demand that adults do her bidding. I don't know how to support my friend who is terrified he'll spend his entire retirement fund on his granddaughter's medical bills before he gets a chance to retire.

Is this privilege or overindulgence? One way to evaluate the granting of a privilege is to hold it against the Test of Four.

If we slip into granting too many privileges, what can we do? We strengthen our backbones, steel ourselves against the fallout, and remove one privilege at a time.

AN OVERBLOWN SENSE OF ENTITLEMENT AND PRIVILEGE IN CHILDHOOD IS A PLATFORM FOR FAILURE IN THE FUTURE.
—Gary Rowland

A WORLD OF ENTERTAINMENT

When I Was Growing Up, My Parents
Made Sure that I Was Entertained

ALL PLAY AND NO WORK MAKE JACK A DULL BOY.
—Folk wisdom revisited

THE mobile sways above the crib. Tinkle, tinkle. Baby coos and waves his arms. Parents start early to entertain their children. They sing and play tapes and CDs. They provide cuddly toys and tickling. Baby smiles. Parents smile. These activities are not only entertaining; they are powerful ways to enhance the development of the brain and to strengthen the parent-child bond. And, of course, they're lots of fun.

DID YOU HAVE FUN TODAY?

Sometimes, as children grow older, adults start to feel that what's most important is entertaining the child, making sure the child is having fun and is happy. This usually turns into over-nurturing and overindulgence. It's easy to forget that those vital brain and attachment functions need to be built not only by having fun, but also by dealing with disappointments and the need to accommodate the family.

> When four-year-old Megan gets home from the sitter's, Mom asks the daily question, "Did you have fun today?"
>
> "Yeah. I played on the swings."
>
> "Good. I'm glad you had fun."
>
> Or the child declares, "I didn't have fun," and the parent responds, "Then we better go to the park. I can finish what I'm doing later. Get your jacket."

Ask the Test of Four questions about the trip to the park.

1. Is Megan getting to master her **tasks** of learning to live with others? How will Megan learn to value activities that are challenging? How will she learn to do unselfish acts for others? Will this constant emphasis on fun keep her from realizing that she is not the center of the world, but rather *in* a world with other people who also need consideration?
2. Is mother **misappropriating her time and attention?**
3. **Who** is the trip to the park really for? Who thinks we need to "have fun" every day? Is Mom a member of the "you deserve a break today" generation? A break that is not earned or may be counter-productive?
4. Does this **harm** others?

THE SLIPPERY SLOPE

The slide down the slippery slope of entertainment is often such a smooth ride that you don't realize you are on it. One of our colleagues took that ride and didn't know it until she hit the bump at the bottom. Here's her story:

> One Saturday, when granddaughter Bobbi Jo was three, I got to have her at my house for the whole day. *Oh, joy, lucky me, we'll have such fun!* I thought. I asked Bobbi Jo, "What do you want to do first?" She looked at me, blank stare, and said, "Snack." Okay, snack. "Now, what would you like to do?" I never once said, "Now we will do . . ."

By five in the afternoon Bobbi Jo was uncooperative and cranky. Nothing seemed to please her. I thought, *This is not right. This is my darling granddaughter with whom I am intending to build a good relationship, and I want to step on her. What am I doing wrong?* I remembered that when children are doing something we don't like, that is a signal that we need to do something differently. But I couldn't think what was wrong or what to do.

At that point my daughter, Bobbi Jo's beloved Auntie Barbara Sue entered. She swooped up the little girl, kissed her, and asked, "Did you have fun with Grandma today?" Bobbi Jo shook her head no. I thought, *Hey, Barbara Sue didn't ask me if I had fun today!*

Barbara Sue continued, "Bobbi Jo, we are going to a restaurant for dinner. We'll meet your cousins Charlene and Marabelle. Whom would you like to ride with? Grandpa, Jiles or me?" I thought, Darn, she didn't ask me who I wanted to ride with.

"You, you," shouted Bobbi Jo. Grandpa Jiles intervened. "I want Bobbi Jo to ride with me. The car seat is already in place and I will take her home after dinner."

"No, no, Auntie Baba Sue." Bobbi Jo started low key, and worked up toward a tantrum. Jiles and Barbara Sue settled the issue somehow while she packed plastic bags of food Bobbi Jo would like. *Hey, she didn't ask me what I would like.*

At the restaurant Barbara Sue produced the bags of food and asked Bobbi Jo whom she wanted to sit by. "Marabelle, Marabelle!" *Shucks, I wanted to sit by Marabelle.*

I watched all through the meal as Bobbi Jo got crankier and crankier and Barbara Sue, bless her heart, continued to do what I had been doing all day. Watching her zip down the slippery slope held up a helpful mirror for me. Good intent, terrible impact.

What was the new course of action? First I apologized to Bobbi Jo's parents for overindulging. I couldn't believe I had overindulged so grossly. Good reminder that the opportunities to overindulge are always present and beckoning. Next I asked them to tell Bobbi Jo, the next time she was to visit, that she was going to help Grandma. I also asked them, when she got home, to ask first, "How did you help Grandma today?"

Then, I thought about how to stop overindulging and take back the leadership during her next visit. I listed (not just thought about) the things we could do.

When Bobbi Jo arrived I said, "I have several things we will do today. I'll draw pictures on stickies and you put the stickies on the refrigerator." She was delighted. Children love to be competent. We posted:

- ❖ clean jewelry drawer
- ❖ read a book
- ❖ swing
- ❖ snack
- ❖ draw a picture for Auntie Faye
- ❖ play with clay
- ❖ visit the baby next door
- ❖ call Uncle Brewster

When the stickies were all up I told her that we had to clean the jewelry drawer first, and then she could move that picture and choose what we would do next. We told Grandpa we were going upstairs for a while so Bobbi Jo could help Grandma. *Family members help each other.* We did it at her pace. Back downstairs, she gleefully moved the sticky and then chose to swing with Grandpa. Wonderful day. We all had a good time. And we grandparents remembered what a self-esteem builder it is for a three-year-old to feel confident.

After her third help-Grandma visit Bobbi Jo enlightened her mom, "I know why I have to help Gamma. It's because she is so litto." (I am. I live in a family of tall ones.) "Of course, she is not so litto as me."

Now, placing the stickies is a dependable, enjoyable ritual. Now Bobbi Jo, at six, insists on it at every visit. Now she draws the pictures and sometimes she adds activities. We all look forward to the visits and she sometimes brings friends. Elly Mae is a favorite.

ENTERTAIN ME! I'M BORED

"Gramma, Gramma, we have to show Elly Mae how to make stickies!" On the day Bobbi Jo brought her friend Elly Mae along, the sticky list included: read a book, fold clean clothes, dollhouse, and craft box. The help-Grandma job was to sort some buttons. That had to be done first: "Here is a box with many divisions. Please sort this bag of jumbled buttons by color. Put each color in one of the sections." Elly Mae protested, "There are too many." Grandma poured out half of the buttons. "Okay, we'll only do half of them today." Two heads bent over the buttons as they started the sort, but after five buttons Elly Mae sprawled back onto the floor and moaned, "I can't do any more. I'm bored." She looked quite pitiful and Grandma felt the powerful tug of the invitation for an adult to attend to her little guest's entertainment.

But Grandma was concerned. This is tragic for this bright, appealing little girl to think she has to be entertained. Without sympathy, but with cheerful firmness, Grandma announced, "Elly Mae, sorry but boredom is not allowed in this house." Elly Mae sat up, shocked.

"Why?"

"Because there is always, anyplace you are, something to look at or do or think about. Boredom is hard on your brain, and it will make it hard for you to learn at school, so there is no boredom allowed in this house. Family members help each other and you are visiting this family today, and I need to have these buttons sorted so help Bobbi Jo finish the job."

"Come on," Bobbi Jo urged. "Then we can go look at the refrigerator." Elly Mae shook her head, as if in disbelief, and the girls finished the button-sort shortly. There was no more mention of boredom, and at the end of the day Elly Mae asked to come again.

ANOTHER CASE OF BOREDOM

The Jacksons placed high value on keeping their school-age daughters entertained. Although the parents were trying to save enough money for a needed new car, a plaintive, "I'm bored!" sends the parents into immediate action. In November a trip to the toy store cost $240.00. Grandma complained, "What do I get the girls for Christmas? Oh well, by that time I expect most of the new toys will be lost or broken."

Would you consider this over-nurturing? Ask the questions:

1. Did this interfere with the children learning some **developmental task?** Yes. Six- to twelve-year-olds are busy learning skills including how to take care of possessions, how to plan their time, and how to entertain themselves.

2. Did this use an unreasonable amount of family **resources?** Yes.

3. Whose **needs** were being met? The Jacksons, with their need to entertain, created a situation where the girls are learning to expect others to meet their demands instead of learning to take care of themselves.

4. Is **harm** being done? Yes, if the car they are driving is not safe.

Are these the girls who will, when they are teenagers, expect to spend spring school break at a holiday resort with other teens and no chaperones? Consider the high school senior who got his classmates to stage a protest on his behalf when he wasn't allowed to graduate. He had been given explicit instructions about past due work he needed to make up during spring break in order to graduate, but he "was stressed out" so he vacationed with his girlfriend instead.

> **C**hildren who habitually turn on the tube instead of creating their own activities or reading can easily become bored.

Over-dependence on any amusement and distraction can create a habit of boredom. This is a habit adults must counter if children are to retain their creativity and learn to take a task through to completion.

Twelve-year-old Harris wanted to earn some money and had been hired to pull weeds out of a small garden. Ten minutes into the job he was playing with a hackey-sack. His employer asked why he had stopped pulling weeds. "I can't do any more," he explained, "because it's boring. I don't need the money this bad. I'm going home and watch TV."

THE NEW ENTITLEMENT—ELECTRONIC DEVICES

Until about fifty years ago, most human beings were responsible for creating their own entertainment. Now that responsibility has been largely given over to those people who create TV programs, and design video games and other chip-driven machines.

Think about the family that really likes TV. There are three sets in the living areas, one in each child's room and one in the van. Last weekend they could not drive to their vacation home, a two-hour trip, because the TV in the van was broken and the children wouldn't have anything to entertain them on the trip.

Try applying the Test of Four to this situation.

Please, parents, let your good intent lead your feet to the bookstore. Get a book of car games for children and connect with your kids.

THE SUBSTITUTE PARENT

Overuse of electronic recreation can come not only from the parents' wish to entertain the children, but also from the parents being just plain too busy, or the idea that working to provide material things is a more important way to nurture a child than to spend time with him. So it's *Go watch television!*

With good intent, the parents may not understand the impact of too much time with the tube, including:

❖ clever advertising, with sex, violence, rude and manipulative children, and adults who are mean to each other
❖ games that feature violence and so much drama that children can find everyday living chronically boring
❖ long hours of physical inactivity and passive observation of other people's lives, and all with problems that can be resolved in twenty-five or fifty minutes
❖ the electronic games where the child solves the problem with finger dexterity and violence rather than empathic or ethical thinking
❖ the Internet with pornography and directions for making bombs

Are all electronic media bad? Of course not, but long hours of unsupervised watching or playing can be. We do not yet know the full impact of TV on brain development, but some pediatricians are recommending no TV for the first four years of life. Think of that!

Someone has suggested that if a stranger came to your house and said, "I'm your new baby-sitter and I will take care of your child many hours every day and teach her my values, not yours," you would slam the door. But many parents have brought TV into their family areas, and sometimes even put a set in their children's bedrooms thereby giving their children over to it for many hours. Remember that American children watch television an average of thirty-five hours a week.

TV does not bring people together, or create nurturing connections. We are Balkanized by the plethora of offerings. No matter who you are or what your interests, there is a show for you, and connecting with real people can be replaced by vicarious connections with people images on the tube.

Monitoring TV and electronic game exposure takes time, but it takes time to rear children and that's what we signed on for when we had them. Two books that you might want to consult to understand the impact of media and how to handle it are *Dr. Dave's Cyberhood* by David Walsh and *Screen Smarts* by Gloria DeGaetano and Kathleen Bander.

VIOLENCE

Listen to a parent's concern about violence on video games.

Robin Brooks's e-mail:
Here's a question about Playstation, the video game thing. Our homeschooling neighbors who occasionally watch my five-year-old son have introduced him to a Playstation game called Spiro. Is anyone else familiar with it? Spiro is this "cute" little dragon in search of treasure. You have to "kill" the bad guys to get the treasure. I am uncomfortable with all this. To me, it is introducing the concept of simulated death and killing in a sugarcoated setting. Yet these games appear to be such a part of the mainstream culture. I personally will not purchase this game/equipment, but I can't prevent my son from playing at his friends' homes.

Now, segue to my husband's high school Film and Media Studies class. A group of boys are huddled around the television screen. One of them has brought his favorite Playstation 2 game to show the teacher how they spend their "free" time. In the name of understanding the media the students consume, the teacher has requested to see the game. It is called "GTA" or Grand Theft Auto. In this game, the goal is to see how many people you can kill. The "game" includes car-jacking, picking up and consorting with a prostitute, and killing police officers. The boys are practically salivating as they call out directions to the student who is at the controls. The excitement is palpable. My first question is "Are their parents aware of GTA and other games like it? Do they know how their kids are spending their "free" time?" I, for one, feel there is NO place for these games in a child's life. WHY is it such a widely accepted recreation? The only purpose these "games" can serve is to teach our children the emotional detachment necessary to commit heinous acts of war and/or criminal acts. These games appear to be highly addictive and occupy our children for huge amounts of time when they could be engaged in real-world activities.

Robin's e-mail leaves us with two questions: *Do you know what your kids are doing?* and *What is the impact of playing these games?* One thing that these games do is render children bored with any activity that does not engender a high level of excitement or drama.

OVERINDULGENCE AND SELF-ESTEEM

Recreation is supposed to be about re-creation. It was never meant to usurp real-time life experiences of learning, struggle, joy, disappointment, and connection. One of the devastating results of over-nurturing children with constant entertainment is that it affects their self-esteem. Perhaps one of the most unfortunate outcomes of over-nurturing is that it encourages dependence on the opinions of others.

Look at the low self-esteem reflected in these responses. Parents who said, "When I was growing up, my parents made sure I was entertained" were also likely to say:[1]

❖ "On the whole, I am not satisfied with myself."
❖ "At times I think I am no good at all."
❖ "I certainly feel useless at times."
❖ "I do not feel that I'm a person of worth."
❖ "I wish I could have more respect for myself."

Building self-esteem really means encouraging children to develop a balance of feeling lovable and being capable; that is, of feeling worthy of receiving unconditional love, and developing the ability to care for self and contribute to others.

During the 1980s and 1990s, there was an unfortunate turn in the public concept of self-esteem. The emphasis was directed to "making sure children feel good," which is a form of overindulgence, of over-nurturing. This preoccupation with telling children they are special, and every little thing they do is wonderful, raises doubts about the credibility of the messages and doubts about those who give them, and results in children's confusion about who they are and what they have or have not done well.

HOW MUCH IS ENOUGH ENTERTAINMENT?

Think of the seven hazards of overindulgence:

❖ *Trouble learning how to delay gratification.* Having enough entertainment is the dessert in life. It is not the whole meal. *You can go to Lytesia's house to play after you have done your homework.*

❖ *Trouble giving up being the constant center of attention.* Enough entertainment lets your child have fun without making his entertainment dominate the family activities. *You can't go to the movie tonight because we will all be helping get ready for Gressa's party tomorrow.*

❖ *Trouble becoming competent in*

✦ *Everyday skills.* Enough entertainment leaves adequate time for chores. *You can ride your bike after your chores are done.*

✦ *Self-care skills.* Enough entertainment supports rather than impinges upon learning self-care skills. *Limit your phone calls to five minutes. You need time to do your laundry and get yourself ready for the party tonight.*

✦ *Skills of relating with others.* Enough entertainment includes each child learning to participate in some activities chosen by other family members. *I know miniature golf is not your favorite, but it is your brother's turn to choose so we are all going to play.*

❖ *Trouble taking personal responsibility.* Enough entertainment adds enjoyment but it does not create an expectation that entertainment should be provided whenever your child wants it. *You have watched TV long enough. Go create something of your own to do.*

❖ *Trouble developing a sense of personal identity.* Enough entertainment does not invite a child to identify with a sports hero or an entertainer instead of her own family. *You know more about the history of* Star Trek *than you do about your own family. You and I are going to find a way for you to learn your own family history and who your family heroes are.*

❖ *Trouble knowing what is enough.* Enough entertainment teaches your child how to make entertainment enriching, not all consuming. *You have been on the Web long enough. Come and make the salad for dinner.*

❖ *Trouble knowing what is normal for other people.* Enough entertainment helps your child understand that although his world is filled with entertainment possibilities, he does not attend every game, concert, or event and he can expect that others will have attended what he did not or won't have watched the TV programs he has watched. *I have never watched that program so don't expect me to know what the characters do. Tell me what you like about the program.*

But, you say, there is so much pressure to entertain children, how can I resist it? The chapters in section IV are filled with helpful clues.

ENTERTAINMENT IS MEANT TO BE A PART OF LIFE.
IT WAS NEVER MEANT TO BE *THE* WAY OF LIFE.
—Paula Pugh

14

THE NURTURE HIGHWAY

The Roadway of Parenting

YOU CANNOT LOVE TOO MUCH,
ONLY IN A WAY THAT'S HARMFUL.
—Gloria Wallace

RAISING children has to be the longest continuous challenge in the universe. It can feel like traversing a road less traveled, but travel it we must, every day, on the days we think we know where we are going and on the days when we are just muddling through. On those good days, when we are driving in the middle of the parenting road, the children grow and thrive and agree and resist. (They are children, after all.) On those good days, the bumps are small and the curves not too surprising, and we are easily building strong bonds and loving connection with our children.

THE NURTURE HIGHWAY

Take a look at the six ways of caring for a child as depicted on the Nurture Highway,[1] which first appeared in Jean Illsley Clarke and Connie Dawson's book *Growing Up Again, Parenting Ourselves, Parenting Our Children.*

HOW MUCH IS ENOUGH?

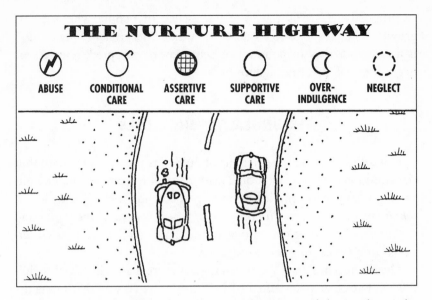

THE NURTURE HIGHWAY

ABUSE	CONDITIONAL CARE	ASSERTIVE CARE	SUPPORTIVE CARE	OVER-INDULGENCE	NEGLECT

Assertive Care and Supportive Care, the center of the road, are the positive ways to nurture, to offer love and care freely and to encourage growth. When children are young, we care for them assertively. We do not wait until they are blue with cold to provide warm clothing. As they grow older we offer more and more Supportive Care. As soon as they are capable of doing for themselves we ask if they want our help. As we keep up with children's growth needs and increasing competencies, we adjust and readjust that balance. We are constantly realigning our parenting to stay in the middle of the highway.

The shoulders and the ditches are less helpful to children than the center positions. Conditional Care and Overindulgence, the shoulders of the highway, keep a connection with the child but also provide burdens.

The ditches of Abuse and Neglect maintain some connection, but the children will be forced to busy themselves with survival tasks, robbing them of energy they need to learn the common skills appropriate for their ages.

THE HEALTHY CENTER

Assertive Care, in the middle of the road, meets needs directly. The caregiver judges the children's need for care, support, and opportunities to learn, and provides for those needs if the children cannot meet those needs by themselves. No overindulgence here.

Supportive Care is the loving presence of people who support growth. They respond to requests for aid or offer to help only if "no" is a safe and okay response. The help may be accepted, rejected, or negotiated. No overindulgence here.

THE UNHEALTHY SHOULDERS

Conditional Care, the price tag shoulder, is the name for care that the child must earn or pay for. This kind of nurturance places conditions on care, with implicit or explicit demands such as, *I love you when you are good,* or *I'll take care of you if you make me look good to others.* One adult overindulged as a child said, *Love was conditional upon accepting the indulgence.*[2]

Overindulgence, the shoulder that gives more than is healthy for children, is patronizing and often sticky. It is given in a way that meets the needs of the giver but undermines the confidence and competence of the receiver. You can see from the chart (page 131) that the shoulders, Conditional Nurturing and Overindulgent Nurturing, which are opposite one another on the road, have similar negative effects on the child.

Sometimes, if we slip onto a shoulder (overindulgence is one of the shoulders) and do things that are not so good for children, we swing back into the center and no harm is done. If however, we plow along the shoulder for many miles, or even head for the ditch, the kids suffer in the long run, and so do we. Overindulgence can be a seductive shoulder. When we have let nurture puff up into over-nurture, we need to be able to figure out where to drive instead without crossing to the other shoulder or one of the ditches.

THE ABUSIVE DITCHES

Abuse, a deep ditch, is typified by harsh contact. It involves physical invasion and/or tissue damage such as shaking, burning, hard hitting, or sexual touch. It includes other invasive non-physical parental behaviors such as humiliation, ridicule, sexual innuendo, threats to harm or abandon, and laughing at pain. What is abuse doing on a Nurture Chart? It's there because, in the absence of positive touch or attention, the child, needing attention, makes use of grossly negative words or touch in the interests of at least staying alive. Many of the people in our first study who were overindulged reported that they were also physically and psychologically abused.[3] Perhaps children feel the wrath when a parent who has been overindulging from good intent is worn down by helplessness and nagging.

Neglect, the ditch, provides nurturance, or lack of it, in a way that ignores or doesn't meet the child's needs. It is a passive form of

abuse. Caregivers may be emotionally or physically absent, too busy or preoccupied to pay attention, or absent because of an addiction. Having an adult physical body in the room is not enough to make good connection. The adult must also be there in mind, spirit, and emotion.

THE WORDS OF EACH POSITION

Take a few minutes to explore each of the six positions as they are presented in the following charts. If you're looking for more helpful information about nurture, we recommend reading Chapters 3 through 7 of *Growing Up Again, Parenting Ourselves, Parenting Our Children,* which has many more examples like the ones that follow. You can use these examples to see the full range of responses to a situation and identify which would be easiest for you to do. If that response falls on a shoulder or in a ditch, you can decide what you need to get back in the middle of the road.

In these common situations, hear the words that are typical of each position on the highway.

Situation: *Dad is making breakfast and three-year-old Hannah wants to help scramble the eggs.*

Abuse: Dad cuffs the child. "Get out of the kitchen when I am cooking!"

Conditional Care: "You can help if you let me brush your hair without complaining afterwards."

Assertive Care: "Get your apron and the stool. I love having an assistant cook."

Supportive Care: "Do you know how to stir the eggs or shall I show you?"

Overindulgence: "I'm in a hurry, but of course you can help."

Neglect: Ignores child's request. Isn't aware that three-year-olds, developmentally, need to be helping with household chores.[4]

The Nurture Chart

Joy, hope, self-confidence, and self-esteem grow from care and support. Despair, joylessness, and loneliness flow from abuse, conditional care, overindulgence, and neglect.

	ABUSE ⊘	CONDITIONAL CARE ◯	ASSERTIVE CARE ⊕
Characteristics:	Abuse involves relating to a child by assault, physical or psychological invasion, direct or indirect "don't be" messages. Abuse negates the child's needs.	Conditional care requires the child to earn care or pay for care in some way. The care the parent gives the child is based on the parent's needs and expectations, not on the child's needs.	Assertive care recognizes the child and the child's needs. The parent decides to nurture in this way because it is helpful to the child, responsive to the child's needs, and appropriate to the circumstance. It is comforting and loving. It is freely given.
Example: School-age child has a badly scraped arm	Parent does not care for wounds. Says, "Stop sniffling or I'll give you something to cry about." Yells at or shakes the child.	Parent says, "Stop crying or I won't bandage your arm."	Parent cares for the wound in a loving way. Says, "Your arm is scraped! I'm sorry."
Children May Hear the Following Underlying Messages:	You don't count. Your needs don't count. You are not lovable. You don't deserve to exist. To get what you need, you must expect pain.	I matter and you don't. Your needs and feelings don't count. You can have care as long as you earn it. Don't believe you are lovable; you have to earn love.	I love you and you are lovable. You are important. Your needs are important. I care for you willingly.
Common Responses of Children:	Pain in the heart, as well as pain in the scraped arm. Fear, terror, rage, withdrawal, loneliness, despair, shame, confusion about reality.	Pain in the heart, as well as pain in the scraped arm. Fear, terror, anger, mistrust of own perceptions, shame, feelings of inadequacy, suspicious of love.	Pain in the arm and warmth in the heart. Feels comforted, accepted, important, satisfied, relieved, secure, safe, loved.
Decisions Often Made by Children:	I am not powerful. I deserve to die, or the reverse, I will live in spite of them. It's my fault, or I'll blame everything on others. I'll be good, or I'll be bad. Big people get to abuse, or I can abuse those smaller than I am, or I will never abuse. I won't feel or have needs. Love does not exist. I am alone; I keep emotional distance from, and don't trust, others. I blame or strike or leave first.	I am what I do. I must strive to please. Big people get what they want. I can never do enough. I must be perfect. I don't deserve love. There is a scarcity of love. I must be strong. Love obligates me and is costly. I don't trust. I do keep emotional distance, or run away, or blame others.	I am important. I deserve care. It's okay to ask for what I need. I belong here. I am loved. Others can be trusted and relied upon. I can know what I need. It's okay to be dependent at times.

HOW MUCH IS ENOUGH?

SUPPORTIVE CARE ○	OVERINDULGENCE ◖	NEGLECT ◌

Characteristics:

SUPPORTIVE CARE	OVERINDULGENCE	NEGLECT
Supportive care recognizes the child and the child's needs. It is care the child is free to accept or reject. It offers help, comfort, and love. It stimulates children to think and to do what they are capable of doing for themselves.	Overindulgence is a sticky, patronizing kind of care. It promotes continuing dependence on the parent and teaches the child not to think independently and not to be responsible for self or to others.	Neglect is passive abuse. It is lack of emotional or physical stimulation and recognition by parents who are unavailable or who ignore the needs of the child. These parents may be "there, but not there."

Example: School-age child has a badly scraped arm.

SUPPORTIVE CARE	OVERINDULGENCE	NEGLECT
[Parent has already taught child how to clean a scrape.] Says in a concerned and loving tone, "I see you've scraped your arm. Does it hurt? Do you want to take care of it yourself or would you like some help from me?" Offers a hug.	Parent rushes to child. Says, "Oh, look at your arm, you poor thing. That really stings! I'll bandage it. Go and lie down in front of the television and I'll do your chores for you."	Parent ignores the scrape. Says, "Don't bother me."

Children May Hear the Following Underlying Messages:

SUPPORTIVE CARE	OVERINDULGENCE	NEGLECT
I love you, you are lovable. You are capable. I am willing to care for you. Ask for what you need. Your welfare is important to me. I am separate from you. I trust you to think and make judgments in your own best interests.	Don't grow up. Don't be who you are (capable). My needs are more important than your's (or) your needs are more important than mine. You don't need to care for yourself; someone will care for you.	Don't expect to be recognized. Your needs are not important. You are not important. You do not deserve to exist. Expect to suffer to get what you need. Be confused about reality.

Common Responses of Children:

SUPPORTIVE CARE	OVERINDULGENCE	NEGLECT
Pain in the arm and a heart filled with confidence. Child feels cared for, comforted, challenged, secure, and trustworthy.	Pain in the arm and uncertainty in the heart. Self-centered satisfaction, temporary comfort, self-righteousness, overentitlement. Later on: confusion, woefulness, helplessness, obligation, resentment, defensiveness, and shame. Not knowing what is enough.	Pain in the heart, as well as pain in the scraped arm. Feelings of abandonment, fear, shame, rage, hopelessness, helplessness, abject disappointment.

Decisions Often Made By Children:

SUPPORTIVE CARE	OVERINDULGENCE	NEGLECT
I am loved. I can know what I need. I am capable. I can be powerful. I am not alone. It's okay to ask for help. I am both separate and connected. I can decide when to be dependent and when to be independent.	I am not capable. I don't have to be competent. I don't have to know what I need, think, or feel. Other people are obligated to take care of me. I don't have to grow up. I must be loyal to my indulging parent. To get my needs met, I manipulate or play a victim role. It's okay to be self-centered. Later on: be wary and don't trust.	I don't really know who I am or what's right. I am not important. I am not lovable. I die alone or survive on my own. It isn't possible or safe to get close, to trust, or to ask for help. I do not deserve help. What I do doesn't count if someone has to help me. Life is hard.

Situation: *Eight-year-old Terry is begging for an expensive new video game.*

Abuse: Dad says, "Ask once more and you'll get it, and I don't mean the game!"

Conditional Care: Dad says, "You'll get the game if you stop bugging me."

Assertive Care: Dad goes to the store with Terry to play the game. If the game supports violence, Terry doesn't get it. If the game is okay, Dad considers how many games Terry already has and whether they can afford it.

Supportive Care: Dad says, "We have this amount to spend on games this year. If you get this one there will be no game for your birthday or Christmas [said lovingly, but matter-of-factly]. Are you sure that is what you want?"

Overindulgence: Buys an even more expensive game that Dad wants.

Neglect: Dad gets the game and is unaware that Terry is spending six or more hours a day playing video games or watching TV.

Situation: *Allegra, thirteen, asks her parents to buy her a ticket to the big concert, drop her and her friends at the entrance, and pick them up afterward.*

Abuse: Mom yells, slamming her hand on the table and glaring at her daughter, "You know I don't like that music."

Conditional Care: Mom says, "Sure, Allegra. Great idea to take your friends. I want you to be popular."

Assertive Care: Mom says, "Get a CD of this group from the library. We'll listen to the lyrics to see if they support our friendly values."

Supportive Care: Mom says, "If I decide the concert is unsafe or too expensive or doesn't support our values, would you like to have your friends here for a party that night?"

Overindulgence: "If that's what you want, Honey, we'll do it."

Neglect: Mom agrees, buys tickets even though she can't afford it. Does not consider safety issues or the messages of the band.

Situation: *Lee, sixteen, didn't show for the Fourth of July family reunion.*

Abuse: When he comes home, Dad smacks Lee to knock some sense into the kid.

Conditional Care: Mom says, "Lee we take good care of you and you are supposed to make our family look good. I was so embarrassed in front of your grandparents and our guests!"

Assertive Care: "Lee, Fourth of July is an important celebration in our family. What you did was hurtful. You need to make amends to us. Get back to us in twenty minutes with your plan."

Supportive Care: "If you need some help thinking of ways to make amends, let me know."

Overindulgence: Parents say, "We missed you at dinner. I suppose you had a better time than you would have had here."

Neglect: Fails to monitor Lee's amend making. Fails to get any help needed.

Situation: *Twenty-nine-year-old Kenny lives at home, spends the income from his good-paying job on himself, and contributes nothing in money or services to the household.*

Abuse: "You lazy, good-for-nothing, poor excuse for a man. You are no son of mine."

Conditional Care: "I will continue to care for you if you will continue to live here."

Assertive Care: "I love you a lot. I am no longer cooking, cleaning, or doing laundry for you. You are to start paying rent and cooking three meals a week."

Supportive Care: "Would you like me to help you look for an apartment?"

Overindulgence: "I clean, I cook, I do your laundry. I want you to be comfortable here. Anything you need?"

Neglect: Fails to notice that son is self-centered and needs to grow up.

You cannot *love* too much. You can cling, you can smother, you can spoil, you can use your wish to train a child as an excuse for abuse, but that is not love. You can't love too much because true love is both respectful and unconditional. Anything that looks like love, but keeps a child from growing into his true self, is not true love.

There is no such thing as too much love. But too much care creates a problem. Listen to the voices about over-nurture from those who experienced it.

As a child did you know you were being overindulged?

Yes. Mother stifled self-determination, self-motivation, and self-respect by attempting to do everything for us. Father was not repressive but lacked child rearing skills and we didn't spend "influencing" time with him.

What childhood decision did you make that affects your life now?

I never as a child learned to try hard, study hard. My parents covered for me. When I was on my own in college, it was a shock. I partied and skipped classes and was stunned at getting poor grades first year. My father chose my first career (teaching). I did not pursue my love—music. I had no idea I could make a change.

WHIPLASH PARENTING

Many parents, determined not to have their children experience the same neglect or pain they experienced, switch to the opposite side of the road from the parenting they received. This is called whiplash parenting. *I was neglected so I overindulge.* Or, *The other parent overindulges so I am strict in an abusive way.* Or, *My partner expects nothing of the children so I make them earn my love.*

The tasks and the challenges are to stay in the center lanes of the Nurture Highway as much as possible. If you stray onto the shoulders of overindulgence or conditional care or into the ditches of abuse or neglect, the parenting trick is to get back in the middle without overcorrecting. Discovering that you have strayed into overindulgence by over-nurturing means you need to grab your good intentions and steer back to the lanes where the impact of your parenting matches your good intent.

As you move from overindulgence back to the middle of the parenting highway, you can expect children to test you. You can expect your children to try to get you to turn back to your old overindulging ways. But, you can also expect them, in time, to tap into their own healthy drive to live up to their own potential and appreciate the effort you made. Of course, you may not hear about their appreciations until they are forty-two years old!

You can also use the Nurture Highway to help you think about how to pull your relationships with adults off the overindulgence shoulder and back into the middle of the road.

ALL BEHAVIOR IS EITHER AN EXPRESSION OF LOVE
OR A CALL FOR LOVE.
—*A Course in Miracles*

FOUR

SECTION

The Pitfalls of Soft Structure— Low Expectations, Soft Rules, and Lax Boundaries

SOFT STRUCTURE

A Blueprint for Insecurity

ON AVERAGE, CHILDREN WANT TEN TIMES MORE ATTENTION,
TOYS, FREEDOM, AND SO ON THAN THEY ACTUALLY NEED.
ABOUT THE ONLY THINGS TODAY'S CHILD NEEDS MORE OF
THAN HE OR SHE WANTS ARE CHORES AND CONSEQUENCES[1]
—John Rosemond

SOFT STRUCTURE

*O*UR overindulgence studies revealed startling evidence that soft structure short-changes children.[2] When kids do not have to do chores, learn skills, meet standards, and follow rules, they miss important life lessons. Add to this parents who are too permissive, who give children too much freedom, and let children rule the family, and you have a blueprint for uncertainty and insecurity. This is definitely not the outcome parents want.

Common Results of Overindulging with Soft Structure

People who were overindulged with persistent soft structure tended:

- ❖ not to know what is enough
- ❖ to have weak social and personal boundaries
- ❖ to be trained in irresponsibility
- ❖ to have a false sense of empowerment
- ❖ to believe and act as if they are the center of the universe

In our research adults who were overindulged as children were more likely to agree with the following statements:[3]

- ❖ "My parents did not expect me to do chores."
- ❖ "I was not expected to learn the same skills as other children."
- ❖ "My parents didn't have rules or make me follow them."
- ❖ "My parents gave me too much freedom."
- ❖ "My parents allowed me to take the lead or dominate the family."

WHAT IS STRUCTURE?

Structure is the firm side, the "how to" of care. It's the bones. Nurture cushions the bones, but it is the bones themselves that are necessary to hold a body up. Jungle gyms with loose and dangling pieces are not fun to play on! You can't trust them. You can't tell what's safe and not safe. Reasonable rules that are consistently enforced, mastery of skills, and learning family values are all part of firm structure. Firm structure not only makes life more secure and predictable for the child, in the long run it makes life easier for the parents as many would-be, could-be misadventures and crises are avoided. Maybe best of all, what the child grows up experiencing, she learns to do for herself. Children learn good boundaries and good self-care.

CHORES AND SKILLS

You thought chores were merely a burden? Not so! They are a highly important way that life-skills are taught within the family setting. Children learn skills for daily living, work skills, skills for individual and group relationships, and the many skills that keep them safe. They learn to respect themselves as important and contributing members of the family. Chores are the grist from which character and confidence are built. They are the construction pieces, glued together by values, with which a child builds his sense of competence and hence his identity. Skills must be taught and learned. They are not inborn, but the need for them is.

No wonder, then, that overindulged adults were so adamant that when they were kids, they should have been required to do chores.

> Structure is the firm side, the "how to" of care. It's the bones.

FAMILY RULES

Rules are parts of the family structures made visible. They are made in consideration of the developmental abilities of the child and the child's level of responsibility and maturity. They are changed to reflect children's growth. Rules are built to protect children and comfort them and show them they are valued and loved.

We use rules to define boundaries, to provide safety and to help us know where one thing begins and another ends. Rules that take into account both the humans and the situation help us draw the line

> Rules are built to protect children and comfort them and show them they are valued and loved.

❖ between what is safe and unsafe (Observe the traffic rule.)
❖ between what is life enhancing and what is not (Eat meals together at least five times a week.)
❖ between what is respectful and disrespectful (No put-downs.)
❖ between what helps and what hurts (No hitting, no ridicule.)

Learning the differences between what is helpful and what is hurtful and deciding where we stand is part of the work we do to define who we are.

FREEDOM

Our studies revealed another extraordinary piece of information. Adults believed they had been given too much freedom when they were children. This means that children need adults who are the leaders of the family. Children thrive when adults make well-considered decisions on how much freedom to allow. Children build sound internal structures from being able to trust reliable and responsible adults.

TOO MUCH POWER

As parents, it's a constant game of evaluation! How do you strike the balance between saying yes and saying no? The overindulged adults say they were given too much say in family decisions. Could this be a case of respecting the rights of the child too much?

RIGHTS AND OBLIGATIONS

Understanding of the difference between rights and obligations is a crucial part of parental structure. A newspaper reported that many high school students were traveling to spring break hot spots (Cancun and Florida) without parents or adult supervision. One mother of a seventeen-year-old was quoted as saying, "I can't stop him. After all, he earned all the money himself and made his own arrangements."

This mother, with positive intent to respect the rights of her child, missed her obligation to be responsible for the impact of her intent. It can be easy to confuse rights and obligations. One way to sort them is to think of rights incurring from obligations met. The child has a right to expect more freedoms as he develops responsibility for self and toward others. He also has a right to parental rules and expectations that are appropriate for his age. Earning money does not mean he has a right to spend it on anything that might put him in jeopardy, delay his development, or stress his family. Earning money only means that he has earned some money, and that brings with it the obligation to learn, with guidance and rules, how to use it wisely. Since he earned the money, if he made his own arrangements to buy illegal drugs with it, would that, too, be okay with his mother?

The boy's mother, with good intent, needs to sort obligations and rights. She has the obligation to provide appropriate parenting. She has the right to expect respect and loyalty from her son. This is an aspect of what David Elkind calls the universal contract between parents and children.

Sometimes children resent safety limits. It may be many years before parents hear children's appreciation for their responsible parenting. Sometimes, however, parents get direct appreciative feedback.

Wanda, also seventeen, begged to do the Cancun spring break trip. She was eloquent. True, her grades were up. True, she was responsible and appreciative. True she was trustworthy. True, she'd be with her friends. It would be so much fun and would make her feel grown-up.

Wanda's parents agreed that she could not go. However, after consultation they decided that her need to feel more grown-up was reasonable. They knew that she wanted pearls and had been saving money to buy some. They decided to add the needed amount of money. Wanda and her mother went shopping and Wanda, while still disappointed about Cancun, was genuinely thrilled to get her pearls. The dramatic twist came when Wanda's best friend came home early. The scene had been far too uncontrolled and dangerous and *definitely not fun*. Her shaken friend shared stories of this misadventure. As for Wanda, she gratefully thanked her parents for not letting her go.

In the next chapters we'll explore each specific area of soft structure and offer you some repair ideas.

IT'S OPPRESSIVE TO NOT GET ANY STRUCTURE
FROM THE OUTSIDE.
—Karuna Poole

WHO WAS YOUR SLAVE LAST WEEK?

When I Was Growing Up, My Parents Did Not Expect Me to Do Chores

WORK IS LOVE MADE VISIBLE.
—Kahlil Gibran

Y OU *don't have to do chores? Are you ever lucky!* Not so, the overindulged adults said. They were asked how they were overindulged, and said, "by having things done for me" and "parents not expecting me to do consistent chores."[1]

THE LABORATORY
WHERE RESPONSIBILITY IS LEARNED . . . AND MORE

If children claim that parents don't have chores, parents can smile just a bit and say, "Nice try." Adults commonly call their chores jobs or work or tasks or projects. Try making a list of all the chores adults do. But not now. Read on.

In hindsight, overindulged adults said they would have preferred to have done chores and get the feelings of pride in helping the family unit succeed.

Donna had Megan when she was thirty-three. Self-described as "plain," she reared Megan on a meager income. Still, she made certain Megan, who grew to be a gorgeous young woman, had every chance to be beautiful. She was to have nothing to do with keeping up the apartment or taking care of her clothes. As an adolescent, Megan began modeling, eventually working at locations all over the world. As a forty-four-year-old, Megan is in therapy saying, "My job was to be beautiful and accomplished, and as I got older I'm called less and less to model, so now what? I don't know who I am. I don't know how to do anything but model. And I'm furious with my mother."

Let's apply the Test of Four to Megan's situation.

Did Megan's mom encourage Megan to master **developmental tasks**? No. Did her mom devote an inordinate amount of family **resources** to her daughter? Yes. Who was Mom's largesse for? Mom. And what **harm** was done to others, to the environment? We don't know because we don't know Megan's costs or the impact of her behavior on others. But we do know that this is a case of overindulgence.

Did Megan's mom intend to cause her daughter pain? Absolutely not. She presumably hadn't a clue that what she did out of love for Megan resulted in pain. This was certainly not what the mother intended.

By the way, it's never too late for Megan's mom to own up to her part, apologize and make good on a new, more respectful way of being with her daughter.

WHAT DID ADULTS WHO HAD NO CHORES BELIEVE?

According to our experts on overindulgence, those who experienced it, aside from not learning the skills that doing chores involves, the following four dysfunctional attitudes were associated with having been overindulged by not having to do chores:[2]

❖ "If you cannot do something well, there is little point in doing it at all."

- ❖ "It is best to give up on your own interests in order to please other people."
- ❖ "When trying to learn something new, I soon give up if I am not initially successful."
- ❖ "I avoid trying to learn new things when they look too difficult for me."

Note: The third and fourth bulleted items are reproduced with permission of authors and publisher from: Sherer, M., Maddux, J. E., Mercandante, B., Prentice-Dunn, S., Jacobs, B., & Rogers, R. W. "The Self-Efficacy Scale: Construction and Validation." *Psychological Reports*, 1982, 51, 663-671. © Psychological Reports 1982.

A CHILD WITH NO CHORES

An interviewee said:

I was so embarrassed about not doing chores that I faked it. After dinner, when my friends came to play, I told them I couldn't come out because the dishes weren't done. That was true. I played by myself or read a book for half an hour. Then I went outside and said that I could play now. That was also true. You see, my parents really wanted us to tell the truth. That was a value I got. I want my children to tell the truth and do chores, but I have a hard time teaching about chores and a harder time holding them to it.

Children continually seek the answers to two questions: "Did I do well?" (Am I a person of value?) and, "Am I okay?" (Do you love me?) Doing chores not only teaches skills, it is one way children elicit that excellent smile that signals to the child he "did good." In fact, neglected and abused children who are moved to homes with positive parents can usually believe in being valued for what they can *do* long before they believe in their value for who they are, and very long before they believe in unconditional love.

The expectation that he will do chores lets a child know that he is valued as a contributing family member.

Doing chores helps children know who they are. Doing chores helps children feel attached and grounded. The expectation that he will do chores lets a child know that he is valued as a contributing family member.

WHAT CHORES AND WHEN

If doing chores is good for children, how do you know which chores and how much to expect? The specific chores that children do and how those chore skills are taught will differ with each family according to their needs and values.

Children generally learn to do chores in three stages. First, with help, during which time they learn the process, the "how to do it," and beginning standards. Second, they do chores on their own with reminding. Finally the chores are done independently, without reminders.

Elizabeth Crary in her book *Pick Up Your Socks* charts the results of a study done in Washington State which indicated parents' reports of the ages at which their children did certain activities. This most helpful chart, found in Appendix C (page 295)

D r. Rossman found that having started to participate in household tasks at ages three and four was a predictor of success in young adulthood (mid-twenties).

gives clues about the question, "What can I expect of my child?" You can compare chores your child does with the chores kids in these 531 families did. Notice that the markers indicate the ages at which half of the children did each task with help (H), with reminding (R), and independently (A). *Pick Up Your Socks* is also a helpful resource on how to teach the many skills that children need.

It is easier to build chores into a routine earlier rather than later. Dr. Marty Rossman, family researcher at the University of Minnesota,[3] discovered that being involved in household tasks at an early age has significant positive outcomes for the children when they became young adults in terms of where they are along the educational path, career path, and family relationship path. Dr. Rossman found that having started to participate in household tasks at ages three and four was a predictor of success in young adulthood (mid-twenties). It should be no surprise that if they didn't start participating until they were fifteen or sixteen, the participation backfired: "You want me to do what?" And these late starters were less successful in their mid-twenties.

YES, VIRGINIA, THREE-YEAR-OLDS *DO DO* CHORES

"Me do that!" Three-year-old Luke thrusts himself into family activities, reminding us that he, like all children, was born to be capable.

Of course, the "be capable" is a long time in be-coming because he has so many skills to acquire, but his drive to learn, which is also a genetic instinct, sustains him, even when we adults think, *Oh, no, not again!* This genetic push to learn is supported when grown-ups present *do-able* tasks in small increments.

DIRECTIONS AND REQUESTS

Laura understood that children's first learnings set long-remembered patterns, so she mixed directions with requests right from the start. Lucky Ah! He *is* little! Luke got to start out with bone-knowledge of both negotiable (requests) and non-negotiable (directive) expectations. Think how much easier that makes the school years and how solidly it sets a pattern for parenting him during his adolescence. When the child is used to having to obey safety rules and mind family values, he has also grown accustomed to choices, problem solving, and decision making.

How did Luke's mother do that? Let's watch.

> Luke is three when Laura's friend Lizzie visits. After greetings, Mom says, "Luke, Lizzie can sit in the big chair, but there's a toy dog on it. Please move the dog so she can sit down." This is a directive, not a request. Laura chose it because Luke already knows how to do that task and doing it is sure to get him a "thank you with a smile" response. Luke gets to show his competence early in Lizzie's visit.
>
> In front of a guest, Laura is careful to ask Luke only to do what she knows he can. Following the thank-you, Laura puts a hand on Luke's arm to get his attention. "Luke, I wrapped a little present for Lizzie. It's on the table. You bring it to Lizzie and give it to her." Another directive. Something Laura guesses Luke will enjoy doing and it gets big thank-yous from Lizzie. A positive notice for competence.
>
> After the gift opening is complete, Mom proudly tells Lizzie that Luke has learned a song. "Luke, would you like to sing your song for Lizzie?" No begging or cajoling, just a straight request. Luke either says yes and sings or says no, to which Mom gives a smiling, "Okay." This is not a directive; it is a request. Luke gets to decide if he wants to show his singing competence or not.
>
> A bit later Mom says pleasantly, "Luke, you may bring some toys in here and play quietly or you may play in your room." This offers a choice but it is still a directive, so Laura doesn't say, "Okay?" If Luke

demurs, Laura draws him toward her with warmth, looks him directly in the eye, repeats the options and adds, "Lizzie and I are going to talk about grown-up things."

What does this have to do with chores? These are early actions in which Luke uses his three-year-old competency to support the family unit, his group.

After Lizzie leaves, the "chores" continue. Mom and Luke are off to do errands. "Luke, I have too much to carry. You carry that bag." Directive. The bag is small and light and Luke gets to be competent again. A three-year-old chore. As Mom stashes the bags she makes sure Luke hears, "You are a good helper." Back in the kitchen Mom is putting the purchases away. "Luke, you carry the toilet paper into the bathroom." Directive. "Luke, would you like to pick the grapes off the stems and put them in this bowl?" Request. Luke decides yes or no. Either choice is okay with Mom.

"Luke, Daddy will be home soon. Be sure your toys are on the toy shelves. Call me if you need help." Directive.

Almost time to eat. "Luke, are you willing to carry the napkins to the table?" Request. Luke decides yes or no.

Notice that Laura gave only one directive or one request at a time. Remember, three-year-olds are still really little and you give them a better chance to be successful if you ask for one thing at a time. Double instructions come later when you say, "Hold up two fingers. I want you to do two things." As you give each direction you touch each finger.

"But, but, but three is so young!" It's too young, you may say. "It's child labor." After our own deplorable period of having young children work long hours in unsafe factories, we outlawed child labor, and rightly so. But that doesn't mean we should expect children to do nothing. Rossman's research reminds us that doing chores is a child's opportunity to develop competence and confidence in herself.

HIGH IN THE ANDES

When Jean visited villages in the high Andes of Bolivia, she noticed that she didn't see any young girls. Young boys, yes. Men? Yes. Women? Yes, always with loaded shawls on their backs. When she asked the California anthropologist who had been living among the Amyra for two years why no young girls, he smiled.

When the little girl takes her first step, the family celebrates.
They pin a little shawl on her back and put a small load in it.
Perhaps a potato. She learns to keep her balance carrying a load
because she will do that all of her life. When she is three, she is
allowed to carry an infant part of the day. When she is four she
learns to care for one small animal, a pig or a goat. (This is part
of the family's financial resources!) When she is five she starts
to herd small animals close to home with an older girl. Soon she
will have her own flock and will herd from about 10:00 until
6:00 every day of the week until she is thirteen in some villages
and fifteen in others. Then she starts school.

Jean was appalled. This is exploitation of little girls! How can the child learn her developmental tasks when she is all day every day with animals? Then she looked at the women of the village. They looked healthy and most of their faces carried pleasant smile lines. And the boys were working too. In the rocky, poor soil strip fields that seemed to run straight up the mountains, these people survive where Jean, a farm girl from the Midwest, could see no possibility of surviving.

Child labor? Yes. Exploitation? You decide. Maybe these sturdy *campesinos* expect far too much of their three-year-olds. Maybe we expect too little. Or maybe we, like they, are preparing our children to live in our culture. Are they preparing producers and are we preparing consumers? Is this what we want?

MORE BIRTHDAYS, MORE CHORES

As children grow, they still need non-negotiable directives, but often those become simple code words.

Six-year-old Kiesen and a friend have stayed overnight at Kiesen's grandma's. Dad arrives to pick them up, visits a bit with Grandma, and then calls out, "Kiesen, Isaac, saddle up!" Directive. The boys scramble to cram their toys and clothes into their backpacks, get on their jackets and appear at the door. "Did you put all the toys away? Did you get all your clothes [a six-year-old chore]? Have you thanked Grandma?" A request and a reminder.

Sounds too good to be true? Sometimes the boys hassle, but most of the time it works. Why? Dad's "Saddle up!" has never been negotiable. It's a wonderful, steadying thing to have a dad who is in charge.

As their self-images as competent persons grow, children start to do things without being asked.

> At a family gathering, when Glenna was two, her grandpa hurt his knee and needed cold packs, fifteen minutes on, fifteen minutes off. Glenna watched her older cousins respond to Grandpa's timer by returning the used cold pack to the freezer or bringing a fresh one. After the older girls went home, observant Glenna did that chore with perfect competence, being a helping family member.

Teaching how to do chores usually involves many more steps. At three, Luke did or did not carry the napkins to the table. Soon he carried the napkins and the silverware. (How soon he can carry the china depends on his parents' position on broken crockery.) By six, Luke could and did set the table adequately. Sometimes the children leave the adults a step behind and acquire skills the adult hadn't noticed. Grandpa was two steps behind five-year-old Luke. They had been playing a game when Grandpa announced, "You find something to play with now. I'm going to get dinner." Luke jumped up with a firm, "I'll help!" and beat Grandpa to the kitchen. By the time Grandpa had the food out of the refrigerator, the place settings were on the table. Pay attention, Grandpa.

By the time children are in middle school, we give several directives at once. We say, "There are several things for you to do. Will you remember or do you need to make a list?"

STARTING LATER:
NO CHORES EQUALS NO SERVICES, NO FUN

> "Jack, I see it's your turn to set the dinner table this month. That means that the table is set by six o'clock." Jack has been taught the table setting protocols and Mom sees Jack is not moving to set the table and it's five minutes before six. "Jack, please set the table now. Grumbling a little, Jack sets the table."

No nagging,[4] no pleading, no doing his job for him without causing Jack some considerable discomfort.

The same thing happens the next night but Mom adds, "Honey, tomorrow night I will not remind you. I'll expect you to remember by yourself." The next night Jack "forgets" again. When he answers the dinner call, the table is set and Mom calmly tells Jack that he now owes her a job because she did his. She offers Jack a choice of one of her jobs that she thinks Jack will not be wildly happy to do, but will serve as repayment for her time and effort.

Author Delores Curran says, "No chores, no fun." In other words: Child, when you withhold your services from the rest of us, so do we withhold services from you. Life is a two-way street. One mom reports, "They often accuse me of bribery or conditional love, but I reply, reciprocity makes the world go around."

Authors Foster Cline, M.D., and Jim Fay offer ways to think about parent positions that are helpful and some that aren't, as well as how to enforce sensible real-world consequences. Cline and Fay say about chores:

> A bigger problem is getting the chores done on your time schedule. Wise parents establish a time frame with phrases like, "by the next time you eat" or "by the time I take you to your soccer game (swimming lesson, or friend's house)." That way the child always knows the ground rules.

PLAYING CATCH-UP

Cecilia joined the family by adoption after living in chaotic and neglectful circumstances from the time of her birth to age three. Cecilia's story illustrates the connection between having to do chores and learning necessary skills. Cecilia and her family were in the midst of bumpy times and had hired an in-home counselor.

The counselor suggested that Mom ask thirteen-year-old Cecilia, who had always gotten out of doing chores, to do the dishes. Terror spread across Mom's face.

"She doesn't do dishes."

"Have you asked her to do them?"

"I have, but she won't," said Mom.

Mom was afraid a request that Cecilia do the dishes would end, as it usually had, in a battle royal. Mom had, with good intent, thought it was her job to convince Cecilia to comply without grumbling, a job at which Cecilia made sure Mom always failed.

"Are you willing to try something?" the counselor asked. Mom nodded agreement. "You've just finished dinner and stacked the dishes and Cecilia is upstairs. Go to her and say firmly but not loudly or with anger, 'Cecilia, come down now and wash the dishes, please.' Then turn and walk away." Mom flinched. "Believe this will work," said the counselor. "Don't stick around to wait for her negative reaction."

Mom did as instructed and rejoined the counselor in the kitchen with a look of apprehension, almost fear. Lo and behold, less than a minute later, Cecilia entered the room with compliance, but not happiness, and went to the sink. "Well, how do I do this?"

Up to this point, Cecilia, at thirteen, had not learned either the basics of contributing to the family, or the skill of washing dishes, among other things. Bummer.

"It isn't that easy," I hear you say. You're right! If a child learns to have power through manipulations and threats that exact a price from the family, changing that pattern at age thirteen takes more perseverance than changing it at age two, three, or four.[5]

WHAT ABOUT REFUSALS TO CONTRIBUTE?

If Cecilia doesn't comply with Mom's requests, Mom has several options, and for some children, they might all need to be used:

❖ Family services to Cecilia might stop. Come to the table expecting a meal and find her place setting missing. Matter-of-factly and with the fewest possible words, Dad could point to a set of separate dishes on the counter and say, "Those are yours. Feel free to join us." Cecilia eats. The meal is followed by a request that Cecilia help wash dishes. If she refuses, her dishes can be stacked, unwashed and ready for her use at the next meal. Parents stay calm, and with any luck, Cecilia is the one who has decisions to make.

❖ Family services like rides to her friend's house, requests for a new this or that disappear into thin air. Favorite food items she asks to be stashed in the family larder are not there. Without anger. Without disdain. All in the line of normal business.

❖ Negotiations about what chores and when they're done can be opened, keeping in mind that the negotiations end at the adults' bottom line.

❖ Devise your own options with your parenting partner. Remember how the real world works. No work, no pay. No sowing, no reaping. Keep balancing give and take.

If children refuse to do their part, they should be dreadfully inconvenienced, not simply by being ignored or punished, but by not being allowed to enjoy the fruits of the contributions of other family members. Will they whine? Maybe. Will they ask why they have to work? Probably. The answer is always the same: "Because you are a member of this family and family members help each other and pull together." No more explanation is needed.

A word here about the distinction between "dreadfully inconvenienced" and punishment. Both provoke change by causing discomfort. Being inconvenienced is a real-world way of not over-adapting to another's disregarding or irresponsible behavior. It is a way of sending a "we are not your minions, expecting nothing in return" message. Life doesn't promise a smooth, unimpeded path where one need only regard oneself as important. Punishment attempts to provoke change by taking away something or even by directly inflicting pain, and can result in the child's becoming more devious or creative in ways that don't benefit the child.

Your child is in charge of the positive or negative spirit with which he works. Sad for the child if he chooses to have a negative attitude, but it needn't let it control you. This will prepare him for many times in his life when he can choose to see situations with negativity or not.

The double mantra should be: Give Options So the Child Can Exert Some Control and Duck Control Battles as Much as Humanly Possible. If you decide to get into a contest, be prepared to stick with it in a good way. Your persistence is likely to pay off. You'll feel better about the child and the child will feel more confident in you and in herself.[6]

THE POWER OF THE CONTRIBUTION

The earlier in life your child learns that he makes important contributions with his good skills, the better for him. The earlier he learns that work is not just a burden or a nasty imposition, the better for him.

Mandi's life-threatening nut allergy sometimes required a sudden trip the emergency room. Older brother Peter was competent to be left with younger Paul and they seemed to take these sudden trips in stride.

When the boys were grown men, Mom asked, "How was that for you? What did you do? What did you decide?" Pete mused, "That's easy. We understood you had to get help fast. We didn't worry because you always made it. But when you got home, you were mad at us if the house was a mess. I guess you were stressed." (Taking a kid on a life-threatening run will do that to a parent every time!) "We figured out what would bug you, cleaned it up really fast, and then went and watched television programs we were not allowed to watch."

Contributing family members, lots of skills, and an illicit reward! Good-hearted, clever boys.

Years later, during a family gathering, Mom heard her grown sons talking about their respective places of work and their angst over dealing with co-workers or supervisors who lacked garden-variety skills. "Why don't they know them?" one son lamented. "They're supposed to learn those at home, not in my shop!"

Chores, guys, chores. Be sure you are teaching chores to your children.

WHAT IF NO CHORES ARE NEEDED?

If the living situation is so proscribed that no chores are needed, how can parents assign chores? Here are some creative ideas you can try:

- ❖ If the halls are vacuumed by building maintenance, the older child can walk around the block daily with his plastic bag on trash patrol.
- ❖ If all meals are prepared by the cook, eaten out, or brought in, the family can arrange one meal a week at home for the express purpose of teaching the child to cook.
- ❖ If all laundry is sent out, the child can learn how and where to put the clean laundry away correctly and some day be taught the laundry process at a self-service laundry.
- ❖ If no pets are allowed, how about an aquarium?
- ❖ If there is no out-of-doors, how about houseplants to tend? Bouquets to arrange or freshen or clean up after?

❖ If the place is small, putting toys away and creating order is a daily chore. If the place is large, an occasional "big play" day when toys can be brought into different rooms for an expanded game of travel. The room is restored to order at the end of the play.

❖ Thank-you notes can be collages or drawings, not e-mail.

❖ If the cleaning person(s) will clean the whole house, the middle school- and high school-aged children are taught to clean from posted directions, standards enforced by an adult. A different room weekly for each month. Why? "Because everyone needs to understand what goes into keeping a room clean and it's our job to see that you learn that."

"But I don't want to and I'm busy."

"I know. So have it done by Sunday at 5:00. Tell me when you are ready to have it checked, and ask for help if you need it."

❖ If the child is a proficient Web searcher, once a week or oftener it is her family task to do a search for something needed or wanted by another family member.

Is not having to do chores lucky? Not in the long run. Chores, regular chores, done to standards, need to be expected of your child and rewarded with thanks, not in return for allowance, because doing chores is an important part of a child's education and family contribution.

■

BECAUSE CHORES TEACH RESPONSIBILITY,
THEY SET A CHILD UP FOR SUCCESS IN ADULT LIFE.
—Marty Rossman

YOU DON'T NEED TO DO THAT

When I Was Growing Up, I Was Not Expected to Learn the Same Skills as Other Children

ALL THINGS ARE DIFFICULT BEFORE THEY ARE EASY.
—Thomas Fuller

WHEN the young bull elephants removed from their family groups and transplanted to a distant preserve began reaching sexual maturity, they terrorized tourists with aggressive behavior and generally wreaked havoc. Their sexual advances were rebuffed by older elephant cows so the bulls took to mating with white rhinoceros, killing several in the process.

Park rangers guessed that some bulls came into sexual heat fully ten years earlier than normal because there were no older bulls to serve as teachers and role models. The youngsters' aggressive behavior subsided when half a dozen adult bull elephants were introduced. They pushed the young bulls around, disciplining them, and taught the teenagers how to be proper bulls.[1]

These young bull elephants exhibited a classic case of bad behavior due to missing skills. As one little boy put it, "They didn't know no better." Of course. In the natural world, the higher mammals teach their young the skills they need to become competent and responsible in their culture groups, which means taking care of themselves and meeting their needs, being responsible to others and for their relationships with others, and learning the countless skills that enable them to be and to feel competent.

THE IMPACT OF MISSING SKILLS

Overindulged adults[2] said they were missing skills, skills that others of their age seemed to have. Some say they were embarrassed and often avoided situations so others wouldn't know they didn't know how to do something. Some charged ahead with bravado, hoping no one would figure out they didn't know what they needed to know, or couldn't do what others expected them to do.

What skills were missing? The answer is different for each person. But, as one person said, "It can be a baffling surprise when you run into something you don't even know you don't know how to do when you always thought you did."

For example, in the area of household skills, Amanda's words say it all.

My growing-up life was perfect. My mom did all the work. I never had to do a thing. Now I have two children and I don't know how to cook or clean and my husband and I fight about it all the time. I'm having to learn now.

In the area of relationship skills:

Imagine being Kevin, who at twenty-five does not seem to know the first thing about getting along with work mates. Even though he usually gets jobs that he wants, he doesn't know how to listen and consider the thoughts and feelings of others. He has either left or been sacked from job after job.

In the area of money management skills:

Chloe, with $25,000 of credit card debt, pleads with a friend, "Tell me how you decide what to buy and what not to buy. I love nice things, but I have to get control of my spending and I don't know how."

These three examples remind us that feeling competent comes from trusting your skills to manage life satisfactorily.

THE UNINTENDED RESULTS OF NOT LEARNING SKILLS

The following disturbing attitudes of adults overindulged as children are related to their not having to learn skills expected of other children. They're disturbing in that they reflect more than "I didn't know how to do something." They are self-deprecating judgments about their worth.[3]

❖ "If I do not do as well as other people it means I am a weak person."
❖ "If you cannot do something well, there is little point in doing it at all."
❖ "If I fail partly, it is as bad as being a complete failure."
❖ "If I ask a question, it makes me look stupid."

Alexis felt "spongy" on the inside. Now and again she even observed her own "fakeness." She was riddled with insecurities.

When Alexis was a child, both her parents and grandparents did everything for her, so she didn't learn many of the skills her friends were learning, but she did learn how to fake it. As an adult, she presented herself so well in job interviews that she'd get hired for positions that were way over her head. Her hidden feelings of inadequacy were constantly reinforced as she struggled to look good out of the fear that others would discover she was an imposter. She had a meltdown at forty-two and entered therapy.

The over-working adults in Alexis's life could have carried through on their good intentions by encouraging her to practice the how-tos of responsibility and relationships. She may have been able to meet life situations with more confidence and less fear. Then, the outcome for Alexis would, no doubt, have matched her parents' and grandparents' intentions.

THE TIME IS NOW

The teachable moment occurs when your child shows interest and is ready to learn. That's often when he discovers he needs a skill, or is frustrated and limited using old skills. Your child may be interested and motivated but she must also have the physical, intellectual, or emotional equipment to carry it off. She must be able. When your child's interest or motivation to learn is lacking, sometimes you have to say, "It's time for you to learn. . . ." These are the children who need nudging.

A child who is pushed to learn skills beyond her interest and abilities is a child in danger of rebelling or shutting down. A child who is prevented from learning skills because others over-function on her behalf or who is not allowed to learn from the consequences of her choices, is in danger of living a diminished or more difficult life.

HERE'S HOW

Children are preprogrammed to learn and we are their teachers. But how? Amazingly, at the very time we feel most inept, when we first find ourselves at home alone with that newborn in our arms, and say, "Help! What do I do now?" we have built in skills that support the baby's learning. We stare at the tiny face, gaze into the bright eyes, and we automatically start to help the baby learn about others and our language. Then we, also automatically, speak in that unique singsong voice that helps her start to differentiate the sounds that are unique to our mother tongue. Months before she can speak she will reveal that she recognizes the language of her people. How does this learning happen? In *The Scientist in the Crib*, Alison Gopnick and her co-researchers explain that process and also describe how, in the infant and young child, every interaction we have with the baby stimulates brain growth. We highly recommend this fascinating book. When children are older we break learning tasks into meaningful, manageable segments. We also remember that the attitudes adults have toward the learning project can be a powerful stimulant or deterrent to the child's learning. Watch Charity with her grandmother.

Six-year-old Charity had quickly learned the leisurely taught, first six sewing and pressing skills in piecing a quilt block. She looked at her grandmother and said, "You really love this, don't you, Grandma?" Grandma, who had been busy with the loving but not thinking about it in that way, looked into Charity's eyes. "Yes, Charity, I really do love to sew. I didn't love it the first couple of years because no one taught me and I made so many mistakes. Now I know how and I love it." Charity looked down at the block Gamma was cutting. "When can I cut?"

"As soon as you can pull a thread cut on the grain line on a scrap." Charity demanded, "Where is the scrap? I've seen you pull a thread."

HOW DO YOU LEARN BEST, MY CHILD?

Later on, when we feel much more confident about directly teaching skills to an older child, we may not be so lucky. Some of us are natural teachers; we intuitively teach to the child's most accessible learning style. But many of us let our presumptions or reliance on our own preferred learning style get in the way of observing how our child learns best.

Mary asked her daughter Lissa to make some muffins for a guest. The ten-year-old looked stricken. "But Mom, I don't know how."

"Of course you do. You have watched me dozens of times."

"Yes, Mom, but you never told me what you were doing."

Lissa is an auditory learner. Watching is fine, but she needs to hear in order for the directions to stick.

Ward, on the other hand, learns best with his eyes. His dad complains, "I tell him and tell him and he doesn't respond. When I remember to give him a list, I can usually count on his doing what I ask."

Ward needs a list, a chart, or a sticky note on the refrigerator. He may even become the dad who reads the directions before he misconstructs the "some assembly required" stroller.

Dick, by contrast, doesn't "get it" until he has "done it," a quintessential kinesthetic learner. His mother, however, starts any project with a trip to the library. She learns best through her eyes. They drove each other nuts until they recognized their differences. Now they laugh about it.

Before you start to teach any skill to a child it is wise to ask yourself:

❖ Shall I tell her?
❖ Shall I show her?
❖ Shall I walk her through it?

When in doubt, do all three. Always do all three if you are teaching more than one child.

It is also wise to observe as children develop a preference for starting a learning with the big picture. "Those small pieces don't mean a thing to me until I know how they are supposed to fit together." Some children prefer to be presented with each small step and figure out how they fit together. "I hate it when you go on and on, blah, blah, blah, about the end product." Offer some of both and then observe. As your children grow older, encourage them to incorporate their less preferred ways of learning. Some teachers and most bosses are wildly innocent of learning style preferences, so adults are stronger when they can learn in a variety of ways.

Probably the most effective way to teach any skill is to love doing the skill yourself. Benjamin Bloom, in *Developing Talent in Young People*, described the three kinds of teachers of the superstars in his study. The first teacher allowed or helped the student fall in love with the subject, anything from baseball to classical music to nuclear science. The second taught standards, the third mentored. And they had to come in that order. Probably the way we most stand in the way of learning is to present a skill as a "hated chore" or a "burden" or something we have to do because the fearful She or He said so. Something to be avoided or gotten through as quickly as possible so we can get on to real life.

LIVING UP, OR LIVING DOWN, STANDARDS AND EXPECTATIONS

Setting standards with the expectation that they be met is a huge part of skill development. When we fail to expect high quality behaviors from our children, they live down to our expectations.

In the following story, the results of flimsy standards for a youngster showed up in later life.

"My twenty-five-year-old daughter is so gifted," says her mother. "When she was fourteen, we thought we were doing the right thing by placing her in an alternative school. The school operated with the philosophy that children learn what they need to learn when they are ready to learn it. Trouble was, the teachers accepted any effort as okay. They didn't have standards that the kids could live up to. When my daughter was a senior, she was assigned to write a major paper. The day it was due she told the teacher she had started it but it was a long way from being finished. The teacher told her, 'That's all right. Don't bother.' I think the message she got from the school was, 'If anything will cause you distress, avoid it.' And as I think about all this, I'm sure her dad and I did our part by wanting to make things easier for her than it had been for us. At twenty-five, she is still telling herself, 'Why should I do it if it requires too much effort?' I can see how she holds back and I wonder how much of her reluctance is about our not having expected much and her not feeling sure of herself."

Let's apply the Test of Four to this scenario.

1. Was the daughter being supported in addressing the **developmental tasks** of the grade and high school ages? The school and parents seem to require little in the way of achievement.
2. Was she a **resource** drain? Apparently not.
3. **Who** were the lax standards for? You decide.
4. Any **harm** done? Probably not to anyone else or to the environment.

Was this overindulgence? Was this a case of missing skills that others her age had acquired? If you say yes, then it's overindulgence.

Yes, kids can learn when they are ready to learn, but they still need the push and encouragement from adults to know they're on the right track. Remember how it felt to do a shoddy job and how different it felt to make a good effort—an effort to be proud of. Adults can insist a child do a job well or insist, if need be, that the child fine-tune her effort until it is one in which she can take pride.

ADULTS TEACH ABOUT STANDARDS IN MANY WAYS

❖ "I'll push the teddy bear back on the shelf so it won't fall off. Now you do that with the truck."
❖ "I can remember when you were just learning how to make scrambled eggs. They were an experience! Now these are really yummy."

❖ "It looks to me like you're not practicing your piano lesson as much as your teacher expects. Have you thought about how to get that done? Let me know what you decide."

❖ "Thanks for the great job you did cleaning the bathroom. There's one more thing to do. Put the dirty guest towels in the laundry and put out clean ones. Here, I'll show you where they are."

❖ "If you leave your homework on the bench by the door when you finish it at night, it will be easy for you to grab in the morning."

❖ "It's time to shop for school clothes. Let's see what you have and what you need and make a list before we head for the mall."

❖ "Hey, look at you! You are doing that way better than you did before!"

For a final reminder of the pain (embarrassment, insecurity) experienced by adults who were overindulged, here are several examples of what they said.

In Their Own Voices

If you missed learning skills that adults are expected to have learned as children, give examples.

✓ Taking care of personal hygiene, like brushing teeth and such. I missed learning the skills of cooking, housecleaning, organizing personal property, getting rid of things that are not needed. I have more fear than trust.

✓ Being in touch with feelings, expressing needs/desires, listening to/for the needs of others, negotiating for win/win outcomes.

✓ Not knowing about my boundaries. I don't know where I stop and another person starts. Identifying so much with others' dilemmas, I forget myself. I take things personally that have nothing to do with me.

✓ Personal time and money management.

✓ The overindulgence kept me close to family and away from others. I didn't know how to be part of a group. I don't know how to join.

✓ I didn't learn appropriate conversation skills. One example: What is discussed in mixed company? I think I learned about arguing, having the last word.

✓ Besides not learning how to set boundaries (saying no), I sometimes feel totally bereft of socializing, intimacy, and communication skills.

Before we go on, and now that you've "heard" the voices of the overindulged, let's review again the seven hazards of overindulgence:

- ❖ trouble learning how to delay gratification
- ❖ trouble giving up being the constant center of attention
- ❖ trouble becoming competent in
  - ✦ everyday skills
  - ✦ self-care skills
  - ✦ skill of relating to others
- ❖ trouble taking personal responsibility
- ❖ trouble developing a sense of personal identity
- ❖ trouble knowing what is enough
- ❖ trouble knowing what is normal for other people

You can use this list to sharpen your skill at seeing the connection between not having to learn skills and the problems of the overindulged. Which ones do you think relate most directly to lack of skills?

A PROMISE MADE IS A DEBT UNPAID,
AND THE TRAIL HAS ITS OWN STERN CODE.
—Robert Service in "The Cremation of Sam McGee"

NO MORE RULES!

When I Was Growing Up, My Parents Didn't Have Rules or Make Me Follow Them

■

WE TRIED SO HARD TO MAKE THINGS BETTER FOR OUR KIDS
THAT WE MADE THEM WORSE.
—Paul Harvey

66 "WE don't need to have rules in our family," one parent explained. "All we need are guidelines. Rules are mean and we are nice." Dream on! Rules and their enforcement need not be harsh, hostile or terrorizing. It is the absence of rules and too much nice that are more likely to produce terror. Of course, rules must be wisely crafted and fairly and firmly enforced. Rules provide boundaries, the edges that mark what is safe and unsafe, acceptable and unacceptable, pro-social and anti-social.

WHAT IS A RULE?

A rule is "a principle or standard to which an action conforms," according to the dictionary.

Traffic rules, work rules, etiquette rules, school rules, sports rules, fashion rules; there is an endless list of areas in which rules guide behavior choices. Rules draw the lines that help families, clubs, work groups, communities, institutions and societies operate to the best advantage of members and the unit as a whole.

Kids are eager to learn the rules.

We say people are in line or out-of-line: that is, within or outside the boundary. There are positive consequences or rewards for complying with a rule (respecting a boundary) and negative consequences or penalties for non-compliance.

Rules are like families; they're made for the nurturance, protection, and safety of the members. Freedom lies within the boundaries set by rules.

RULES FOR SUCCESS?

Read these belief statements that closely relate to having been overindulged as a child by not having rules or not having to follow them:[1]

❖ "If I fail partly, it's as bad as being a complete failure."
❖ "If I do not do well all the time, people will not respect me."
❖ "If you cannot do something well, there is little point in doing it at all."
❖ "My happiness depends more on other people than it does on me."
❖ "If someone disagrees with me, it probably indicates he does not like me."

RULES AREN'T RULES WITHOUT CONSEQUENCES

A rule isn't truly a rule unless there are consequences, both positive and negative. Children learn from experience. The "positive" rewards for following rules reinforce children's ability to acculturate. Allowing children to experience the "negative" consequences that naturally follow from a negative behavior or decision and expecting them to apologize, acknowledge, make amends or

> Rules are like families; they're made for the nurturance, protection, and safety of the members. Freedom lies within the boundaries set by rules.

restitution, and change their behavior, gives them a great chance to think and to learn.

Some parents believe that children will naturally respond positively without the need for rules or consequences.

Three-year-old Jasmine refuses to ride in the grocery cart seat. She takes things off the shelf she wants her mother to buy. If Mom says no and Jasmine pitches a fit, Mom either gives in or promises her something else instead. Mom reminds her daughter not to touch stuff or says, "Jasmine, come here," which Jasmine totally ignores. This goes on all the way through checkout. As they leave, Mom looks fried and Jasmine looks as if she's having fun.

What is wrong with this picture? There are no consequences for Jasmine because there are no rules or they are not being enforced. The adult who is being a child's everlasting "reminder service" is not doing the child any favors. Without respect for her safety or a trustworthy authority figure, what might Jasmine's behavior be like when she's fourteen or eighteen? By then, we expect youngsters to be much more responsible for themselves. Responsibility is learned in the context of relationship with parents who demand responsible behavior. Observe Mom's new behavior.

"Jasmine, in the cart or we go home now. Which will it be?" Mom is prepared to go home or she doesn't offer the alternative. If Jasmine won't choose, Mom chooses going home matter-of-factly and without lecturing. This teaches the child that Mom knows how to be in charge of what's good for her and her daughter.

Some parents have rules but get mushy when it comes time to enforce them.

Blake bought his son a car. Blake's rule was, "I buy this one car, you take care of it. After this car, you're on your own." His son totaled the car. But the family lives six miles from town and it didn't take much pestering before Blake replaced the car saying, "My boy has to have a way to get around."

When Blake's son totaled the second car, Blake anteed up one more time and complained to his friends about the hazardous conditions of the roads.

> The adult who is being a child's everlasting "reminder service" is not doing the child any favors.

There are no consequences here. The rule is there, but the boundaries are lax and get undermined or mutilated by a "nice" adult or, perhaps as in this case, for an adult's convenience. Adults overindulged as children tell us they lacked confidence in the good judgment of their parents because their parents seemed so uncertain about what was or wasn't good for them.[2]

FROM LAX TO FIRM RULES

Lax: The history paper has to be a minimum of five pages long, but no points are deducted for turning in a four-page paper.

Firm: At the time the assignment is made, the instructor announces clearly how points will be deducted, then does as he promised.

Lax: The group's meeting begins promptly at 7:00. The important announcements are always made at the very beginning. Those who arrive late ask what happened before they got there and the chairperson takes ten minutes to repeat the announcements.

Firm: The announcements are not re-stated for those who were not there to hear them. "Please ask a friend to bring you up to date after the meeting."

Lax: The spelling test is on Tuesday. Ten-year-old Jonathan gets most of the words wrong because he didn't study. When Dad sees the spelling paper, he says nothing and goes back to his computer.

Firm: Dad says, "If you know how to handle this problem, Jon, I hope you do it right away. I'll be happy to help you work it out if you need that."

Lax: "What time should I be home?" asks thirteen-year-old Natalie. "Nine o'clock. It's a school night," comes her mother's reply. No argument, but Natalie gets home at ten and because her mother isn't home, Natalie tells her friends the next day, "I got by with it, no trouble."

Firm: Next time, Mom is home to enforce curfew. If Mom can't be home, she makes other arrangements or says no to her daughter going out at all.

CONSEQUENCES OF BREAKING RULES

If the consequences do not involve injury, permitting consequences to take their course allows children to experience both negative and positive consequences. When consequences cause emotional distress like worry or guilt or remorse, allow your child to experience the distress of the poor decision. Indeed, he can also experience the rewards of a wise choice.

> Aaron grew up with a rule that children dress for weather conditions. But Aaron, fourteen, thought he knew better. Aaron's dad drove him and his buddy to a late-fall high school football game. Dad noticed his son wore no jacket but Dad said nothing. Midway through the game Dad noticed Aaron hunching over in the cold or running in place to keep warm. Dad said nothing. Aaron brought his jacket to the next game.

Diane Wagenhals, director of a parent education center, has this to say about consequences:

> *I think there are negotiable as well as non-negotiable consequences. I am encouraging parents to design "open-ended consequences" in which the child needs to convince the parent that he or she has accomplished the necessary learning, has made the necessary amends and has earned the right to return to life as usual. This can be replacement for "You are grounded for a week!" Instead, "You are grounded until we sit down and talk this through and you come up with a plan we both agree will make things right again. You also need to convince me that you have a viable plan for making sure this won't happen again. Once you have convinced me, the grounding is over. When you are ready, we will sit down for a preliminary conversation." This way the child has a lot of healthy power and the parent is less likely to punish himself or herself by taking on too much of the responsibility for solving the problem.[3]*

When a child has violated or exceeded some boundary, appropriate consequences need to slow the child's life way down until he uses good thinking to get the problem solved or the situation corrected.

WHEN BREAKING RULES BREAKS A TRUST

To say we don't trust someone is to say we can't count on them.

Savannah baked and carefully decorated her daughter's birthday cake. Her sister, Hailey, whom Savannah describes with some resentment as the overindulged, the Special Child, the one who was favored and treated differently from her siblings, dropped by on her way to a concert. She announced that she would not be staying for the birthday party. On seeing the cake, Hailey asked Savannah if she could have a piece to take with her.

"No," Savannah replied, "at least not until "Happy Birthday" has been sung and the birthday girl has cut the first piece." Savannah left the room, returning shortly to find a chunk of the cake missing, along with her sister.

Savannah was taking good care of herself and others when she said no cake until later. That Hailey took the piece of cake signals Hailey's disrespect of Savannah, the birthday girl, and in this case, most everyone else, including herself. Respecting boundaries is crucial in earning and maintaining others' trust.

MY PARENTS WOULD KILL ME: WHEN A PARENT HAS NO WAY TO EFFECT A CONSEQUENCE

For the times you don't have direct knowledge of your youngster's breech of your rules, that is no reason not to make the rules. This is particularly true as children get older. Studies tell us that the most effective way to say "no" to drug use is for the youngster to say (and believe), "My folks would kill me." In other words, they know their parents would strongly disapprove and there would be negative consequences. Big ones.[4] For the kids who are sure about their parents' values, the biggest negative consequence is the knowledge that their parents would be grossly disappointed by a decision that allowed harm to come to themselves or others.

When it comes time for a child to make a choice or decision, the rules in the head, the voices of loved ones saying, "I'll stick by you if you say no to this drug—it's bad for you and I love you," can strengthen the child's position to do the right thing. A parent message of "I don't expect you to drink until you're twenty-one, when the laws say you can decide," makes it likely that a decision to drink would be made with considerably more thought than if there were no message about drinking at all. Or to hear "All kids drink before the legal age anyway." No, they don't, and implicit permission to engage in potentially harmful activities should never be a parent's message.

WHEN PARENTS HAVE DIFFERENT RULES

Dad always got the boys gum from the gumball machine whenever they were out together. Mom did not approve because she believed gumballs should be for very special occasions or for a reward for something. One day her boys (two- and three-year-olds) began pestering her for gumballs at the store where Dad always got them. Mom said, "Sorry, no." The boys begged, "But Dad gets us gum." Mom replied, "But the rule in our house is that Mom doesn't." The boys never bothered her again about gum.

YOU CAN'T HAVE EXCEPTIONS WITHOUT RULES

Sometimes we indulge ourselves and our children by occasionally breaking a rule. Both adult and child should know they are going beyond the rules intentionally. "Tonight we will break the rule and read an extra story. We can sleep late tomorrow morning." Breaking rules on purpose can make both parent and child feel good and does not constitute overindulgence unless it is done so often it no longer qualifies as occasional. "Having limits does not mean saying no to every request a child makes."[5]

STAYING OUT OF THE WAY OF A CHILD'S LEARNING

It's quite normal for parents to want their child not to be in distress. When this feeling is about to launch a parent into action, parents should ask themselves: Is this my problem or hers? If it is the parents' problem, they take action to correct the problem. If it is the child's problem, the healthy parent tolerates any distress the child feels, giving the child a respectful chance to learn. This distress is the child's cue that he needs to pay attention. If the child doesn't solve the problem, the parent can support the child's ability to take action while not removing the stress.

Seventeen-year-old Fred received a traffic ticket by going forty-five miles in a 30-mph zone. Kids at school were free with advice about contesting the ticket. "You don't want to go to DumbDumb Driving School. Make something up. Their equipment isn't that accurate, you know."

Fred's mother was expected to accompany him to court on the assigned date. Mom asked her son how he intended to handle the situation and he told her about the advice he received. "And, do you think that would be wise?" Mom's tone of voice indicated what she thought. She left the ball in his court.

At the old courthouse, they and about thirty other pairs of parents and miscreants filled the courtroom to hear the judge deliver an hour-long, no-mincing-words lecture. As the bailiff called each teen's name, parents and teen were ushered into an old-fashioned glass-enclosed office in the back of the courtroom. One by one, the waiting parties heard the muffled sounds coming from the judge's office. The voice of the judge. Sometimes the voice of the teen. But mostly, the voices of the parents. And then the "sentences" being meted out. Suspended licenses. DumbDumb Driving School. One after another, dejected teens and agitated parents left the office. Fred's palms were sweating.

When it was Fred's turn, the judge looked at Fred's traffic report and then turned to him. "Well, if this doesn't take the cake." A picture of her child being marched off to jail passed quickly through Mom's mind. The judge queried Fred, "Did you, in fact, exceed the speed limit on Hampshire Avenue?"

"Yes, sir."

The judge continued very seriously, "Well!" Then, gruffly, "You're the first one to admit it today." Pause. "The arresting officer noted you were courteous and didn't deny you were speeding. Is that correct?"

"I think so, sir."

"Are you going to exceed the speed limit again? Have you learned your lesson?"

"No, sir. And yes, sir," replied a hopeful Fred.

"All right. I will believe you. Drive carefully, son." And he nodded toward the door. They left in silence, descended in the elevator and exited the building. Halfway down the block, Fred spoke.

"That was almost a good experience."

Fred had broken a rule that had consequences. He chose not to evade and his mother did not get in the way of his learning.

PERSONAL BOUNDARIES ARE RULES FOR OURSELVES

Setting personal boundaries, the ability to decide what's good for you and what is not, is a matter of identifying a rule that protects your own health, safety, and emotional well-being. Many who were overindulged complained of having trouble setting and keeping boundaries.

A way to determine where your personal boundary lies is in the answer to this question: "How would I be taking good care of myself?"

> At an evening meeting, Steph asked Brittany to have breakfast with her the next morning. "What time should I pick you up?" asked Steph. Brittany replied, "Nine o'clock." Steph looked dumbfounded. "I was thinking of seven o'clock."
>
> Brittany liked Steph but seven was too early. She had meetings beginning at eleven that morning that would run until ten that night. Mindful of taking care of her health, she told Steph she was unwilling to be up at seven. "How about 8:30?" offered Brittany.
>
> Steph agreed. "I'll pick you up at 8:30."

Brittany negotiated a rule, a boundary, if you will, when she agreed on 8:30. If she had agreed to seven o'clock, she would have violated a personal rule based on what was healthy for her, and if she had violated what was good for her, she could end up resenting her friend.

A forty-three-year-old talked about personal boundary problems this way:

> *My mother felt that it was her duty to ridicule her children to get them to comply. My father withheld love and himself from me, expecting our relationship to go through my mother. Shame was a big part of her discipline. Secrets were always kept, even from each other. I felt it was my duty never to express any real feelings at home, being fearful of losing my parents' love. The skill I didn't learn that's affected me all my life is how to set boundaries. I often find myself in a triangle situation.*

WHAT IS TRIANGULATION?

Being in the middle of parent relationships was a problem for many who were overindulged. Laurie Simons has a clear and simple definition of relationship triangulation: *When a third person gets involved between two people who ought to be talking to each other, you have a triangle. Also, when a third person takes sides or tries to solve the problem between two other people, you have a triangle.*

This woman (we'll call her Betty) speaks about finding herself in a triangulated situation, which was not of her making. It is true that many who grow up being overindulged can have a hard time knowing who is responsible for what and find it difficult to set the boundaries that keep them out of triangulation.

Similarly, Mom may get mad at Dad but not want to get mad at him directly. So her daughter gets mad at him instead. Dad is surprised by the strength and anger of Betty's reaction to what seems to him a small provocation. And Mom is silently pleased that Dad is feeling Betty's anger. Betty is triangulated in her parents' relationship, largely because the adults are not being responsible for their own business.

As an adult, Betty, accustomed as she is to the lack of clarity of her parents, may decide to correct what is now her problem by getting good help.

Betty says, "I think 'boundaries' are vital and so many of us girls have been brought up to please others. I still struggle to set healthy boundaries. I have found learning to set personal boundaries very liberating."

In Their Own Voices

When your parents overindulged you, what feelings resulted?
- ✓ I felt neglected. They didn't care enough to set curfew for me like my friend's parents did. I was proud I could "mother" my brother ten years younger than I.
- ✓ I felt confused as this treatment was not consistent.
- ✓ I was mad because I wanted my parents to stand up to me and say, No.
- ✓ I felt ignored because attention wasn't paid to my needs for structure and limits.

continued

✓ I felt good (powerful) because I got to do what I wanted, but this would usually end up with bad feelings because when the limits were finally expressed it was done with anger and/or punishment.

Were you overindulged in most things, or were there some areas in which you were given structure (guidance, rules, boundaries)?

✓ At times there were rules as to where I could go and when to return, but they were inconsistent. Past age thirteen there were none.

> *In your case, were there rules?* Yes.
> *If yes, who set them?* Unspoken rules.
> *If yes, were you expected to follow them?* Yes.
> *If yes, did you follow them regularly?* No.
> *If yes, were they enforced?* Yes.
> *Who enforced them?* Father.
> *If yes, were there consistent consequences if you broke them?* No.

✓ I had curfews and was expected to do household tasks. I knew not to ask to do things that would inconvenience Mom, like ask to have a slumber party. I learned Mother was "in control" and expected her control to be maintained.

> *In your case, were there rules?* Yes.
> *If yes, who set them?* Mother.
> *If yes, were you expected to follow them?* Yes.
> *If yes, did you follow them regularly?* Yes.
> *If yes, were they enforced?* Yes.
> *Who enforced them?* I did.
> *If yes, were there consistent consequences if you broke them?* No.

✓ I learned how to behave when visiting older people.

> *In your case, were there rules?* Sometimes.
> *If yes, who set them?* Mom.
> *If yes, were you expected to follow them?* No.
> *If yes, did you follow them regularly?* No.
> *If yes, were they enforced?* No.
> *If yes, were there consistent consequences if you broke them?* No.

WHEN CULTURAL RULES HAVE BEEN BROKEN

Every culture has rules that help that culture function in its own unique way. Those cultural mandates provide for stability and safety. In William Ury's book *The Third Side*, he describes how Botswana Bushmen deal with conflict.

> *When a serious problem comes up, everyone sits down, all the men and women, and they talk and talk—and talk. Each person has a chance to have his or her say. This open and inclusive process can take days . . . until the dispute is literally talked out. The community members work hard to discover what social rules have been broken to produce such discord and what needs to be done to restore social harmony.*

It's not possible for us to talk for several days to resolve a problem, but when a child has broken a cultural rule we can ask:

What needs to be done? How do we help disputing individuals comply with the social rules? Or if the rules need to be altered, how do we go about that?

Social rules provide stability and define what is normal, and children need to know what the social rules of their culture are and how to comply with them.

I NEVER KNEW WHAT WAS NORMAL

"I never knew what was normal," complained an interviewee. One definition of rules is that they define the pervading custom or standard, the normal state of things. Understanding the role of rules and their place in the cultural norms is a lifelong learning task for all of us.

"Drive on the right side of the road" (except for those countries where they insist on driving on the "wrong" side) is an up-front rule every driver knows. Some cultural rules, however, are unspoken and therefore are learned in informal ways. One of the challenges of moving forward is figuring out the unspoken rules.

David C. Pollock and Ruth E. Van Reken in their book *Third Culture Kids* describe in detail the confusion that children who have grown up in more than one culture can experience when they enter or re-enter a culture after some years absence. For example, they tell of a young girl who was growing up in a country where water was scarce. She learned the rule, if it's brown, flush it down. If it's yellow, let it mellow. A spoken, up-front rule. During a visit home to the states when the child "let it mellow," her grandmother shamed her for being a thoughtless girl. The flush rule of the states had never been clearly stated to the granddaughter and she was deeply embarrassed. Not grandmother's intent at all. *Third Culture Kids* is a profoundly helpful book for anyone who is raising or knows someone who grew up in more than one culture. The experience of the child, it turns out, is very, very different from the adult business, missionary, military, or government parents whose work or lifestyle causes them to move their children from one culture to another.

Parents teach hidden rules informally, usually over a long period of time; rules such as when to hold our tongues, and when to tell a white lie. Just remember that it takes children a long time to learn some of these rules (some of us who are socially inept never do) and you can avoid ridicule or shaming as you point them out.

Rules set and enforced with a loving heart transmit love to children. Even when they resist in the short haul, the long haul tells the tale.

■

SHE TOLD THE GROWN-UPS IN THE WORLD WHAT TO DO
AND THEY DID IT. SHE WILL HAVE TO LEARN
TO COLOR INSIDE OF THE LINES.
—Nancy McKelvey

DO AS YOU LIKE

When I Was Growing Up, My Parents
Gave Me Too Much Freedom

YOU often hear kids complain that their parents don't give them enough freedom, so it's particularly interesting that as adults, those who were overindulged said that they resent having been given too much freedom as children. What could they mean? What is too much freedom?

What is *freedom*? Try these modifiers on for size:

❖ having the power of self-determination
❖ emancipation
❖ liberty
❖ lack of restriction

These conditions are not all bad . . . when you're an adult. Even in adulthood, however, we learn that pure freedom can go from positive to negative in a heartbeat, depending on how you use your freedom.

Freedom granted or allowed too soon, allowed before the child has the skills to handle it, is not a great gift, as the adults overindulged as children told us.

Many youngsters say, "I want to do what I want to do, and I don't want any authority telling me otherwise." "Freedom" to them is excitement, self-indulgence, exceeding social or conventional rules, and acting with no restrictions. But a child who has more freedom than responsibility is in a precarious place. So is anyone in his or her path. Terrorists think this way. Criminals think this way. Anarchists think this way. "Your rules don't apply to me! I can do what I want to."

THE HAZARDS OF TOO MUCH FREEDOM

Children are not equal in all ways. They are equally valued for who they are, but they are not equal to adults in discernment, experience, skills, and responsibility. And freedom given to one child may not be wise for another. Children who are given permissions beyond their demonstrated responsibility level are at risk. And so is everyone who comes in contact with them.

Howard Light, a Harvard University professor, has been studying how students can make the most of their four years of college. He says, "Most colleges and the people that run them tend to think: Let's admit the best students we can, and then get out of their way."

Light advises students to get to know at least "one faculty member each semester fairly well." His advice was guided by student responses to being asked how their college experience could be improved. "I was horrified," he said. "Students told us that in order to make the most of college we—the faculty, their advisors—need to get in their way. They wanted us to get in the way."[1]

Too much freedom for children occurs when wants and desires outrun maturity and good judgment. Too much freedom is scary for a child who is ill equipped and inexperienced in the handling of it. It puts the child in jeopardy by expecting the child to be able to handle people and situations without having learned how he or she can do so with safety and responsibility. Adults need to get in the way of too much freedom for their children.

BELIEFS OF ADULTS WHO HAD TOO MUCH FREEDOM

Adults who had too much freedom as children tended to agree with the following:[2]

❖ "I feel insecure about my ability to do things."
❖ "I do not seem capable of dealing with most problems that come up in my life."
❖ "If a person asks for help, it's a sign of weakness."

Note: The first two bulleted items are reproduced with permission of authors and publisher from: Sherer, M., Maddux, J. E., Mercandante, B., Prentice-Dunn, S., Jacobs, B., & Rogers, R. W. "The Self-Efficacy Scale: Construction and Validation." *Psychological Reports*, 1982, 51, 663-671. © Psychological Reports 1982.

Of course, we would never intend for our children to believe so little in themselves, yet the study results indicate they do.

GETTING TOO MUCH FREEDOM

How do children get more freedom than is good for them? Some children work in groups, put together a plan, and then figuratively move arm in arm to apply enough pressure on their parents to get restrictions dropped. Some children work singly and very effectively to wear adults down. Some adults are quicker to cave in than others, wanting to please the child or to insure the child is not left out or shunned. Some parents give in, even when it is against their better judgment.

A parent who, in order to be pleasing, compromises the health and safety of a child by changing a rule, is overindulging. Children push the limits but some parents need to stiffen their backbones in order to be pushed against and still hold to what they know is best for the child.

NOT TOO MUCH TO HANDLE

The wisdom of a thirteen-year-old, Annie, who was allowed to be the boss, helps us to know how much a parent's warm sturdiness counts.

> Both Mom and Dad grew up in homes with addicted, unskilled parents. Determined their daughter would not experience the deprivation they experienced, they allowed her far too much to say about everything from a very early age. She told the grown-ups what to do and they did it.
>
> When she left the house without permission to be with her friends and didn't return until she was good and ready, often the next day, Dad would hit her in punishment. She responded by leaving again.
>
> Forced into therapy by her own out-of-control behaviors, a therapist asked Annie, "How long have you been too much to handle?" Surprised, she answered without a moment's pause, "Always."

No matter how they may fuss and stew, children yearn for adults who are wise and strong and sure. Giving kids too much freedom, giving in to their demands just because they're making them, sends the wrong message. Parents should consider a child's opinions and wants, but the adults make the choices and set the boundaries.

ADULTS ON DUTY . . . OR NOT?

"Good" freedom allows children to explore or experiment within the bounds of safety and their abilities. "Good" freedom allows for creativity without destruction and "good" freedom allows for learning important lessons from experience.

"Sure you can go to the party." These are the words of a fifteen-year-old's parents who did not expect answers about Who, What, Where, When, How much, What time, What if, Who else, What about a ride home, and Who's supervising, before answering the "Can I go" question. Too much freedom. Adults not on duty. Scary for kids.

"Sure you can go to the party." These are the words of a fifteen-year-old's dad who *did* find out all information and in spite of misgivings,

HOW MUCH IS ENOUGH?

says yes under pressure. Too much freedom. Adults not on duty. Scary for kids.

"Sure you can go to the party." These are the words of a fifteen-year-old's parents who did the checkout for information, called a couple of the other parents of partygoers and said yes with some conditions that were negotiated with the teen, such as the coming-home time. Adults on duty. Security for kids.

When children (and all of us) repeatedly bump into authority that is too harsh or unreasonable, that is a sign that it's time to review the situation and negotiate and determine necessary changes.

> "**G**ood" freedom allows children to explore or experiment within the bounds of safety and their abilities. "Good" freedom allows for creativity without destruction and "good" freedom allows for learning important lessons from experience.

HOW MUCH FREEDOM?

What is the right amount of freedom? When in doubt, parents and others can ask themselves these questions:

- ❖ Is it an amount of freedom the child can handle responsibly?
- ❖ Will giving the child this freedom help him accomplish his developmental tasks?
- ❖ What accountability is built into this increased freedom?
- ❖ Whose needs are being met?

One of the biggest challenges in parenting is reconciling the joint needs of children for nurturance and limit setting. Researcher Diana Baumrind[3] and others have explored what kinds of families rear the most competent children. Using the dimensions of responsiveness to children and demandingness of children, they developed categories of families. "Responsiveness" equates with nurture and "demandingness" equates with structure. The categories are:

Authoritarian. Low in responsiveness and high in demandingness. These parents impose rules and expect obedience. They use punishment to ensure compliance. They restrict autonomy of children. Too little freedom.

Permissive. High in responsiveness and low in demandingness. These parents impose few demands on children. They are supportive and nurturing, but avoid exercising control over children's behavior. Too much freedom.

Rejecting-neglecting. Low in responsiveness and demandingness. These parents are detached. They are not supportive and nurturing and place few demands on children's behavior. Too much freedom.

Authoritative. High in both responsiveness and demandingness, they set limits and consistently enforce them while explaining their reasons. They value a balance of self-will and conformity. "Good" freedom.

Any number of studies based on this work agree that competent children are more likely to spring from families with authoritative styles, the one with high nurture and high limit-setting.

HIGH NURTURE AND STRUCTURE
FOR APPROPRIATE FREEDOM

In the home

Danielle, who is four, uses all her best "move-the-adults" skills when Dad leaves for an errand and Danielle wants to go with him. It's eight o'clock in the evening and Dad says, "No, you may not go with me this time. It's too near your bedtime." Danielle erupts in a full-blown tantrum. Dad says, "I love you, Danielle. I'll be back later," and leaves her with Mom. Danielle's squall subsides quickly when Mom waits calmly until Danielle "gets a hold of herself." Then Mom says, "Come sit with me for a minute," and reads a book or they just sit and snuggle until Danielle pops off the couch to play with her sister.

Is high nurture and limit-setting (structure) at work here? Yes. Adults on duty. Security for the child.

The four Willis kids, ages three to fourteen, watch TV and play Nintendo pretty much when and for as long as they want to. Their parents sometimes know what kids are watching what programs, but they have few yesses and nos. The three-year-old, if he's interested, watches the programs the older kids select. The Nintendo is set up in the twelve-year-old's room and someone is playing most of the time. The parents announce when it's bedtime, which is the signal to turn off all "screen machines."

Too much freedom? No question. This situation is also low in nurture because nurture is about meeting children's needs. Whose needs are being met in the Willis home? It's low structure because structure is about limit-setting to provide healthful and safe situations for children's growth. The Willis parents seem to have vacated healthy limit-setting.

A college student was heard to say, "We were in front of the TV all the time when I was a kid. I wish that hadn't been the case."

"Why?" Connie asked.

Because I would have learned to do things much earlier. I didn't start learning to do a lot of the things I love until I was nineteen.

At the school

The school faculty and staff were being drained by demanding and disrespectful students. The staff's increasing resentment should have been a big clue there was a problem that needed solving.

Isabella went to her son's high school to tutor a recent immigrant. She was taken aback by a haze in the hallways, the result of students smoking in one of the bathrooms. The floors were dirty and littered with refuse.

Isabella peeked into that bathroom between classes to discover it was an empty tiled room. The plumbing had been capped, the stalls removed. She asked a teacher what was going on and was told that the students who smoked kept breaking the fixtures so the fixtures were removed.

"Why are they smoking in the building?" she asked.

The response was a shrug of the shoulders and an "I'm not sure." The principal said he'd tried to respect the kids' desire to act on their convictions, but they pushed more and more and he didn't know how or where to stop saying okay. "Most of the faculty doesn't like where we've gotten."

Adults are clearly not on duty. Low structure, low nurture. Scary for kids. Whether at home or at school, kids want parents and authority figures to be in charge. Will they bump against that authority? Yes. If they are challenging the boundaries as part of figuring out who they are, they need empathic and sound authority to bump against. The school story continues:

The next year a new principal implemented changes after taking a stand, getting the support of the staff, and having several meetings with the parents. No smoking in the building. No more litter and disgusting behavior in the hallways. Changing the paradigm to one of mutual respect. More smiles all around.

Because the principal led the way in seeing that both the teachers and the students had an environment where they could get their needs met, this is a situation of high nurture. And because boundaries were set in consideration of making the learning environment healthy (physically and emotionally) and safe. This is the structure side of good freedom.

Adults back on duty. Security for the students (and the staff).

Laurie Simons has written a super-helpful book, called *Taking "NO" for an Answer,* which is filled with directions for playful games and family activities that teach and help families practice an array of skills, including family leadership, in a fun way.

ADULTS ON BOARD WITH ONE ANOTHER

The best decisions about who's in charge of how much freedom and when, are the ones the parental units agree on. In this family, the parents disagreed, but sadly, one deferred without discussion.

> "Why didn't you say no when I told you I was going to Jerry's house to see his new camera?" Brooke was twenty-two when she asked this question."I was only eight years old and he was fifteen. How was I to know?"
>
> When she'd asked if she could go to Jerry's house, Mom had said no, and her husband, standing nearby, said, "Oh, let her go." In spite of misgivings signaled by a clutching under her heart, Mom deferred. Brooke went into Jerry's house and was molested.

Adults not on duty. Too much freedom. Unsafe for Brooke. Not developmentally ready to protect herself. Needed more skills, more guidance. Forced into growing up too fast. Wronged development. Harm. One doesn't need the Test of Four to know that too much freedom in this case was overindulgence and the overindulgence caused pain.

Much later, in joint therapy, Mom told her daughter, "I'm sorry I didn't protect you. You needed me and I failed you. I'm so sorry that I didn't stick with my first answer. I'm so sorry I didn't stand up to your dad. That was my responsibility and I blew it. I will do whatever I can do to earn back the trust I lost when you were eight."

HELP IN DECIDING

Again, consult the Ages and Stages charts (page 275) for more help in deciding if your rules and boundaries need to be tighter or looser. Ask yourself if you are enforcing your rules. When you ask for information from the child and hear fuzzy, irrational or suspicious replies, consider tightening your rules and limits. Be sure you are doing on-going monitoring to check for adherence to the rule and evaluate whether or not the rule continues to serve its purpose. Negotiate rules that need changing. This is how you teach your children to think and develop the tools to make responsible decisions about their own freedoms.

BYSTANDERS ON BOARD

In this current cultural atmosphere of "Don't say anything to other people's children," parents who are trying to limit misbehavior are denied the support of the larger community in reinforcing the need for socially appropriate behaviors. Years ago, when Jean misbehaved, the nearby adults did not call the police or phone her parents. They just stopped the unwanted behavior and no more was said about it. Now people often ignore children's misbehavior or reinforce it by smiling. We are not talking about an infant crying, which is natural, or the tantrum of a two-year-old, which is sometimes the response of a child who is thwarted. These situations deserve only a sympathetic glance to the parent. We're talking about children's behaviors about which the parent should be authoritative, like whining, pushing, hitting, kicking, throwing things, yelling, and screeching. Parents need the support of bystanders who signal to the child that certain behaviors are not appropriate.

When other people's children are misbehaving, we sometimes walk away. Often we don't know how to help. But sometimes we can't walk away. What do we do when we are in a small space with a misbehaving child (as is the case with passengers on an airplane). They are trapped. They can't walk away from unwanted behaviors. But the things they can do are similar to things we bystanders can do in other close-quarter situations, like on a bus or a train or in a small restaurant.

Those kids are bothering me!
"I'm exhausted!" Ralph complained. "This trip shouldn't have seemed long, but it went on for ages. There were a couple of kids running up and down the aisles of the plane, crawling under the seats,

bumping my arm, yelling, and those high-pitched screeches pierced my ears. I couldn't concentrate on the report I needed to write and I couldn't read, never mind trying to sleep. What can a passenger do when the parents aren't managing their kids and won't even make eye contact with you?"

Many of us feel helpless when people a quarter of our size are making a plane ride miserable. But we do need to do something. Miserable we may be, but helpless we are not.

When asked what passengers should do, a young mom who flies regularly with her children said emphatically, "Don't let a single incident pass." That means:

- ❖ Don't act as if it is okay.
- ❖ Don't make sympathetic remarks like, "He sure is active," or "Children need to move; what can a parent do?" or "My son did that too."
- ❖ Above all, don't smile or chuckle at the misbehavior. That tells the child he is finding successful ways to interact with strange adults.

You can:
- ❖ Call the flight attendant and request help. Remember that if the seat belt sign is off and the child is not disturbing the flight attendant's service, the attendant is not required to do anything about the child unless a passenger complains.

When you speak to the flight attendant, be specific:
- ❖ "This child is bothering me. If there is an empty seat farther from him, I would like to move."
- ❖ "This child's behavior is bothersome. Please take him to his seat."
- ❖ "I have a headache and the screaming really hurts my head. Please do something."
- ❖ "Could you ask the parent to keep the child in her seat most of the time? This running and bumping is really distracting, and I must finish this report."
- ❖ "What is your airline's policy on children being out of their seats and bothering other paying passengers?"
- ❖ "I'm wondering what you would do if I were running down the aisles and yelling. Something immediately, I bet. Can't you do the same with these children?"

HOW MUCH IS ENOUGH?

Since the flight attendant may have no authority to enforce a request, there are things a passenger can do:

❖ Do not smile at the misbehavior; frown at the child.
❖ If you are bumped, say, "Ouch," and shake your head "no."
❖ If the child in the seat behind or in front of you is annoying you, say firmly to the child, "Please don't do that. It bothers me." Don't smile.
❖ Use your intuition about whether to speak to the parent. Remember, the parent is trapped too and may not know what to do. Consider what approach might be successful with that particular parent.

If you are scorned for objecting to a child's misbehavior, that is because our whole society suffers from the sickness called "too much freedom." It does not mean you are wrong; it means you are the only one helping the child.

TRUE FREEDOM

Too much freedom is harmful for the children, their parents, and other people. True freedom occurs within safe spaces. That safety is created by understanding the boundaries in a familiar setting and then gaining the understanding of them in strange places.

CHILDREN DO NOT NEED PARENTS WHO ARE FRIENDS.
THEY NEED PARENTS WHO ARE FRIENDLY.
—Ada Alden

THE STRUCTURE HIGHWAY

Six Ways of Structuring Children's Lives, Two that Are Helpful

YOU CAN'T CHANGE THE WAY A CAR STEERS
BY GIVING IT A NEW COAT OF PAINT.
—M.C.K.

ANY road is designed to take a car and driver safely from here to there. "There," for the parenting road, should lead a child into his or her own fullness. This is when they realize their own competence, confidence, skillfulness and admirability. That is our intention.

The "here" from which we begin the journey is not always a solid starting place. It can be spongy or brittle or only half-there. Nonetheless, if it's what we have to launch us on the journey, and launch the journey we must, we use it, that is, until we slip off the road and feel the drag and the bumps of the shoulders.

When we get off track, no matter the reason, the bumpiness serves as a signal that adjustments to bring us back to center are called for.

"If what I'm doing is not working out well, what on earth am I supposed to do instead?" I hear you say. This chapter is about what to do instead.

THE STRUCTURE HIGHWAY

Just as there is a Nurture Highway, we can think of structure in that way too. These structure positions are aligned horizontally like the chart (pages 197–98), Rigidity at one end and Abandonment at the other.

The Structure Highway provides a big picture of the ways to set rules. As you read, keep in mind that Marshmallowing is the way to overindulge with rules. If the word "rule" has a negative connotation for you, use a more neutral word or phrase that means the same to you, such as "our way." Period.

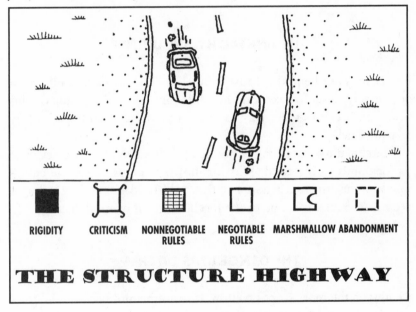

RIGIDITY   CRITICISM   NONNEGOTIABLE   NEGOTIABLE   MARSHMALLOW   ABANDONMENT
                          RULES   RULES

THE STRUCTURE HIGHWAY

The Highway illustrates six ways to manage children and ourselves by establishing rules. The positions are arranged from most strict to least strict. The four outside positions are destructive or less effective than the two center positions, Nonnegotiable Rules and Negotiable Rules. When these two center positions are implemented considering the child's age and stage of development, they offer the most workable ways to create safety for a child and set boundaries for oneself.

Here are the descriptions of each of the six positions on the chart arranged as a Highway.

THE HEALTHY CENTER

Nonnegotiable rules are helpful. They define what is safe and makes a child feel secure. These rules must be observed and are enforced with appropriate consequences, both negative and positive. The adult does all of the thinking when setting the rule, but takes the developmental ability of the child into account.

Negotiable rules are also helpful because they teach children to think by expecting them to collect and evaluate information, and to be responsible by allowing children to learn that their behavior choices have consequences.

THE UNHEALTHY SHOULDERS

Criticism is not helpful because it involves ridicule, name-calling and grandiosity, and focuses on the child himself rather than on his behavior. It can signal a way to fail. "You will end up being as lazy as your Uncle Joe."

Marshmallow parenting is not helpful. It patronizes or gives in to the demands of the child. Marshmallowing compromises the child's safety or health. It teaches that the child need not follow rules or become capable. It is one of the mechanisms of overindulgence.

THE DANGEROUS DITCHES

Rigidity is the most strict position. It is not helpful because the rules are set by one who does not consider the child's needs or abilities. The person who sets the rule does not negotiate.

Abandonment is certainly not helpful. It happens when adults fail to make or enforce rules to protect children. It does not teach children how to keep themselves safe and does not teach them skills they need to be successful.

The chart on the next two pages gives additional information about the positions on the Structure Highway. We encourage you to read Chapters 8 through 15 of Jean and Connie's book *Growing Up Again, Parenting Ourselves, Parenting Our Children* for more information and many more examples of ways to provide children with structure.

The Structure Chart

Children internalize protection, safety, freedom, success, and self-esteem from nonnegotiable rules. Despair and failure come from rigidity, criticism, marshmallowing, and abandonment.

	RIGIDITY	CRITICISM	NON-NEGOTIABLE RULES
Characteristics:	Rigidity, supposedly for the child's welfare, springs from fear. It consists of old rules "written in concrete" sometime in the past and usually for someone else. These rules often ignore the developmental tasks of the child. Rigidity threatens abuse or withdrawal of love to enforce compliance; it doesn't believe children should have a say in working things out.	Criticism labels the person with bad names rather than setting standards for acceptable behavior. Criticism often includes global words such as "never" and "always." It negates children and tells them how to fail. Ridicule is a devastating form of criticism that humiliates and invites contemptuous laughter from others.	Nonnegotiable rules are rules that must be followed. Children count on these rules to put order in their lives, to provide safety and security, to help them know who they are, to help them make decisions, and to build their own self-esteem. Even though nonnegotiable rules are firmly set and firmly enforced, they are not "rigid" and can be rewritten for the welfare of the family and its members.
Example: Thirteen-year-old Drank Alcohol:	Parent says, "If you ever touch alcohol again, don't bother coming home."	Mother says, "You're always doing something stupid. Now you are drinking. You're just like your dad."	Parent says, "You may not drink alcohol until you reach the legal age. We expect you to honor this rule. If you do not honor the rule, there will be very tough consequences."
Children May Hear the Following Underlying Messages:	You are not important. Don't be. Don't think. Don't be. Don't exist. You will be punished or abandoned if you make a mistake. Don't trust your own competence.	Don't be who you are. Don't be successful. Don't be capable. You are not lovable.	Your welfare and safety are important. Your parents expect you to be law abiding. Your parents are willing to be responsible and enforce the rules.
Common Responses of Children:	Feels oppressed, distanced, angry or rageful, scared, hopeless, imperfect, discounted, mistrusted, abandoned, no-good, powerless.	Feels powerless and diminished, rejected, hurt, humiliated, squashed, angry or rageful, unimportant, inadequate, scared, discounted.	Feels safe, cared for, powerful, helped, responsible, confident, accounted for. May feel frustrated, irritated, and resistant at times. Learns to follow rules and be responsible.
Decisions Often Made by Children:	Rules are more important than my needs. I am not wanted. My parents don't care about me. I will let others think for me. I will comply, rebel, or withdraw. I will blame myself.	I'm supposed to know what I don't know. I won't ask for help. I will try harder, be strong, be perfect. If I don't do things right, I am a bad person. I can't be good enough. I am hopeless. Why bother?	There are some rules I have to follow. I can learn from my mistakes. I am a good person. I'm lovable and capable. They care about me and take care of me.

The Structure Chart (continued)

	NEGOTIABLE RULES	MARSHMALLOW	ABANDONMENT
Characteristics:	Negotiable rules teach children how to think clearly and to solve problems, helping them raise their self-esteem. These rules are negotiated. The process of negotiating provides children an opportunity to argue and hassle with parents, learn about the relevancy of rules, assess data on which to base decisions, and learn to be increasingly responsible for themselves.	Marshmallow parenting grants freedom without demanding responsibility in return. It sounds supportive but it implies the child does not have to or is not capable of following rules. It discounts the child's ability and gives the child permission to be irresponsible and to fail, to be helpless and hopeless. At the same time, it lets the parent look good or play the martyr or feel in control.	Abandonment consists of lack of rules, protection, and contact. It tells children that adults are not available for them. If teasing is used when a child needs structure or approval, that teasing constitutes abandonment.
Example: Thirteen-year-old Drank Alcohol:	Parent says, "There are kids whose number one priority is drinking. When do you think it is okay to be with kids who drink? How can you find kids who don't drink so you don't spend all of your free time with the ones who are drinking?"	Parent says, "If all the kids drink, I suppose you can," or "You're too young to drink and drive, so you can have a kegger here," or "Kids will be kids!"	Parent says, "I don't want to talk about it." Parent is not available (either physically or emotionally), is drunk or mentally ill, or ignores or teases the child.
Children May Hear the Following Underlying Messages:	You can think, negotiate, and initiate. Your needs are important and others' needs are important. You must deal with how things really are. You are expected to be powerful in positive ways for yourself and others.	Don't be competent or responsible. Don't be who you are. Don't grow up. You can have your way and be obnoxious and get by with it. I need to continue taking care of you. My needs are more important than your needs.	I am not willing to care for you. I don't want you. Your needs are not important, mine are. No one is here for you. You don't exist.
Common Responses of Children:	Feels respected, cared for, listened to, powerful, important, loved, intelligent, safe, and sometimes frustrated. Learns to evaluate rules and participate in the making of rules as well as to follow rules and be responsible.	Feels patronized and encouraged not to grow up, remains incompetent in order to please parent. Feels unsafe, undermined, crazy, manipulated, discounted, unloved, unsatisfied, and angry.	Feels scared, terrified, hurt, angry or rageful, rejected, discounted, baffled, unimportant, upset. Perhaps suicidal.
Decisions Often Made by Children:	It's okay for me to grow up and still be dependent at times. I can think things through and ask others to think with me. I continually expand my ability to be responsible and competent.	I must take care of other people's feelings and needs, or I don't need to care about anyone but me. I am not capable of learning how to value and take care of myself. If help is offered, I mistrust it or at least expect to pay a price for it, but I don't expect helpful structure from others.	Don't ask for or expect help. No one cares. If I am to survive, I will have to do it by myself. If help is offered, mistrust it. Help and trust are jokes.

THE WORDS OF EACH POSITION

Here are some examples of the six structure positions. Reading them should give you an idea how structuring messages apply to each situation. The nurturing messages for the same situation may be found on pages 133 to 137.

Situation: *Dad is making breakfast. Three-year-old Hannah wants to help scramble the eggs.*
   Rigidity: "No"
   Criticism: "You don't know how and you're too messy."
   Nonnegotiable Rules: "You can watch how I crack the eggs and I'll show you how to stir them."
   Negotiable Rules: "Do you want to stir the eggs or put the shells in the garbage?"
   Marshmallowing: Lets the child do whatever she wants, but hovers nervously, picking up the pieces.
   Abandonment: "Go watch TV."

Situation: *Eight-year-old Terry is begging for an expensive new video game.*
   Rigidity: "Never."
   Criticism: "You never take care of the stuff you have now. I'm not wasting any more money on you. You sit and play too much already. Get up and move, Mr. Lazy."
   Nonnegotiable Rules: "You know the rule about the number of games you can have. When you get a new game, you give an old game away or sell it in a garage sale."
   Negotiable Rules: In Terry's family, this rule is not negotiable.
   Marshmallowing: Buys the game and sets a limit on time to play, but doesn't enforce the limit.
   Abandonment: Buys the game, no questions asked.

Situation: *Thirteen-year-old Allegra asks her parents to buy her a ticket to the big concert, drop her and her friends at the entrance, and pick them up afterward.*
   Rigidity: "No kid of mine is going to a concert like that. Don't even think about it!"
   Criticism: "All you do is want, want, and want. What's wrong with you?"
   Nonnegotiable Rules: "I trust your big sister's judgment to

decide if the band is okay. You can go if your sister and her friend go with you."

Negotiable Rules: "How do you plan to pay for the ticket? Would you like to ask your friends' parents to call me or shall I call them?"

Marshmallowing: "I don't really think you should go, but as long as your friends are going, I suppose you can go."

Abandonment: "I don't care as long as I don't have to pick you up."

Situation: *Lee, sixteen, didn't show for the Fourth of July family reunion.*

Rigidity: "You know we expected you to be at the reunion. Hand over your driver's license. I'll decide after six months if you get it back."

Criticism: "You did it again! You never think of anybody but yourself."

Nonnegotiable Rules: "In this family we don't disrespect one another. By tomorrow morning I expect you to have thought about the impact of what you did and to tell us how you will restore our trust in you."

Negotiable Rules: "How will you apologize to this family?"

Marshmallowing: "I know you are getting older and you think your cousins are boring. Try to make it next year."

Abandonment: Doesn't mention the absence. Pretends like it didn't happen.

Situation: *Twenty-nine-year-old Kenny lives at home, spends the income from his good-paying job on himself, and contributes nothing in money or services to the household.*

Rigidity: "I'm fed up! Pack your bag and get out."

Criticism: "You always take the easy way, Prince Kenny. You'll end up sponging your whole life."

Nonnegotiable Rules: "It's time for you to be out on your own. Find your own place by the end of next month."

Negotiable Rules: "It's time for you to be out on your own. Until you leave, what will you do to contribute to your keep?"

Marshmallowing: Complains to friends but lets things go on as they are.

Abandonment: "You can live here as long as you like."

Depending on the age of your child, you have probably experienced all six ways and have parented with all six. Most adults usually have a home base, or one way they use most often or revert to when they're stressed. The point is this: Recognize where you are and ask yourself if you want to be there. If not, move!

IN A NUTSHELL

Okay, here goes. Take a breath. The helpful ways to establish structures are: to set limits, boundaries, and standards with rules, and to enforce the rules with rewards for compliance and discomforting consequences for noncompliance. All rules are **nonnegotiable** until the children demonstrate the ability to handle the increased responsibility that leads to greater freedom. All rules are established with an understanding of children's development (what can be expected at different ages). The older the child, the more rules are **negotiated**. (If the child is doing good thinking!) They can be modified as ability and mastery increases. A new nonnegotiable rule, complete with consequences, results from a negotiation. Again, refer to the Structure Chart for the nuances of the structure positions (pags 197–98). If you want more help in setting and enforcing rules, consult *Growing Up Again* by Jean and Connie.

MORE REAL-WORLD APPLICATIONS OF THE STRUCTURE HIGHWAY

How this process works in the case of the child pushing the limits is illustrated in these three examples.

When a four-year-old pushes a nonnegotiable rule:

> "Time for bed, honey. Bring a book. I'll meet you in your room." (Mom reads two books.) "Time for a good night kiss."
> "Read this one. Just read this one more. Paleez and I'm not tired." (Said with great brightness and conviction.)
> "You can watch the stars on your ceiling or close your eyes. Take good care of Mr. Bear. I love you and I'll see you in the morning." (Leaves.)

Mom is in charge of bedtime because she's the best judge of the sleep her daughter needs. When her daughter is older she can negotiate a bedtime.

A ten-year-old negotiates:

"Dad, can I go home to Brian's house on the bus after school tomorrow?"

"Jacob, you know we only do visits with Brian on the weekend because he lives so far away."

"Brian's mom said she'd drop me off on her way to a meeting. Remember, Dad, tomorrow's a half-day at school."

"What time would she drop you off and what about your homework?"

"I'll find out what time she'll bring me back and I promise if I have homework, I'll do it at Brian's because we have the same teacher, remember?"

"Jacob, you check with Brian's mom and then I'll check with your mom. If you'll be back by 8:00, it's probably all right, but I don't know how your mother will vote. She may want to talk with Brian's mom."

The steps in this negotiation are:
Request
    Statement of limit
Child's assertion
    Request for information
Child provides information
    Parent decides *yes*
New or restated limit or rule
    or
Parent decides *no* and the negotiation continues or the parent calls a halt.

A fifteen-year-old negotiates:

"Dad, remember how I helped clean the garage? I really need a favor."

"Yes?"

"Well, I have this paper due tomorrow and I haven't gotten very far yet. I really need help. I'll be in a world of hurt if I don't turn this in tomorrow."

"I don't do your homework. What's it on and how much of it have you done?"

"It's on earthquakes in Japan and I am just getting started."

"Son, you want more help than I'm willing to give, but I know you'll figure out what to do."

Request
    Limit
Child's assertion
    Request for information
Child provides information
    Parent decides no
New or restated limit or rule

A seventeen-year-old pushes for a negotiation:

"I know you and Dad are going to be gone this weekend. Can I have the guys over here for a while on Saturday night?"

"Other kids aren't here when we're not here." (The family's non-negotiable rule.)

"But you know all these guys and it's my turn."

"Will there be any drinking or smoking? And who, exactly, will be here?"

"No, I'll tell them there's absolutely no drinking or smoking. Tim, Eddie, Justin, Fabio, and I will be here."

"If someone wants to crash the party, what will you do?"

"Tell them they can't. Anyway, that's not going to happen. C'mon, Mom. Why are you being so difficult? Don't you trust me?"

"I want to, but I'm not convinced you can enforce the no-smoking-or-drinking rule because I know Justin and Fabio do both. I can't imagine spending a relaxing weekend away without being worried. My answer is no. Do you want to check this out with your dad or do you want me to?"

Request
    Limit
Child's assertion
    Request for information
Child provides information
    Parent decides no
New or restated limit or rule

THE HAZARDS OF OVER-CORRECTION

An overwhelming response to "Why do parents overindulge their children?" was "Because they want them to have a better or easier life than they had." When adults who grew up with rigid rules come to developing rules for their children and themselves, they seldom want to repeat what they experienced. *I'm never going to do that to my kids.* Trouble is, such an adult has not experienced and learned how to establish and enforce rules in more successful ways (from the Nonnegotiable and Negotiable Rules positions). But they do wish for what they wanted and didn't have. In rejecting what they experienced, parents may over-correct and move to a position that is opposite and still find themselves unsatisfied with the results.

For instance, a child experiencing the negative effects of rigidity may grow up to parent from Abandonment, which has similar negative effects. The same is true for adults who marshmallow in an attempt to change the harmful effects of the criticism they experienced as children.

Remember, the ditches are the places to avoid. When we find ourselves there, it's a sure signal we need to move to a safer place. Rigidity and Abandonment are the places that can have a profound negative long-term effect on children.

Criticism and Marshmallowing also negatively impact children. They are the soft shoulders of the Highway. Children of the shoulders manage to grow up and function well in their lives, but they can have difficulty and miss the more rewarding aspects of life, such as emotional intimacy, feeling truly confident in themselves and their skills, and being able to experience child-like joy.

The center two lanes are the places of greatest security for children. They teach children to think and to be responsible. Because we are human, it's safe to say that none of us conducts business exclusively from these most-productive positions. But when we find ourselves doing our parenting from an unproductive or downright hurtful place, we can use the Structure Chart and the Highway to help us know where to head: straight to the middle of the road. Remember, over-correction means you're moving. Your good hearts and minds are acting on a wish to do better. Do it. Refine. Do it again. Evaluate. Do it again. Improve. Celebrate!

IT HELPS TO HANG WITH OTHER FAMILIES
WHO DRIVE IN THE MIDDLE OF THE ROAD.
—Jim Jump

21

THE HIGH ROAD—
COMBINING NURTURE AND STRUCTURE

A Powerful Parenting Tool

FOLLOW THE THREE R'S: RESPECT FOR SELF.
RESPECT FOR OTHERS. RESPONSIBILITY FOR ALL YOUR ACTIONS.
—Unknown

Nurture without structure is as sticky as a marshmallow. Structure without nurture can feel as harsh as criticism. Nurture and structure hold hands, dance with each other, flow together like day into night. They are the safe, loving, supportive, center lanes of the highway. "But," you say, "it isn't always easy to see those center lanes. What if the situation is sticky or if the same old problem is here again?"

Combining the nurture and structure highways can offer some clues about what needs to be done, or what is going on. Here's how to do it:

❖ Identify a situation or problem you want to address. Or use one item from the Parental Overindulgence Assessment Tool (page 293). If you have more than one problem, put each on a separate page.

❖ On the Highway chart (page 209), fill in your probable or

possible response for each of the center lanes, the shoulders, and the ditches. There may be slots where you say, "But I never do that!" Of course you wouldn't, but make up what you might do or have seen someone else do. Fill every slot.

❖ Now look at the center lanes. The course of action should be there. If a reasonable possible solution doesn't show up there, think some more, or ask someone else for ideas.

❖ Identify what you need to do and do it.

❖ But wait. If you say, "I know what I should do but I just don't do it," help is on the way. Look at the shoulders and the ditches and identify which response you are in the habit of doing, or are likely to do, or want to do. If that response wasn't written down, write it down now.

❖ Study that thing you want to do, that thing that doesn't work. Don't blame yourself; don't bother to feel ashamed. Just study it. Study it fearlessly so you can move to the middle of the road. After you have looked that thing squarely in the face and examined it, get yourself a little distance from it and ask yourself:

What do I need so I wouldn't have to do that thing any more or at least so often?

Here are some examples:

Abuse: "I abuse because I get so angry. I need some help, not only with controlling my anger, but also with being more powerful to resolve what is under my anger."

Marshmallow: "I marshmallow because I want to be popular with my kids. Wow! Parenting is not a popularity contest. Ada Alden says, 'Kids don't need parents who are friends. They need parents who are friendly.' Where can I learn to set boundaries and limits in a firm but friendly way?"

Abandonment: "I realize that I have bought into the myth that you can't set limits for children after they are thirteen. Where can I learn about teenage development and how to mentor and monitor my son?"

Criticism: "I vow not to criticize and then I hear the same ridiculing words that were said to me pop out of my mouth. I need to put those old parent tapes to rest and replace them with new language."

Overindulgence: "I like to overindulge, but I know that it isn't good, so where can I get those good feelings without hurting my children?"

❖ Try it. Go the mile! Get whatever you need so you can move from the shoulder or ditch where you find yourself into the center of the Nurture/Structure Highway and let the impact of your parenting match your good intent.

Here is an example that combines a situation we met in Chapters 14 and 21.

Situation: *Allegra's favorite teen idol is coming to town. Allegra and her friends are panting with desire to go. Allegra, twelve, asks her parents to buy her a ticket to the concert, drop her and her friends at the entrance, and pick them up afterward.*

Abuse: "I don't trust you or these friends. You are looking for trouble and you are the one who'd be sure to find it." (Psychological abuse, character attack.)

Conditional Care: "Sure, Allegra. Great idea to take your friends. I want you to be popular." (Price tag—pay me by being popular.)

Assertive Care: "Get a CD of this group from the library. We'll listen to the lyrics to see if they support our values."

Supportive Care: "If I decide it is unsafe or too expensive or doesn't support our values, would you like to have your friends here for a party that night? You know you are important to me." (Shows loving support and offers an option.)

Overindulgence: "If that's what you want, honey, we'll do it." (Lacks concern for child's welfare.)

Neglect: Parent agrees, buys ticket even though she can't afford to. Does not consider safety issues or the messages of the band. (Fails to assess the situation and the family's needs.)

Rigidity: "No kid of mine is going to a concert like that. Don't even think about it!" (Doesn't consider child's point of view.)

Criticism: "All you do is want, want, and want. What's wrong with you? There will never be enough to satisfy you." (How to fail.)

Nonnegotiable Rules: "If the band is okay, you can go if you have an adult with you. You can pay for the ticket and I'll need a check-in with your friends' parents." (Sets boundaries.)

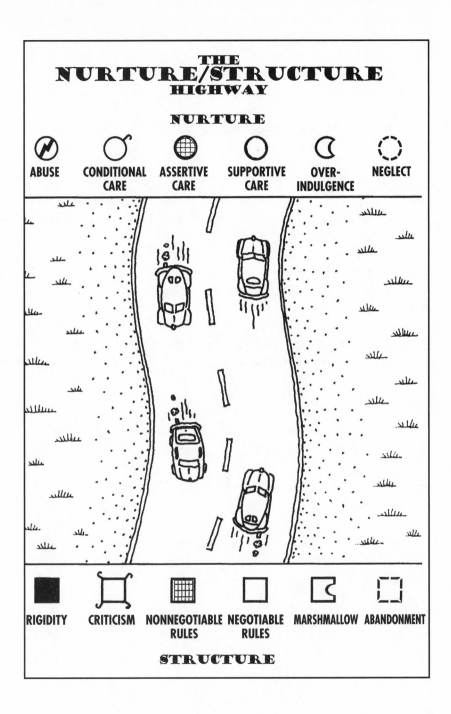

Negotiable Rules: "Would you like to ask your friends' parents to call me or shall I call them?" (Promotes an option.) "Which adult would you like to have that you can persuade and who is okay with me?" (Involves child in finding a solution to the problem.)

Marshmallow: "As long as your friends are going, you can go." (Abdicates responsibility.)

Abandonment: "I don't care as long as I don't have to pick you up." (Parent fails to function.)

Is this easy? It wasn't for Jean. When she had her first child and asked her mother, "How will I know how to be a good parent?" she replied, "Oh, it just comes to you." She waited for the blazing light of understanding. It didn't come. It's not easy for most of us. It's easier to blame the children. But, we are the leaders of our families, so when situations need to be addressed, it is up to us adults to do it. We need to get our own needs met. Not our band-aids for needs, not our own excesses of food or shopping or sex or work or play or control or gambling or alcohol or drugs or excitement. Our true needs. Our needs for love and recognition, for structure, for stimulation, and for quiet.

Remember to get help as often as you need it. Find your village and use it.

RAISING CHILDREN IS FAR TOO IMPORTANT AND TOO COMPLEX
TO BE DONE BY ONLY ONE OR TWO PEOPLE.
—Pat Daunt

TAKE ME TO YOUR LEADER

When I Was Growing Up, My Parents Allowed Me to Take the Lead or Dominate the Family

WHO IS THE BOSS IN YOUR FAMILY?
THE COUNSELOR ASKED.
I AM, REPLIED THE EIGHT-YEAR-OLD.

SOMEONE MUST LEAD

WISE boy, that eight-year-old. He recognized that leadership is essential for any group and if his parents aren't leading the family, he must. Leadership is essential for any family. If parents don't lead the family, one or more of the children will.

When parents abdicate areas of leadership to children, family members don't get what they need. Children don't have the maturity or the life-skills to lead a family, and it is not their job. This eight-year-old is being cheated and so is his family.

Leadership is the parents' job. When parents let some of the leadership roles slip to their children, the question becomes how to take them back.

DINNER WITH THE CHILDREN?

Over the years, Hal, Betsy, and their teenage son Tyler had developed a painful pattern of interaction that nearly destroyed their family. Tyler would demand. Hal would criticize the boy. Betsy would step in to make Tyler feel better. Hal would criticize both his wife and Tyler. Mom would protect Tyler further and glare at her husband. After each round, Tyler skated free and clear, while Mom and Dad endured another of their silent times. Meanwhile, Tyler was rude and even obnoxious, blew off most of the rules (even if he'd been involved in negotiating them), and refused to participate in extended family gatherings. He routinely came home whenever he pleased, and violated the family rules by failing to let his parents know his whereabouts. Perhaps most dispiriting was the uncommonly disrespectful language with which Tyler spoke to his parents, especially his mother.

The day Tyler skipped out on Thanksgiving dinner, Dad had had enough. When Tyler wandered in that evening, Hal wrestled his son to the floor and sat on him, repeating, "Who's in charge here?" After his father had asked the question over and over for ten full minutes, the boy finally said, "You are, Dad." Only then did Hal let his son get up off the floor.

From then on, Hal followed up with stiff consequences whenever Tyler spoke disrespectfully or blew off his responsibilities.

Today Tyler is in his thirties, and he is an agreeable son and a successful man. His mother says of the wrestling incident, "That was a huge turning point for both Tyler and me. I regret that we let our son run our lives. We should have done something much earlier. Taking a stand made a huge difference for Tyler and for us."

It has been said that nature abhors a vacuum, that an empty space begs to be filled. When adults don't take on their natural leadership role, they leave a gap—a gap that is filled by children because a family has to have leadership. After all, a primary goal of children is to keep their families together, so they will do almost anything, endure almost anything in order to take care of the parents and see to the survival of the family unit. They will take over responsibility and leadership whenever their adults fail to do so and even though they don't have the experience to know how to lead well.

DINNER WITHOUT THE CHILDREN

When friends suggested that their two families stop at a restaurant for dinner after the boat races, Dick and Stephanie declined with a made-up excuse. The truth was that whenever they took their five- and seven-year-olds out to eat, the kids acted up and the parents wound up stressed, embarrassed, and very angry at their children. After that evening, however, they agreed that something needed to change. They consulted several books and an aunt, then made a plan.

The next week Dick and Stephanie asked their children to get into the car. As they drove, they explained that they would be going to the same restaurant where the kids had made a scene a few weeks before. But instead of driving straight to the restaurant, they made a pre-arranged stop at the cooperating Auntie Rachael's house and announced matter-of-factly that the children would be staying with her until Mom and Dad finished enjoying their dinner without the children's uproar. Then they drove off.

The aunt made no attempt to entertain the children. The children had a nutritious but austere dinner and then helped to weed the garden.

After their hassle-free dinner, the parents picked up the children. They resisted the temptation to nail the lesson to the wall with a lecture, but spoke pleasantly about how much they had enjoyed themselves.

The next time they planned to go out for dinner, Dick and Stephanie wondered aloud if the children had grown up enough to go along. Both children jumped around and yelled, "We're ready, we're ready!" Oops, same stop at Auntie Rachael's house. Same austere snack.

That evening, on the way home, the children asked, "What do we have to do?" The parents acted skeptical, but promised they would have "practice dinners" at home until they thought they would enjoy having the children join them in a restaurant.

POSITIVE INTENT, POSITIVE OUTCOME

Can single parents do all this? Absolutely. By identifying (or creating) a team of family, friends, child-care providers, and support groups, a single parent could do the sort of things Hal, Dick, and Stephanie did. The principles are the same, although the details will differ.

The following situations signal that parental figures must assume or resume family leadership:

- Children try to be in charge way before they have the training and experience to do so.
- Children are behaving badly in ways that are self-defeating or that push others away.
- Children's energy goes to maintaining family stability; as a result, their own development suffers.

Sometimes parents let leadership slip to their children because they value living in a democracy and want their children to learn democratic principles. But being democratic does not mean there is no leader. In fact, a healthy democracy requires strong leaders.

All of us, including adults, need leadership to help us meet our basic needs for structure, recognition, and stimulation. A good leader provides for all three—the structures that make life predictable, the recognition that each person in the group is important, and the stimulation and contact that encourage growth. The family is the primary group in which children learn about leadership with parents who provide strong leadership for the children and for themselves.

THREE FUNCTIONS OF STRONG LEADERSHIP

Three functions of leadership are essential to the welfare of any group, including families. We can call these three roles the *responsible leader*, the *effective leader*, and the *psychological leader*.

The *responsible leader* is the person with the title. In a family the title is always Parent. If something goes wrong, this is the leader who is called to account by higher authorities.

The *effective leader* is the one whose questions are most likely to be answered, whose directions are most likely to be followed, and who actually makes the decisions. The effective leader may also be the one who does things or makes sure things get done.

The *psychological leader* holds a special position of power in the group. That leader is the one who is irresistible, omnipotent, indefatigable, and fearless. The psychological leader must always be pleased or placated. (No wonder children who are regularly allowed this leadership function are often referred to as the Little Emperor or the Little Princess.)

Generally, parents need to perform all three of the leadership functions in a family. However, sometimes one or two of the roles can be temporarily delegated to a child for a specific reason and a limited period of time—provided it is developmentally appropriate for the child.

THE CHILD AS TEMPORARY RESPONSIBLE OR EFFECTIVE LEADER

In a family, special circumstances may thrust a child into the responsible or effective leadership role. Some children find this a burden, but if the parents are clear about why and for how long, many children use it as an opportunity to show competence. Sharing leadership with children as they are developmentally capable of shouldering it builds self-esteem and helps them become competent.

Miguel, whose parents do not yet speak English, went with them to school for a conference with his teacher. When the teacher called the parents' name, Miguel stood up, momentarily taking on the responsible role. During the conference he translated; here he was playing an effective role, making the right things happen. After the conference the teacher thanked him for doing a good job during the conference. This was a signal that those functions were finished for the time being, and that he would be a regular student in class the next day. At home his parents also thanked him for doing a good job. Then they said, "Now, son, as your parents, let's talk about what we learned from your teacher. We are proud of how you are doing in art and in history. First tell us how you made art and history successful. But we also want you to work harder and improve at math and science. What can you do to be a better student in those classes?" The parents thus reasserted their leadership of the family, defining Miguel as a contributing family member, but not the leader.

Sometimes a family emergency requires a child to assume one or more of the leadership roles for a time.

Clara's mother needed to go out of town for a few days to care for a sick grandmother. So she delegated effective leadership to thirteen-year-old Clara for that time. "Clara, Grandma is sick and I need to go to her. I'll be gone Thursday through Monday. I would like to take you children out of school to go with me, but I can't take Benji into the hospital with me and I need you to be here for him. Your dad's job is very demanding right now, but he thinks he can get off early on Thursday.

You'll need to be excused from your last hour of classes and your after-school activities on Friday and Monday. I'm sorry to have you do this, but family members help each other and Grandma needs me. You and I will plan menus and I'll grocery shop before I go. We'll also plan some things you can do with Benji, and I'll show you how to comfort him if he worries. Your dad will be home every night and on the weekend."

Clara's mom provided structure, recognition, and stimulation. As a parent, she was the responsible leader. Her effective leadership was evident in the plans she made to help Clara. Her strong psychological leadership came through in the confident way she made clear what she wanted and that she expected Clara to comply. Mom didn't say, "Okay?" or "Are you willing to?" or "Would you please?" Mom's strong "I expect you to," her attitude, and her confidence in Clara's capability invited Clara to turn an inconvenience into an act of honor, a special way to help her family by temporarily taking on the job of effective leadership. All children of all ages need to know and feel that they are contributing family members.

SHARING RESPONSIBLE, EFFECTIVE, AND PSYCHOLOGICAL LEADERSHIP

In some families, all three of these roles are held by the same person—usually the mother, the father, or a grandparent. In other families the parents hold all three roles, but divide them—for example, with the father as the responsible and psychological leader and the mother as the effective leader.

All children of all ages need to know and feel that they are contributing family members.

Sometimes some of the leadership comes from outside of the family. When Wanda, a single mom, became ill, several members of her support group shared effective leadership by bringing the family meals, taking Wanda to doctor's appointments, and driving her daughter to child-care. One member, Annette, took over the psychological leadership role, calling daily, cheering Wanda on, and making sure she was taking care of herself.

In some families the roles alternate in different areas of family life. In the Rutgers family, for example, both parents are responsible leaders, but the father is the psychological leader in athletics. He expects the children to become competent in certain sports. The mother is the effective leader. She drives the children to practices and games on time and makes sure their uniforms are clean. In the area of household chores, Mrs. Rutgers plays all three roles. Mr. Rutgers is the effective leader of schoolwork. He attends school conferences and tracks homework. The parents share psychological leadership in setting standards for schoolwork and giving recognition and rewards for work well done.

CONFLICTING GOALS OF FAMILY LEADERS

This sharing of functions works well as long as parents are in agreement about the goals of the family. Sometimes, however, parental leadership falters when parents are not clear about their goals or are not in agreement on them. This is sometimes the case with divorced parents. However, if parents with differing goals articulate them clearly and respect the other parent's goals, the children need not be confused. They learn that there are different goals, different norms, and different behaviors expected in the two homes.

Martha Farrell Erickson, director of the Children, Youth and Family Consortium at the University of Minnesota, asserts that:

Research on the consequences of divorce has been overstated and the methodology often is problematic. Most children of divorce don't have serious problems. And most negative consequences for the child are mitigated when divorced parents agree to cooperate when it comes to parenting, making sure their child has close, positive, ongoing involvement with both parents.[1]

Strong equals structure, loving equals nurture.

In fact, conflicting parental goals may be most confusing to children when parents are living together in one home.

Elizabeth and Robert had many areas of contention in their marriage. Each sent strong messages to their kids about what was important—messages that were sometimes mutually exclusive, and therefore confusing. Robert thought Elizabeth's rules about responsible behavior toward the community were too strict. Elizabeth thought Robert's expenditures on the children's sports equipment were overindulgent.

When a counselor asked them each to articulate the goals of their family, the difficulty became crystal clear. They had never discussed the topic. Each had assumed that the goals of their own childhood families would be the goals of the family they were creating.

Growing up, Elizabeth lived by her family's goals, which were, in order:

❖ Make the world a better place.
❖ Support and stand by your family.
❖ Make education a lifelong priority.
❖ Earn enough to live as well as you can.

In the family Robert grew up in, however, the goals were, in order:

❖ Earn enough to live well.
❖ Support and stand by your family.
❖ Make education a lifelong priority.

When Elizabeth announced that she planned to run for city council, Robert vetoed her plan. "You shouldn't do that. Your family comes first. It will take too much time. Stay home and take care of us."

Elizabeth was preparing to take an effective role in the community to meet her first goal. Robert used his effective and psychological leadership functions within the family to promote his own first goal, to live well. Elizabeth acquiesced but wasn't happy about it. In the face of this conflicting leadership from the parents, one of Elizabeth and Robert's children took on part of the psychological leader's role.

Young Tim's goal was different from either parent's first goal, however: It was to have fun. Tim pushed for family fun whenever he could. Soon he developed engaging ways of suggesting play activities—and became stubbornly angry if his parents did not comply. (Remember, the psychological leader is the one who must be obeyed.)

To avoid conflict between themselves, Elizabeth and Robert—both of whom liked fun—soon found themselves living in service of Tim. They used more and more of their effective leadership functions to support and manage the recreation the child lobbied for. They played miniature golf, went to the zoo, attended sports events, played cards and board games, bought new electronic games, and acquired new equipment for active games in the backyard. Family chores and lessons were soon neglected. As a result, Tim was short-changed on learning life-skills—and his parents felt anxious about what wasn't getting done. The whole family became out of balance, and Tim became overindulged with soft structure, too much freedom, and too much power.

Children need parents who have their oars in the water together, pulling toward the same goal. This allows children to be free to attend to the job of growing up.

YOU CAN BE THE LEADER, OKAY?

Sometimes adults inadvertently invite a child to become the effective leader, and to make decisions, by incorrectly using the word "okay" (or "all right") as a question. Children (and adults as well) typically hear "Okay?" as meaning "Do you agree?" even though what the parent means to ask is, "Do you understand?" So, when the adult says, "Okay?," gets a "no" response from the child, and then makes the child do it anyway, the child can feel confused or even cheated.

> Children need parents who have their oars in the water together, pulling toward the same goal. This allows children to be free to attend to the job of growing up.

Put yourself in the place of your child for a moment. Assume you're asked each of the following, and you don't like the idea. You don't agree, and you say so, but your parent insists that you comply anyway.

* ❖ "I'm going to belt you into the shopping cart, honey. Okay?"
* ❖ "It's time to go to bed now. Okay?"
* ❖ "Don't forget your bike helmet, okay?"
* ❖ "Call me when you get to your friend's house, okay?"

Did you feel recognized and acknowledged? Did this help you trust the adult?

Your parent's intent was probably to make sure you heard and understood. But since "okay" asks for agreement, the word puts you, the child, in charge. A better question would be "Got it?" or "Do you understand?" Better still would be one of the following:

* ❖ "I'm going to belt you into the shopping cart, honey. Hold up your arms."

- ❖ "It's time to go to bed now. Race you!"
- ❖ Don't forget your bike helmet. Protect that great brain of yours!"
- ❖ "Call me when you get to your friend's house. We need to know where you are."

Listen again to your emotions. Do you feel recognized and acknowledged? Does this help you trust the adult?

WHEN ADULTS DON'T FUNCTION WELL

When, due to an adult's illness, addiction, absence, or neglect, the running of a household frequently or consistently falls to a child, that child has to take on some of the making-it-happen functions of the effective leader.

> Eleven-year-old Mina's mother was alcoholic. Most days, Mina shopped for food on the way home from school, got her mother—already drunk—off the sofa and into bed, straightened up the house, and prepared dinner (mostly snack foods) for herself and her younger siblings. No adult seemed to notice. As a result, Mina did not get the structure or recognition she needed. And running the household took precious time from her own important developmental tasks.

This abdication of parental leadership is easy to identify. This example is clearly one of neglect, but it also is overindulgence, because Mina has too much power.

Sometimes the turning over of effective leadership to a child is much more subtle.

> At age two, Jacob showed the usual two-year-old tendency to be demanding and resistant. But Ruth, his mom, believed that a good parent doesn't say no to a child. She also believed it is the parent's job to keep the child happy. As a result, she over-nurtured him.
>
> Now, at age five, Jacob is loud and clear about what he wants. His mother has become the servant to his demands, and she can't understand why he is unappreciative and often unhappy.

Ruth looks like the effective leader because she is so busy doing things to make the family work. But remember, the effective leader is the one who actually makes the decisions. That's Jacob. Jacob has lost the security that comes from firm parental structure.

RECLAIMING PARENTAL LEADERSHIP

If you realize that, wittingly or unwittingly, you have given up some of your leadership to one or more of your children, here is a checklist you can use to help you take it back again:

1. Get clear about your family's goals and values. An especially helpful book is Harriet Heath's *Using Your Values to Raise Your Child to Be an Adult You Admire.*
2. Tell your children what the goals of the family are. Feel free to post them. Remember the modern-day dictum, *If it isn't written down, it doesn't exist.*
3. Identify what part of what leadership role has been given up.
4. Tell your children that you have been making a mistake by letting them lead and that you are going to correct this. From now on you will make the decisions. "I've been letting you decide too many things. From now on I decide when breakfast is. You can decide what to wear to school if you get dressed and are ready to eat your breakfast on time. If you aren't dressed, I choose what you wear. And I still expect you to eat some breakfast." It is a good idea to add, "I may not do it well at first, but I am going to do it."
5. Turn an absolutely deaf ear to their objections and escalations.
   If they say, "Don't change. I'm used to you the way you are," reply, "I'm going to change. I'm the parent and that's my job."
   If they say, "I hate you," say, "Maybe you do right now, but I still love you."
   If they say, "I'm going to report you to the child protective services," say, "Here's the number; I can use the help of a good social worker."
   If they say, "I don't want you to change," say, "I expect you don't; I wish I had done it sooner."
   If they rant and rave, say, "You'll get used to it, and it won't be so bad."

Most children settle down very quickly and act much happier when they get a strong message that their parents are taking back the leadership role.

Remember, abdicating one of the family leadership functions to young children is a form of overindulgence. Giving children too much power or inappropriate levels of responsibility can interfere with their learning age-appropriate developmental tasks, which is item number one on the Test of Four.

SHARED LEADERSHIP

As children grow, they need to assume effective leadership in many areas of their own lives. Teenagers will be taking over more getting-it-done aspects year by year. And when children buy into family goals and add their psychological leader energy to the family pool, the family becomes more effective as a unit.

With young adult or older adult children, sharing leadership functions often becomes a dance, with flowing roles or role swapping.

> When Cameron, who had been on his own for a time, returned home, the family made clear contracts about shared effective leadership. His parents (responsible leaders) indicated two areas they expected him to take over: caring for the cars and doing certain lawn work (effective leadership). Cameron, whose computer competence exceeded his parents', also asked to be the computer expert in the home (effective leadership). Laundry, cooking, and house cleaning were divided on a weekly basis (effective leadership). Cameron exerted (psychological leadership) energy to get some areas of the house repaired—jobs that his parents had let go due to their "house blindness."

THE CIRCLE OF LIFE

Later, in the life cycle of a family, an adult child may have to take over effective leadership if there are things his parents are no longer capable of doing. Sometimes mental impairment makes it necessary for adult children to become full responsible leaders, as the family cycle goes full circle.

PARENTING IS FOREVER. . . . SO IS GRANDPARENTING

Sometimes parents have to reassume leadership when adult children die, are ill, or are not functioning responsibly.

Grandmother Emma took over all three leadership functions in order to get legal custody of her grandchildren, because their drug-addicted mother was abusing and neglecting them. Emma expended considerable psychological leadership within the extended family to make this change happen. She became the responsible leader, the guardian, and the effective leader, the one who set the goals and made things happen. This is not what Emma had wished for her family and her grief was great, but she did what was necessary for the welfare of her grandchildren.

Sometimes the leadership roles parents have to reassume are dramatic and life-changing. At other times they provide welcome short-term support.

Faith, a competent middle-aged daughter, was losing her hearing. Her doctor urged her not to do any heavy lifting because that might cause a change of fluid pressure and do further damage to her inner ear.

Her parents asked her what she planned to do about taking down her storm windows and redesigning her garden. Not wishing to give up her adult independence, she announced adamantly that she would be doing her own work, but very carefully. She would roll the concrete rounds for her garden walk and do only one storm window per day. Her tone made it clear that there would be no more discussion. Mom and Dad conferred. "How do we parent a grownup? Clearly this is an appropriate time for us to intervene. How can we do that in the most respectful way?"

They handed Faith an envelope with a check in it and told her, "We know how independent you are. We like that, but in this instance we want you to go along with your parents and hire someone to do the garden and storm window work. We're making an investment in your hearing." Faith laughed and cried and hugged her parents. "You know me too well! Okay, I'll do as you ask."

Faith's parents intruded with a bit of effective leadership, making a gift of money without overindulging their daughter, and without assuming effective leadership in areas where they were not needed. Good intentions, good outcome.

CHEERS

As the family ages, adult children will swap and share leadership roles according to the situation. When this is done with mutual respect, it can make for a smooth running extended family. The toast "Cheers" applies here, a toast that has come to us from the early Greeks:

Cheers

Not above you,
Not below you,
But beside you.

■

OUR DEEPEST FEAR IS NOT THAT WE ARE INADEQUATE, OUR DEEPEST FEAR IS THAT WE ARE POWERFUL BEYOND MEASURE.
—Nelson Mandela

For Parents Who Were Overindulged as Children

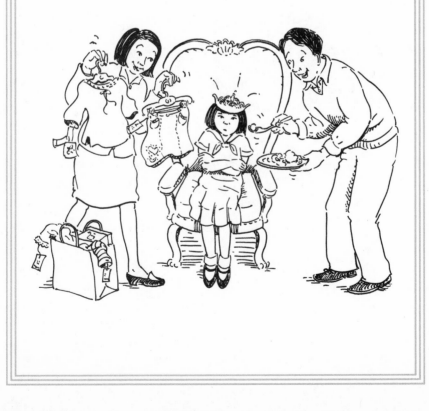

I'LL NEVER DO THAT!

How Having Been Overindulged Affects Parenting

■

I WILL NEVER DO TO MY CHILDREN WHAT MY PARENTS DID TO
ME, I SAID. OOPS, I JUST DID IT AGAIN.

THE LEGACY

LUCKY are those who were parented well, for they have been handed a legacy, a bone-knowledge of how to parent their children well.
But the rest of us, all who received uneven parenting,[1] by our birth
parents or any adults who were caring for us when we were young,
have a job to do. We need to sort the helpful from the unhelpful, keep
the helpful, and figure out how to replace the unhelpful parenting
skills and beliefs.

Our job is to stop overindulging children.

But it may not be easy to change. Why? Because all of the parenting we received is natural to us. That is how it was. And all of the
skills we learned are automatically on tap to be used at any time.
Most especially, when we are under stress, we can find ourselves
doing something our parents did, even though it didn't feel right
when we did it then. And it didn't work either.

DOING THE OPPOSITE

Some strong people decide to do the exact opposite of unsuccessful childhood experiences and succeed in doing that well. Some adults who were beaten never hit. Some who were the victims of incest are rigorously vigilant to assure that their children are safe. Some who grew up in alcoholic families find spouses and friends and whatever other help they need to break out of the addictive system, even if that means becoming distanced from some of their family members. Some who were overindulged in childhood do not overindulge their own children, but some find themselves doing so.

If you recall the Nurture and Structure Charts (pages 134–35 and 197–98), the arrangement of the six ways on each chart give clues about how you can make changes that really benefit children.

Here's how it works. If I feel that the nurture I received was predominantly conditional and I want my children to feel loved, instead of offering assertive and supportive care, I might offer the opposite of conditional nurturing and overindulge. Remember good intent and unexpected impact or outcome. Or if I want to change critical parenting, I swing on the Structure Chart from the shoulder of criticism to the shoulder of marshmallowing, thinking I am smoothing out what I experienced as a child.

By being mindful of the qualities and behaviors of the center positions of both charts, when I find myself parenting in a way I now know as unhelpful, I can aim for the center positions of the road.

In the research, here is what parents who were overindulged as children said about the ways they parent.

In Their Own Voices

If you have children, do you overindulge them?
- ✓ "It's what I do best. It keeps me in control and on the move."
- ✓ "I usually overindulge them when my needs are not being met."
- ✓ "I want them to have as much as I can give them. I enjoy them having it."
- ✓ "I overindulge my time with them for intellectual and recreational activities because my parents didn't spend enough time with me and because they couldn't afford to provide me with the intellectual stimulations that I would like to have had."

✓ "My parents usually felt the indulgence was necessary and I knew no difference."

✓ "I bring home a 'surprise' for him when coming home too late from work. I want him to learn things quickly."

✓ "I can't seem to enforce rules and feel bad, especially if I mishandled a situation. Then I let my son off the hook, sometimes giving him money when we don't have it, so my son fits in."

✓ "I don't think I have a good understanding of where overindulgence begins and stops and where just 'being okay' actually begins."

RECOVERING FROM OVERINDULGENCE: THE FOUR STOPPERS

Breaking out of a pattern of overindugence has not been easy for some. There is much that mitigates against it, holds us back, or stops us cold.

❖ First. there is the *secret* they must keep to avoid ridicule.
❖ Second, if they have not recognized overindulgence and *named* it, they may not know what they are wrestling with.
❖ Third, they don't intend to hurt their parents, who had *good intent*.
❖ Fourth, they may have *not a clue what to do* about it.

Let's replace each of the four stoppers.

First, *Secret*. We are beyond the secrets. We are speaking openly and without blame; we are talking about overindulgence.

Second, *Naming*. We can do something about a pesky problem once it is named. We are naming this monster condition overindulgence and getting insights into our beliefs and behaviors so we can talk about it, become reasonable, and sort out our feelings.

Third, *Intent*. We are respecting the good intent behind overindulging, recognizing that in all areas of life there are times when one's good intentions do not have the impact one expected.

Fourth, *Clue*. Not a clue what to do? We can stop discounting.

DENIAL—THE GLUE THAT KEEPS US STUCK

An easily understood way of identifying why we don't do the things we say we want to do is to think about denial, a process of discounting.

Discounting is the way we keep ourselves from solving problems, from getting our feet unstuck from the mud. We may not be aware we're discounting to keep a problem at a distance. Part of why we're unaware is that discounting and denial are a part of our culture. Everyone does it. It's so common that we don't see it. However, when we carry an understanding of what discounting is; it's easier for us to change it.

Understanding levels of discounting helps us know how to counter it. Consider this situation. Mom, newly aware of overindulging, tells Dad she's concerned that he's overindulging their son.

Problem: *She says, "I'm afraid your spending may be overindulging Jerry."*

Level 1: Discounting the existence of the problem.

He says, "The neighbors do it but I don't." (The problem does not exist.)

Level 2: Discounting the severity or negative impact of the problem.

He says, "Okay. I spend a lot on Jerry, but he really likes and uses all the stuff I get him." (Recognizing he may have a problem, but believing that it has no negative impact for him or for his son.)

Level 3: Discounting the solvability of the problem.

He says, "Maybe he has too much, but look, with all that his friends have, there's no way to fight this." (Recognizing the problem and its impact but feeling that there is no solution.)

Level 4: Discounting one's personal power to put a solution into effect.

He says, "For all the things I get for Jerry, he always wants more. I'm not getting a kick out of it anymore, but what can you do? All kids are like that now. Maybe some parents, or even a counselor, know what to do about this, but I sure don't." (Recognizing the problem, its impact, its solvability but still not taking responsibility for the last step.)

Eureka! Empowerment

"Neither Jerry nor I are really having fun anymore. I'll find out how to change what I'm doing so I stop contributing to the problem and start liking my kid again."

PARENTAL BEHAVIORS AND ATTITUDES
TOWARD A CHILD—PITFALLS IN PARENTING[1]

Our third overindulgence study gave us some clues about the pitfalls in present-day parenting that are the legacy of having experienced overindulgence as a child. We identified parental attitudes and behaviors that indicated whether the parents expected their leadership in the family to come from within themselves or to be controlled by outside forces. The findings are divided into three areas:

❖ parental behaviors and attitudes toward a child
❖ parental behaviors and attitudes about themselves
❖ parents' underlying beliefs and attitudes

The more parents had been overindulged, the more they agreed with the following nine statements that are about ways of handling children.[2]

❖ "Parents should not address problems with their children because ignoring them will make them go away."
❖ "Sometimes when I'm tired I let my children do things I normally wouldn't."
❖ "I allow my child to get away with things."
❖ "My child usually gets his/her own way, so why try."
❖ "It is often easier to let my child have his/her own way than to put up with the tantrum."
❖ "If your child throws tantrums no matter what you try, you might as well give up."
❖ "If a child frequently has tantrums, a parent gives up."
❖ "I can't deal with my child calmly when my child gets angry."
❖ "When I make a mistake with my child I am not usually able to correct it."

The statements could look daunting at first, but remember:

❖ Not every item applies to everyone who was overindulged.
❖ The more a person was overindulged, the stronger their agreement with a statement, so those overindulged in childhood range along a continuum from somewhat to always.

❖ Any overindulged person may have identified a parenting attitude or behavior that is not included in these items. Feel free to
add items from your own observations to the above list. Your
items may parallel these items, some may be the opposite, and
some may reflect strengths that have grown out of experience.

Now, reread the items while thinking about the parent as leader.

Now, consider each item with the following questions in mind:

❖ Does this feel/sound familiar?
❖ Do I do this often? Seldom? Never?
❖ Is this something I need to attend to?

If so, ask yourself, "Do I need to increase my Responsible leadership, my Effective leadership, and/or my Psychological leadership?"

HOW TO CHANGE OLD BEHAVIORS AND ATTITUDES

Since each of us owns and is responsible for our own behaviors and
attitudes, we can change them if it seems best to us to do so. There
are many kinds of entry points to the process.

1. **Pick one** attitude or behavior to change at a time. Only one.
   Stay under-whelmed.
2. **List** all the ways life would be **better** for your child and for you
   if you were to change that attitude or behavior.
3. **List** the **disadvantages** to changing. Everything from "My child
   will throw more tantrums" to "My child might not like me" to
   "I've not a clue what to do instead."
4. If you decide you do want to change, do whatever **grief work**
   you need to do—everything from letting go of familiar but loser
   attitudes and behaviors to acknowledging the sadness and
   regret that you kept the loser attitude and acted on it so long. If
   you don't know how to resolve griefs, try the suggestions in
   Good Grief Rituals by Elaine Childs-Gowell. If you'd like to
   know more about grieving, among the many books that can
   help is *Connections: The Threads That Strengthen Families* by
   Jean Illsley Clarke. Make room for new learning. The gardener
   pulls a weed to make room for a flower.

5. Make a **description** of your new attitude or behavior by turning around the old one in words that make sense to you. "I allow my child to get away with things" might become "I do not allow my child to get away with things." Or, "I hold my child responsible for his behavior." Say it aloud five times morning and night. Post it on a mirror, on the dashboard of the car, in your wallet.

6. In the morning think of **one little way** to act on your new attitude or one small way to behave in a new way that day and do it.

7. When you are ready, choose **one big way** to act on it each week and do it. Get help if you need it.

8. If you **fall back**, congratulate yourself for being on the journey. No beating yourself up.

9. When you notice a **positive shift** in your own attitude and behavior, celebrate. When you notice a positive shift in a child's behavior or attitude, celebrate, but don't overindulge.

10. Go back over the list and notice how many other things have changed in a positive way. **Celebrate.**

PARENTS' BEHAVIORS AND ATTITUDES TOWARD THEMSELVES

The next six items of the Locus of Control Scale refer to how parents regard themselves. Any time a parent who is being an effective leader of the family makes decisions, he or she thinks, *How will this decision impact me? My child? The whole family?*

Look at the following items and notice the extent to which the parent has turned over control of his or her life to the child.[3]

The behaviors and attitudes parents have toward themselves:

❖ In order to have my plans work, I make sure they fit in with the desires of my child.
❖ My child influences the number of friends I have.
❖ My life is chiefly controlled by my child.
❖ My child controls my life.
❖ I feel like what happens in my life is mostly determined by my child.
❖ It is not easy for me to avoid and function independently of my child's attempts to have control over me.

Look again at each item and ask yourself the question, *If I were saying yes to this item about myself, would I be giving effective leadership of the family to the child by over-nurture, by soft structure, or both?* Now re-read the items while thinking about the parent as leader.

PARENTS' UNDERLYING BELIEFS AND ATTITUDES

The following seven statements can be looked at as underlying beliefs and attitudes parents can hold about their children and about their relationships with children. The greater the degree of overindulgence people reported, the stronger their agreement with these statements. Look at each item and notice how it relates to the parents' power.[4]

❖ Without the right breaks one cannot be an effective parent.
❖ Heredity plays the major role in determining a child's personality.
❖ I have often found that when it comes to my child, what is going to happen will happen.
❖ Success in dealing with children seems to be more a matter of the child's moods and feelings at the time rather than one's own actions.
❖ Neither my child nor myself is responsible for his/her behavior.
❖ When something goes wrong between me and my child, there is little I can do to correct it.
❖ When I set expectations for my child, I am almost certain that I cannot help him/her meet them.

Holding these underlying beliefs can create a propensity on the part of the parent, who is by definition the Responsible leader (Chapter 20), to give the Effective leadership position to the children. If parents don't make decisions and rules and create structures and activities, children will. That is definitely not helpful for the family or for the children's healthy growth.

One way to deal with disempowering beliefs like these is to reclaim power by rewriting them. You can rewrite each one or you can read on to see how one parent rewrote them.

WHAT ONE PARENT WROTE

❖ *Without the right breaks one cannot be an effective parent.*[5]

"No parent is perfect. I can continually learn how to be more effective."

❖ *Heredity plays the major role in determining a child's personality.*
"And the environment (the parents) can help a child use his/her personality traits in positive ways."

❖ *I have often found that when it comes to my child, what is going to happen will happen.*
"I can help my child learn how to cope and I can mold my child's behavior by teaching the skills he/she needs to learn. I will evaluate my child and the situations and decide what to accept and what to do something about."

❖ *Success in dealing with children seems to be more a matter of the child's moods and feelings at the time rather than one's own actions.*
"Success with children means taking their moods into account and helping them name and deal in positive ways with their feelings."

❖ *Neither my child nor myself is responsible for his/her behavior.*
"My child is responsible for her/his behavior and I am responsible for my behavior and for holding my child accountable for his/her behavior."

❖ *When something goes wrong between me and my child, there is little I can do to correct it.*
"When something goes wrong between me and my child it is up to me as the adult to figure out how to resolve it and to get help if I need it."

❖ *When I set expectations for my child, I am almost certain that I cannot help him/her meet them.*
"When I set expectations for my child I can make sure they are reasonable and then encourage him/her to meet them."

HOW TO CHANGE BASIC BELIEFS ABOUT SELF

Since each of us owns our own basic beliefs, we can change them if we want to. Apply the ten change guidelines on page 232.

If you recognized yourself in any of the stories you've read so far, look for the "what to do insteads" that appear there. Find other adults who were overindulged and talk about the secret: What may have looked good didn't always feel that way. Be compassionate with yourself and others, and resist the temptation to get stuck in blaming or whining.

❖ Recognize.
❖ Apply what you've learned.
❖ Claim who you are.
❖ Let go of erroneous beliefs.
❖ Claim the power of knowing what is true.

PUSHOVER PARENTS

If you have been a pushover parent, keep a list of things to say when your children try to push you back into the old ways. Here is a starter list:

❖ *I'm the adult and I make the decisions.*
❖ *Why do I have to do that? Because I'm your parent and having you do that is my job.*
❖ *I'm the mother and I said no.*
❖ *I'm the father and I said no.*
❖ *Both of us say no.*
❖ *Parenting is not a popularity contest.*
❖ *Adversity and frustration are an inevitable part of life. You'll get used to it.*
❖ *This is a family and we all need to pitch in.*
❖ *Family members help each other.*

If you need to change, today is the right time to start. It's worth it for yourself and your children. Remember, strong parental leadership helps a child know who he is. You can create the legacy you want for your children, and thus for their children.

PARENTING IS A CAMPAIGN,
NOT A ONE-TIME ENCOUNTER.
—Karen Zimmerman

Turning Down Invitations to Overindulge

HAZARDS IN THE HOME

Dealing with Circumstances that Can Turn Good Intentions into Overindulgence

THE LITTLE WORLD OF CHILDHOOD WITH ITS FAMILIAR
SURROUNDINGS IS A MODEL OF THE GREATER WORLD.
THE MORE INTENSIVELY THE FAMILY HAS STAMPED ITS
CHARACTER UPON THE CHILD, THE MORE IT WILL TEND TO
FEEL AND SEE ITS EARLIER MINIATURE WORLD AGAIN
IN THE BIGGER WORLD OF ADULT LIFE. NATURALLY THIS IS
NOT A CONSCIOUS INTELLECTUAL PROCESS.
—Carl Jung

In the midst of many life circumstances, the shoulders of the highway can be filled with gremlins, pulling at us to leave the road. It's unavoidable. But when your vehicle is aware of the gremlins, and awareness is the key, you can activate your gremlin sweeper and steer your true course back to the center once again.

Participants at workshops on overindulgence never fail to ask questions that begin with "Don't you think . . . ?" The rest of the question usually spells out circumstances *they* think make well-meaning families vulnerable to overindulging children.

Here is a list of conditions that may lead to overindulgence in a home. It is drawn from the insights of the many people we spoke with.

- ❖ working parents
- ❖ unresolved conflicts between adults
- ❖ divorce, separation, stepfamilies, and two homes
- ❖ helping children whose friends' divorced parents are overindulging
- ❖ presence of addictions
- ❖ overcompensating for child's loss, neglect or abuse, chronic illness or disability, or adoptees and foster children
- ❖ death of a family member
- ❖ lack of knowledge of child development
- ❖ wealthy parents/poor parents
- ❖ parental immaturity, parents meeting their own unmet needs through children
- ❖ only child, only grandchild, youngest child, or long-awaited child
- ❖ lack of good parenting skills

This looks like a formidable list, but in any family only one or a very few may apply. Use the list to increase your awareness of the many circumstances that can invite overindulgence, not to judge, but to support every person who is attempting to avoid or stop it.

WORKING PARENTS

John Q. Public's first response to *Why do adults overindulge?* is, *I think it's because parents are working.* This common assumption is a misperception, but it is still worth mentioning as a hazard.

Working parents need to pay attention to guilt. Feeling guilty tells you that something is out of sync. Your behaviors or choices are not matching your values, your goals, your intentions. There are two ways to deal with this guilt discrepancy. One way is to re-arrange your lifestyle so your choices are congruent with your values. *Voila!* No more discrepancy. Relief of guilt. Another way is to keep your choices and use sound structure and nurture to give your children what they need and give yourself what you need, making your behaviors congruent with your values.

Mandy and Joe, although they were loath to admit it, sought to give their kids privileges and possessions to compensate for their long hours working away from home. When they became uncomfortable with the situation, they sat down together to look at options. Here's the list they made:

1. One of us quits working outside the home and becomes full-time parent.
2. We both look for jobs closer to home, perhaps with some flexibility about hours.
3. One or both of us works from home full- or part-time.
4. We move to a less expensive house, sell the good second car and replace it with a reliable but cheaper one.
5. We stop buying out of guilt and use the Test of Four to check out overindulgence.
6. We do a reality check to determine if we are shorting the kids by both working at the jobs we have now.
7. We check out situations to see if our guilt meter means "Change what you're doing" or "This is not a reason for guilt."

When choosing the options that work best for your family, changing your values or your behaviors, still pay attention to loving and teaching your children without overindulging them out of guilt.

What we call guilt may be shame. Shame is a "You are a bad person" message we give ourselves when we are paying homage to a very deep and probably old message. If you have such a message, identify it. Who first said it? Do you still believe it? Could who said the message have been saying it about themselves? Is it really true that you are a bad person?

Kids are expert at "hooking" our shame. "I don't have to vacuum the living room. You both work. Get a cleaning lady." An old message about "good mothers don't work outside the home" can hook shame. "Teflonize" yourself so that the hook slides right off you. If you bite, you may find yourself in one of those "Philadelphia lawyer" discussions with your child. It's an exchange that you will probably never win. One mom says, "Nice try. Lucky for you that your parents provide ways for you to get stronger. Lucky for me I have such a sharp kid. Now vacuum!"

Consider the "Case of the Bad, Bad Mother."

> Thirteen-year-old Mackenzie had her mother's permission to stay at her cousin Rebecca's house for the weekend. Rebecca was excited because she planned that they would go roller skating on Friday night and stay till the rink closed. When Mackenzie found out that the closing time was past her usual curfew time, she told her uncle that her mom probably wouldn't let her go. "What?" he reacted sharply. "Your mother is too much! She treats you like a baby. What on earth is wrong with her?"

An adult who has a problem involving another adult should deal directly with that person and not involve the children. The uncle could have called his sister to request permission for Mackenzie to stay out past curfew on this occasion.

As if dealing with the extended family isn't already enough of a challenge, one parent undermining another parent's authority to set limits is a serious problem. In families where the adults have problems they are not addressing with one another, it is common for their resentment or anger to go through the children, and that sometimes leads to overindulgence.

In Their Own Voices

Ĭn general, why do parents overindulge their children?
✓ My parents had a dysfunctional marriage and indulging us was a way to get us away from the other parent.

Listen to the story of the Princess:

> Dad told his three-year-old daughter, as she sat on his lap, that she was the princess, he was the king, and Mother, who was in the kitchen making dinner, was the Wicked Witch of the West. This was reinforced in many ways. Daughter would allow only the king to comb her hair, but screamed and carried on when Mother tried. King whispered confidences in the princess' ear while both glanced knowingly at Mother.
>
> When this child was eleven, she asked her mother if she could get her ears pierced. Mom told her she'd have to wait a year or two. But

Dad gave permission. The following day the princess showed Mom her new ear piercing with a haughty "Ha, I got my way" look.

At fourteen, daughter was yelling angrily at Mom who was helping her older brother make dinner. Mom said, "I can't hear what you're saying when you yell at me." Dad walked by and chided, "Now, now, girls." Son curled his lip and sputtered. "He's always interfering."

When the child became an adult, she entered therapy to straighten out the crooked goings-on in her family.

When a child's anger is expressed far in excess of the incident that triggered it, it might represent not only his or her anger, but also the unexpressed anger of the parent with whom that child is allied. In the story above, the daughter "carried" her father's anger at her mother. In this case, the daughter's older brother spoke out the anger of his mother toward the father. This can support a seemingly stable relationship for the parents, but at a high price for the kids. Parents are responsible for themselves and for addressing their conflicts without involving the children. Better the parents had entered therapy or somehow resolved their mutual anger while the children were very young. Better yet, before they were born.

SEPARATION AND DIVORCE, STEPFAMILIES AND TWO HOMES

Except under the most amicable of circumstances, separated partners sometimes use an adversarial tone in making references to the other party. The adults are often angry and resentful. They may be filled with anxiety about the uncertainties that lie ahead. It can be hard for them to keep anger directed toward the partner, where it belongs. Instead, the child can become the victim in a destructive game of "Choose me, I will make you love me best." But the child is not benefited by any ensuing overindulgence.

Cody has visitation with daughter Melissa every other weekend and on Wednesday nights on alternate weeks. When he arrives, Melissa is dressed in school clothes, packed and waiting. Cody usually seizes the opportunity to roundly criticize his ex-wife for not dressing Melissa in better clothes and not keeping her hair "the right way." Then he and Melissa go off to buy a piece of clothing or two or three and Cody does "Disney Dad" for the remainder of the visit.

Mom says that Melissa is developing a "You can't tell me" attitude and she is worried about what Melissa is beginning to think about herself.

When children come home after a visit with one parent and tell about the great things that parent does for them or buys for them, a pernicious game of one-upmanship can get started. Doing special favors, buying whatever the children want and some things they don't even know they want, not holding children accountable, not expecting chores duty, accepting substandard effort or work, and giving too much freedom and power are not doing the child any favors. While the children may like and boast about what they receive, they also develop a distorted picture of reality and an inaccurate sense of their own importance.

Carlos and Vanessa have regular meetings to work out problems that came up in the course of co-parenting in different houses with new spouses. One parent can afford to take the children on extended trips while the other plans activities, but buys more of the children's clothes. When one parent wants to get a birthday present that's on the costly side, they discuss the purchase first with the other parent. The children have different "goodies" at each home and different ways they are expected to contribute to each family. A comparison game doesn't work here because the parents don't let it work.

Anyone who has children signs on for the long haul. Divorce does not change that obligation. When separated parents have a conflict, they need to keep it between themselves. However, if an ex-spouse refuses to recognize the overindulgence or stop doing it, what are you to do? Listen to a parent educator's suggestions to a parent who is frustrated with an ex-spouse's overindulgence of their nine-year-old son.

Dear Frustrated,

First, it seems to be very difficult to change ex-spouses, so unless this seems serious enough to go back to court, I suggest that you accept this as a part of your child's learning experience. It will be just that, as I gather that your son spends some time with you. His brain will record your words and he will retain somewhere in himself the skills you teach him. When he is older and sees how positively the world responds to your input, I expect he will not only use it, but will value you highly as well. Here are some of the words you can use when he is with you:

- Nine-year-olds are expected to put away their clothes. Do you need me to show you how to do that here?
- Now that you are nine, I see that you are becoming more responsible. I notice that you hung up your coat, put the dishes in the dishwasher, ...
- For *I can't* or *I don't know how*, try, *I bet you can. You try and I'll cheer.*
- Do be able to stand his pain when he gets frustrated. That's part of growing up. Don't comfort him if he tantrums. Give plenty of love other times, and never, never end a sentence with 'Okay?' That lets him think he is in charge.

I wish you well.

HELPING YOUR CHILD WHOSE FRIEND'S DIVORCED PARENTS ARE OVERINDULGING

This story of a sensitive mother's response to her envious daughter illustrates how you can help your child keep perspective.

My daughter told me yesterday that a good friend of hers is moving to a southern suburb to live with her dad. My daughter is very sad that she wouldn't be seeing her friend each day at school. We've had difficulty in coordinating out-of-school get-togethers, yet we want this friendship to continue, so we'll do what we can.

After my daughter talked about her disappointment, she continued in a brightly spirited voice about how her friend's dad was going to get her a computer and printer and maybe even a laptop. She could redecorate her room and she'd be getting new bedroom furniture. She's also getting a cell phone and a whole new wardrobe. My daughter's eyes were wide with amazement.

I said that all of those things didn't guarantee her friend would be happy and that presents can't buy love and attention. My daughter said, "I know, but it'd still be cool to get it." I agreed that it might be cool to get, but I was glad she knew the difference between love and stuff.

I'm not worried about my daughter; she has a pretty good head about things like this. I do worry about her friend as it seems to me that the competition between her parents is increasing and this young girl is being swayed by the offer of a "princess" life."

THE PRESENCE OF ADDICTIONS

Whenever a family member has a primary relationship with a substance or process instead of with himself, another person, or people, we say that person is addicted. The list of addictions is long. It includes drugs (alcohol and marijuana are drugs), work, sex, food, gambling, the Internet, relationships, religion, television, exercise—any substance or process with which a person develops a consuming relationship.

Ordinarily, family attention is over-focused on the behaviors of the addicted one and under-focused on the needs of other family members. The children's developmental needs fall by the wayside as they assume responsibilities for under-functioning adults. Children may be out-and-out neglected and/or abused when addiction is present. Then they can be overindulged as compensation, or out of guilt.

In Their Own Voices

If you have children, do you overindulge them?
- ✓ Often. I felt guilty due to divorce and pain caused by my abuse of alcohol and drugs early in my child's life. I also felt guilty when I went back to school because I missed time for being together.

Dealing forthrightly with the addiction and the family's recovery means taking steps to unravel and repair the damage. Family relationships are at the top of the repair list, especially the couple relationship and the parenting lapses.

OVERCOMPENSATING FOR A CHILD'S LOSSES, NEGLECT, ABUSE, DISABILITY, CHRONIC ILLNESS, ADOPTION, OR FOSTER PLACEMENT

Children recovering from trauma need understanding and empathy along with sound nurture and structure. The same is true for children with chronic illness or disability. The first order of business is to see that the children's basic needs are met; needs for a safe and caring environment, needs for proper medical care, and so on.

However, if you overdo empathy, it can become over-nurture and soft structure. Out of a sincere wish to compensate for your child's pain and to make their life better, you can give the kind of care that becomes overindulgence.

Melanie and Alex had prepared a nicely furnished room, complete with astronaut motif, colorful wallpaper, spaceships, toys, and stuffed animals, for the five-year-old Russian boy they were adopting. They showed him how to brush his teeth, taught him English words for things, and acquainted him with the features of his spiffy new jacket. Ivan had no chores, few rules, and no consequences.

Imagine their surprise when they discovered broken new toys under Ivan's bed, pieces of wallpaper he'd picked off the wall, and drawings scratched in the surface of his new desk. Baffled by his seeming rejection of their loving approach, his parents were confused by the disappointment and anger they felt. They'd done their best to receive him and make him feel welcome. When he ripped apart his best teddy bear, Melanie and Alex quickly found a therapist who could help them figure out what to do . . . and what not to do.

For the child who experienced early abuse and neglect, including those coming from institutional care of one sort or another, getting too much stuff, nice stuff, and too much attention is unfamiliar. Whatever is unfamiliar signals possible "danger." If a situation is unfamiliar, it is unpredictable and the child is flooded by feelings of fear. The bizarre and destructive things he does in reaction to having too much stuff or love are an attempt to regain a feeling of being in control in the face of the fear.

In Melanie and Alex's case, the therapist recommended taking everything but the bed and a chest of drawers out of Ivan's room. Ivan came from stark orphanage conditions and was not equipped to be in a place with so much. This home was so different from Ivan's previous experience, he was afraid he didn't belong there. In addition, Ivan couldn't make sense of why he had so much when he felt so bad about himself. Ivan needed to learn that he could trust his new parents. They simplified his room, implemented a few simple rules with consequences, expected him to contribute to the family by doing chores and working alongside Mom and Dad. Ivan's anxiety lessened over time. The stuff in his room was gradually re-introduced as Ivan became able to tolerate the "richness" of his new home.

DISABILITY DOES NOT MEAN INABILITY

The best approach for parenting someone with a disability is to expect what you would expect of a child that age, considering the particular limitations of that child. This also applies to children who have been abused and neglected and those who are recovering from alcohol and drug dependency, or have chronic illnesses or were born drug affected.

In Their Own Voices

If you have children, do you overindulge them?

✓ Often. This is a major problem in my family for both me and my husband. We have twins, age seven. One is hearing impaired. Both were medically frail as babies. We overindulge, pamper to keep them happy. We don't let them be unhappy.

✓ Often. My wife is chronically ill. I have often overindulged the boys to make up for the lack of attention from my wife and my lack of being there because of work.

Kimberly had never worked with disabilities before she began her job as a camp counselor at a summer camp for physically disabled children. Trying to do the job well, she helped kids who didn't need it and didn't want it. And they told her so. She learned to ask if they wanted help and to let them tell her what kind of help they needed. And she learned which camper needed what help routinely and provided that help matter-of-factly so she didn't have to ask each time.

Kimberly learned that the Care and Support positions are the best places on the Nurture Chart from which to relate with those for whom many of us would be tempted to over-function.

DEATH OF A FAMILY MEMBER

We are learning more and more about how children grieve the death of a loved one. When a family member dies, adults support grieving children through all the many forms that grieving takes. Caring, however, moves into overindulgence if the adults try to care for their own pain by over-caring for the child.

> Aunt Michelle gave Sean an expensive train set that she thought would make him feel better after the death of his mother. What Sean really wanted was to talk about his mom. He already had a train set.

> Evan, age nine, was protected from the stress of school by being kept home from school during the two weeks following Grandpa's funeral. Evan missed his friends and wondered why he was being kept home and worried about how he would make up his work.

> Jenna became the only grandchild when her older sister died. After the sister's death, her grandparents and parents began treating Jenna like a princess, not expecting her to do any work around the house, allowing her much more freedom than usual, giving her lots of attention, and buying expensive clothes and art lessons "to make her feel better." Jenna didn't understand the change but decided to enjoy it. At the time, she didn't even relate it to her sister.

Regularity is comforting to children all the time but particularly during a grief period. They are reassured that adults they count on will still be there and available to them in times of loss, fear, and need. Children are reassured by a parent who can see when they need comforting and give it, or who relate a story about a special past time with the person whose loss is being grieved (Assertive Care). Or the adult can ask the child if he'd like some snuggle time or would like to remember that person by recounting a story he knows (Supportive Care). This is middle-of-the-road parenting.

LACK OF KNOWLEDGE OF CHILD DEVELOPMENT

When you don't know what is age-development-appropriate, you are vulnerable to overindulging your children with too much, too soon, and by giving freedoms without expecting responsibility to match.

Aunt Molly gave baby Briana a rattle and was disappointed that the one-month old wasn't interested and didn't play with it.

One month of age is too soon for babies to begin playing with rattles.

Mason, age two, is allowed to throw his toys at furniture or people.

Two-year-olds have more thinking power than one-year-olds and need to be starting to develop some internal restraints. Mason is being treated like a baby.

Nora's mother is delighted her four-year-old daughter is dancing like a twenty-one-year-old sex kitten, and buys her mini-skirts and tight strapless tops.

Four-year-olds are big-time into figuring out role and power relationships with others. Sexually provocative clothing sends wrong signals to both the girl and others.

When eight-year-old Brittney begged for make-up, Dad bought her an eyebrow pencil, mascara, and lipstick. He shows her off to his friends when she wears it. He has a "glamour shot" appointment scheduled.

Six- to twelve-year-olds are examining the values on which rules are based. Brittney should be learning to differentiate between wants and needs. Dad is wishing her into adolescence.

Seth lives at the edge of a city. Seth's parents have given him permission to drive his snowmobile within two miles of his house. Seth is twelve.

At the age of twelve, Seth should have learned about the freedom and safety that come from having rules and skills to depend on. In this example, we wonder how the parents made the assessment that they could have confidence in Seth's ability to handle himself and the snowmobile two miles away and alone.

Max watches X-rated movies at home with his dad.

No matter what Max's age, this activity supports none of Max's developmental tasks.

All these examples are related to not knowing the developmental tasks of the child. In each case the kids are being encouraged not to grow up or to grow up too fast.

In *The Hurried Child*, author and child psychologist David Elkind wrote in 1981 about a subject even more timely at present:

If child-rearing necessarily entails stress, then by hurrying children to grow up or by treating them as adults, we hope to remove a portion of our burden of worry and anxiety and to enlist our children's aid in carrying life's load.

The chart in Appendix C (page 279) will help you remember the jobs of kids at each stage of development.

PARENTAL IMMATURITY

Parents who have holes in the navigation of their own development may be vulnerable to filling those holes at the expense of a child. Age alone is not the only determiner of maturity. We all know a forty-five year old who can act as immature as a fifteen-year-old.

Let's start with this. Infants and very young children survive by being symbiotic. That is, they are unable to care for and protect themselves. They depend almost solely on being attached to another who will care for them, protect them, and do things for them. As they grow and as they learn more about themselves, they learn how to take care of themselves and extend their caring to others.

At the end of adolescence, we expect to see a young woman or man who has passed through self-absorption and not only considers others, but thinks about his or her relationship to family, community, nation, and world. People who choose to be parents during adolescence are pressed to grow up fast and assume adult responsibilities before their time.

The sixteen-year-old mom props the bottle for her baby while she reads a fashion magazine. She spends money intended for food on stuff, like fancy dresses for baby Leslie so she can show her off to friends.

Parents need to promote communication and connection with an infant by holding the baby in a face-to-face position while feeding a bottle. Babies need soft, comfortable clothing and should have parents who are attuned to their needs.

We need to be careful to choose activities that match our children's needs, not just our wishes.

Adolescents who are parents need to put skillful parenting ahead of their own wishes. Then they need to guard against transferring their unmet wishes and needs to their children, perhaps overindulging one child and neglecting others.

When Luis was an adolescent he desperately wanted a motorcycle. Luis wants his boy to have the boyhood he didn't have because of his alcoholic father. Luis gets his son a junior-size motorcycle when he's only eight, and the two of them spend every Saturday at motocross events. The two girl children in the family are left at home.

Luis's effort to be the father he wanted dominates Luis's family time and attention. Luis could buy his own motorcycle and find a skillful adult rider who would mentor him.

We need to be careful to choose activities that match our children's needs, not just our wishes.

THE ONLY CHILD, THE ONLY GRANDCHILD, THE YOUNGEST CHILD, OR THE LONG-AWAITED CHILD

In Their Own Voices

In general, why do parents overindulge their children?

✓ I was the baby and only girl—the little princess—they couldn't do enough. They didn't understand the effects of their behavior. They wanted to protect me so they kept me sheltered.

All of the following situations have this in common: They are circumstances that can lead from treasuring a specialness to overindulgence.

The Only and Long-Awaited

Grandpa and Grandma see Sabrina, their two-year-old youngest grandchild, the one who lives some distance away, only twice a year. They take a stuffed animal and a book for her each time. Between visits, she hears their voices on the telephone and they hear hers. They send pictures and postcards.

The other grandparents also live at a distance from Sabrina. A long-awaited grandchild, Sabrina gets expensive presents from them on every holiday during the year. Often the presents are too old for her. During their frequent visits, their entire and complete focus is on Sabrina, with little or no time spent on connections among the adults.

Both sets of grandparents are trying to connect with the child, but the second set have fallen into the trap of overindulgence.

If her parents aren't careful, Sabrina is in danger of being kept at the center of the universe or of being caught in the double bind caused by opposing messages: "Grow up fast," here are gifts that are too old for you; and "Don't grow up," stay the complete center of family activities.

The information in this book works as well for only children as it does for children with siblings. Think of a line of fluffy ducklings swimming behind Mother Duck. The ducklings follow the leader in a straight line where the mother's large feet protect them from creatures that nip little duck feet. If the ducks get out of line, Ms. Duck sees to getting them back in order. This is the way that is best for ducks. If there is only one duck, he's in the line, just a much shorter line. It is the same for children.

The Youngest

The youngest child or any children who are overindulged are often resented by siblings. *She's too much to put up with. I'm tired of his screwing up and the folks rescuing him. How come she has nine lives with Mom and Dad and I had to make a go of it the first time? All he can think of is himself. She's like a bull in a china shop and is clueless about what a pain she is. I don't even want to be around him.*

Nora's good friend has a sister who does things that have repeatedly provoked the ire of her sibs. Nora, having been to a workshop on overindulgence, thought it sounded like a case of overindulgence and told her friend about the overindulgence studies. "Oh my! You're talking about my sister. I can see it isn't all her fault. As I think about it, my parents seriously protected her from consequences. They babied her. I see her getting frustrated by all the dead-end jobs and relationships that have gone wrong. She complains or makes excuses and it drives us all nuts. I need to learn to react differently and not just get mad at her."

LACK OF GOOD PARENTING SKILLS

All people learn an original set of parenting skills from the way they were parented. But now you are parenting for a different world than the one you grew up in, and you need more skills, especially if you tend to overindulge.

In Their Own Voices

When your parents overindulged you, what feelings resulted?
- ✓ I felt insecure because my parents didn't seem to have things under control or didn't seem to know as much as other parents about how to raise their children.
- ✓ I can remember at age ten really being worried about how I'd grow up because I knew that neither one of them knew what they were doing.

How can you improve your parenting skills? Try following these two steps:

Step One: Assessment: Inherited and borrowed parenting skills
   a. How did my (mother, father, parent figure) handle this kind of situation when I was growing up?
      Was what they did helpful? Keep that.
      What would have been more helpful? Think about that.
   b. Think of someone whose parenting you admire. Observe that person and identify attitudes and behaviors you want to copy.
   c. Identify attitudes and behaviors you want to improve.

Step Two: Change
   a. Choose one thing you want to change, only one thing at a time. Stay underwhelmed.
   b. Collect information to help you. Use the ideas in this book, see the Recommended Reading section, read other books, attend classes, ask friends, ask a parent educator or a parent coach, ask the person(s) whose parenting you admire, see a therapist, use other sources you have.

Here are some strong leader parent messages:
   (To a fifteen-year-old): "Amy, I'm happy to drive you and your friends to the mall when you've finished the dishes . . . if it's before seven o'clock."
   (To an eleven-year-old): "I'm sorry you don't have your six-week project ready to turn in tomorrow. What will you do about that?"
   (To a two-year-old): "Honey, I understand you are having fun and don't want to go to the store with me but I can't leave you alone. Come now." Child continues to play. "I see you have chosen not to come when I ask you to. You can come under your own power or under mine. You choose." Child ignores. Dad picks up child. "Come on, honey. We'll be home soon." Dad carries child with sureness and without anger, to the car, no matter how much the child protests.

You may want to review Chapter 22, Take Me to Your Leader, again. The earlier in a child's life you establish your leadership, the better. Convincing a youngster of fourteen to suddenly pay attention to your "No" is a lot harder than getting it straightened out when she is two. Using the developmental information in Appendix TK and the Nurture and Structure Charts will be helpful.

The moral of these stories and this chapter? It is the grown-up's responsibility to be grown-up and the child's responsibility to be growing up. Staying in the center of the road can get you to the places you want to go. The problem areas we cover in this chapter were identified by the people who took part in our studies. There undoubtedly are many more. We've recommended a few of our favorite books if you're seeking further information, but many more covering overindulgence situations can be found in your local library and bookstores.

WE NEED TO RAISE CHILDREN WITH THE EXPECTATION OF SERVICE, NOT THE EXPECTATION OF ENTITLEMENT.
—Kaara Ettesvold

HAZARDS ON THE ROAD

Outside Pressures to Overindulge—
Consumerism, the Media, the Community,
Other People

GOODNESS HAS A PLACE AT THE TABLE.
—Fred Mednick

T HE overindulgence shoulder of the societal highway is cluttered
with sometimes alluring and sometimes annoying invitations to drift
over. Some days they beckon but some days they jump out and grab
our children, and, yes, us too. Some days the clutter makes for very
hazardous driving. And some days we have to do repair work after
some of the clutter has grabbed our children or us. Let's identify
briefly some of these societal shoulder hazards.

Let's remind ourselves that avoiding overindulgence takes a keen eye
and a steady hand. Sometimes a quick slam on the brakes keeps us
from sliding onto the shoulders. Other times, in order to bypass an
overindulgence side trip, we have to put the pedal to the metal, regard-
less of the backseat pleas to slow down and pull over. Let us forgive
ourselves if we do slide over, and get back in the middle as soon as possible, so that the outcome of our parenting matches our good intent.

THE CHALLENGE TO RESIST THE "NORM"

"Members of the class of 1994 will long live under the shadow of the widest cheating scandal ever to scar the U.S. Naval Academy," reported the *Minneapolis Star Tribune*. The twenty-one-year-old brigade commander, highest rank among 4,200 Naval Academy students, was quoted as saying:[1]

> It used to be that people just came here and all these things were assumed. The idea of integrity wasn't that hard to grasp. Now, institutionally we've hardly changed. But the whole world has turned upside down. Our class . . . grew up at a time when nobody in our entire lives, in any institution, was ever there to tell us what's right or wrong.[1]

Each of you will have your own opinions about what the brigade commander said. Is he blaming institutions and not holding midshipman accountable for their cheating or is he trying to understand how this could happen at the institution of which he is an important part? What the commander *does* highlight is his perceived lack of moral fiber in contemporary role models and authority figures. He may also be commenting about what some call living in a time of cultural rationalization. If this is so, it leaves most of us wondering, *How did we get this way?* But the real question is: *How do we get to the middle of the highway now?*

In this chapter, we raise the issue of "norms" by pointing out a few dilemmas facing parents—dilemmas involving overindulgence.

DILEMMAS

❖ the influence of media and consumerism
❖ community pressures to overindulge
  ✦ schools and peers
  ✦ courts
  ✦ police
❖ others who give too much
❖ others who smother
❖ going against the current
❖ identify overindulgence
  ✦ prom

+ graduation
+ a pile of leaves
+ curfew

THE INFLUENCE OF MEDIA AND CONSUMERISM

Taking care not to overindulge within the walls of your home is one thing. Your children, however, in their wider world, often find it hard to maintain their integrity in the face of the "You're entitled to it" mentality presented by the outside world. The pressures to overindulge by excusing, justifying, or glamorizing grim, low-standard behaviors seem to be everywhere.

Refraining from overindulging can also result in a parent's feeling alone and beleaguered. As one mom put it, "I'm known as Mean Mother in my neighborhood." Many parents, it seems, have yielded to the overwhelming pressures to adopt the "popular" norms of behavior, norms that are set by marketers and media. Parents with squishy nurture and wobbly structure who are pressured by tenacious children often give in.

When a group of parents discuss the media and its effect on family buying decisions, you're likely to hear something that echoes the thoughts of a mother reported in the *Christian Science Monitor* in 2001.

> The Gunning children, to their mother's dismay, are lobbying for a new XBox video game system, a product Gunning curtly describes as "not very stimulating." Yet she admits it is all but a foregone conclusion that her kids will eventually own it, given the tidal wave of hype—including a $500 million advertising budget promoting the game console.

Like the Gunnings, many parents are growing increasingly frustrated with a culture of consumerism that seems to be slipping beyond their control. As recently as fifteen years ago, experts say, toy selection came from the top down, with parents doing most of the choosing. Since then, the decision-making power has shifted drastically.

That raises the question: Who is in charge? If parents have yielded to perceived pressures by kids and advertising and they don't like it, they can ask themselves the four questions.

Test of Four

1. Will this support the healthy physical and emotional **development** of our child?
2. What proportion of our **resources** do we want to devote to entertainment, toys, lessons, and so on?
3. Will this meet our **needs** or the child's?
4. Might this be **harmful**? Is it congruent with our values?

Many children will emphatically declare that to give them what they want is good for them. But, when they are adults, if they buy whatever they want when they want it, the result of not knowing what is enough and not learning to be realistic about what they can afford is called large credit card debt.

A mother of two sons, ages ten and seven, and a daughter age five, wrote this story and gave it to us:

> *It is often difficult for me when I am not able to overindulge my children. So many other children have the things my kids want. I feel frustrated at the conflict between the common standard and what I am either able or willing to provide.*
>
> *Every once in a while I get clear about a situation, though. For example, last week I took my little ones to an indoor playground. They complained the whole time about one thing or another. They wanted to spend time on arcade games that would cost a great deal of money and were unhappy with the little toys they got for the arcade game tickets they won. Now I remember why it has been a year since we went there last. It may be another year till we go again, next time with a few more ground rules.*
>
> *We can go to the park with a picnic cheaper and be happier. There are several other choices they enjoy more so why do they still ask to go to the indoor playground? I believe it is the advertisements. They are sold on the fantasy and disappointed when it isn't as they expect. Another day. Another lesson for Mom.*

Advertising is advertising. Buying is the decision of the ones who can buy. Is it that simple? Yes, simple, but not always easy. It is easy for children to get pulled into wanting the stuff that's advertised. It is not so easy for parents to avoid taking what is often an "easy way out" by acceding to the child's demands. The questions to ask yourself are:

- Do I need it?
- How will acquiring this item, taking this trip, paying for this experience improve the quality of my life? My family's life? My child's life?
- Am I clear about what constitutes my quality of life?

Adam, who is ten, asks Dad, "Why can't we ever get anything? George and Charles each have a TV in their room and they each have a great computer set-up. How come I can't have that? You've got as much money as their dad has."

Dad explains that families spend money according to what's important to them. "We chose to buy a cabin we can all use during vacations. I suppose we could have bought TVs for you and your brother, but your mother and I believe your room is for doing schoolwork and sleeping. When we watch TV, we watch in the room next to the kitchen."

Adam looked like he was about to try another tack, but instead, rolled his eyes and walked away with an "Oh well" look.

Some eight-year-old girls are wearing clothes that are appropriate for their age. Sierra, however, wants to be associated with a peer group that has bought the look-older media message.

Mark complained about his eight-year-old daughter, Sierra. "When she went shopping for school clothes with her mother, Sierra absolutely refused to consider outfits her mother wanted to buy. Called them 'little girl stuff.' She went right for the clothes that are slinky, tight, and like some twenty-four-year-old entertainer's clothes. Spaghetti straps and bare midriffs. My wife is no fun when she comes back from a shopping trip with Sierra. Before the next trip we'll set some rules and I'll go along as the enforcer. Sierra will not run this family! Also, I'm concerned about her choice of peer group. I know that can be terribly important in a child's life."

Sierra's story applies just as well to boys who are following a dress and behavior standard set by male entertainers. Whatever kids see and hear in the media and on the stage can become a norm that violates family values. Swearing. Disrespect. Violence.

The role models in the media or the pressures from advertising or the "All the kids are . . ." pressures can push us into overindulging. Bit by bit they push. And bit by bit parents need to hang onto their values and stand firm.

COMMUNITY PRESSURES TO OVERINDULGE

Schools and Peers

Eleven-year-old Isaac found a twenty-dollar bill in the school playground. A bunch of kids gathered quickly and as Isaac headed off to the principal's office to turn it in, the kids yelled: "Keep it! Are you crazy? What's wrong with you, man?"

Mom heard twelve-year-old Colin swear a blue streak at his younger brother. Anger welled in her, "Colin! If you use that language when you're not at home and where I can't hear you, I'm not able to stop you, but you should stop yourself. If I hear you, I will collect a quarter from you for each swear word."

She continued. "If swearing is usual among kids your age, I expect you to outgrow it speedily!"

This mother identified a rule and an enforcement of a rule for Colin. She also has a personal rule that she does not accept any behavior that results in her being angry at her son. If he is disrespectful, she does not provide services like rides or money or accommodation to his wants as long as she's feeling resentful of him. She also rewards him for following rules, usually with a smile or a squeeze that says, *Colin, I'm so proud of your self-control.*

A customer in a gift store overheard a conversation about the pervasive school and peer effects of overindulgence. She said:

Excuse me. I'd like to say I agree with you. I'm a teacher and it is very challenging to have students in my junior high classes who feel entitled to be uncooperative and dare me to do my job. I think they know there are no consequences for them, except school failure, and grades don't seem to be a motivator. I don't know where the parents are.

Ask experienced educators how students have changed over the years and they will say that while many schools have added advanced courses to their curricula, in other ways many have "dumbed down" their academic and behavioral expectations, and that many more students now are not particularly interested in working hard, and many are more defiant.

It's a classic chicken-or-egg scenario. Which came first, dumbed-down schools or overly entitled students and overindulging parents?

Do school faculties and boards relax their policies and standards in an attempt to please, thereby offending no one? Do they back off from holding students accountable at least partly because of parental lawsuits or threats of lawsuits? Are parents demanding that the school assume some of the responsibilities that belong to the parents and then criticizing the school for doing so or for not doing it right?

Have the teachers succumbed to the idea of having only a "positive" response to children for fear of damaging their self-esteem?

❖ "Even if they're annoying, don't say anything to hurt their feelings."
❖ "If you want her to feel good about herself, don't evaluate anything negatively. This applies to her art *and* her behavior."

Have parents stopped supporting the teachers and the learning process?

❖ "You don't like that assignment? Well, that teacher always makes dumb assignments."
❖ "Good grades are not a measure of a person's value."
❖ "That teacher just doesn't understand you."

When did self-esteem become "self-excusement?" How did entitlement turn into disregard?

Arguing about who is at fault is ridiculous. We are all part of a community/school system, and there is general agreement that some schools are not functioning in the way they could if they received more widespread constructive parental support, if they received the help they needed to serve their many constituencies, and if parents insisted that homework be done and children be respectful.

The Court System

Another important institution that may have experienced an off-balancing of rights and responsibilities is the legal system. Many court programs have been instituted that attempt to hold miscreant youngsters accountable for changing their anti-social behaviors instead of excusing them. However, the courts, which are, after all, a reflection of the community's will as defined by law and procedure, have become places where technicalities sometimes outweigh truth and where excuses have resulted in failure to hold people accountable. Could applying the

Test of Four bring us greater clarity about separating justice from overindulgence?

The Police

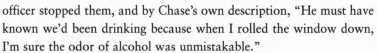

Chase and his date were on their way home from a formal school dance. Both had been drinking. A police officer stopped them, and by Chase's own description, "He must have known we'd been drinking because when I rolled the window down, I'm sure the odor of alcohol was unmistakable."

"Had a little to drink, huh?"

"Yes, sir. One or two." The reality was they had had a lot more.

"How far are you from home, Son?"

"Only a couple of blocks." Actually, two miles.

"Can you make it there safely?" asked the officer.

"Oh, yes sir. No problem."

"All right then. Go along, Son, but be careful."

As an adult, Chase maintains if he had gotten a ticket or been taken off to jail, bad as that would have been at the time, perhaps he would have become aware of the seriousness of his problem with alcohol much sooner. As it was, he was thirty-five before he got help.

Pressured by "go soft" and "be tough" public opinions, police are caught in the middle. The public says, *Let the demonstrations take place.* Then when all hell breaks loose the public cries, *You shouldn't have let that happen.* Damned if they do. Damned if they don't. That's called a double bind. That makes it harder for the police to make decisions based on protection and safety. As it is, the police are often concerned that they will be hung out to dry for taking an action that is the right action in the service of public safety. With that in mind, we all must be careful about blaming, and actively support and demand that the police act responsibly.

DEALING WITH OTHER PEOPLE WHO GIVE TOO MUCH

In a wish not to appear ungrateful, and assuming the gifts came from a good heart, the recipient of too- or overly lavish gifts may feel caught in a double bind.

Diana's friend of six months, a loving and generous woman, gave Diana an obviously expensive gift for her birthday. Diana was discomforted by the gift, but said nothing. As her friend's birthday approached, she found herself in a dilemma. Should she reciprocate in kind? Diana did not ordinarily exchange pricey presents with friends, but she also had a "matching" rule in her head. She decided to give a present that she was comfortable with.

A few months later, her friend invited her to a holiday gift exchange saying, "We all bring ten small gifts for each of the four others. The gifts are around a dollar or so each."

Reluctantly, Diana brought ten gifts for each person and the exchange began. When her friend brought out an especially stitched four-foot-long stocking to hold the presents for Diana, Diana didn't know how to respond. There were at least twenty gifts from her friend and most cost between five and fifteen dollars. Diana's heart sank.

After becoming clear about her thoughts and feelings, Diana spoke with her friend. "I want to tell you that while I have appreciated the thoughtfulness behind your gifts, I do not want you to do that for me. I have no trouble accepting a small gift, but when I get so much from you, I have the feeling I should owe you in some way that isn't clear to me. I don't want to feel that the connection I have with you is that I owe you. It isn't good for our friendship."

During a follow-up conversation, her friend confided that as a single person, she was afraid if she didn't give gifts, she wouldn't receive any. Diana's response: "You will not be loved for the gifts you give. You are loved for who you are. Tears welled up in the friend's eyes and the over-gifting ceased."

Overindulgence is not a substitute for true love and caring.

DEALING WITH OTHER PEOPLE WHO SMOTHER

It can be a touchy situation when your child is smothered by people outside your home or extended family, but when your child has regular contact with someone who is doing things for him that he could, or should be able to do for himself, it's a concern that must be addressed. Think of these situations:

A new child-care worker took the four-year-olds' coats off and hung them up before they had a chance to. Before long, they stood there and waited for her, even though they could have begun an activity if they had gone ahead on their own.

Cole is in trouble with his boss. Routinely late for work, last week his immediate supervisor smelled marijuana on his clothes. The boss suggested Cole get to work at eight and Cole agreed he'd be there on time. His boss didn't follow through to see if Cole made good on his promise. Two days later, Cole ran a stoplight while under the influence, and killed the passenger in another car. Cole's employer was mortified, thinking that if he had used his employee drug-use policy to get Cole help much earlier, an innocent person wouldn't have died.

Over-protection is over-nurture. When it occurs, in home or in the community, it is overindulgence. For each of the situations above, you can apply the Test of Four.

GOING AGAINST THE CURRENT

The director of a summer camp located on a good-sized river was also a swimming coach at a big city high school. Every year he hired his most promising swimmers for camp staff and saw to it they trained by swimming against the current. On days when the river's flow was normal, they would dive in and swim upstream for thirty minutes, making about two hundred yards before they hit the beach. However, after a hard rain, when they surfaced from their dives, they were already thirty feet downstream. After thirty minutes of hard swimming, they barely made it back to the dock.

Parenting without overindulging can be like serious swimming against a fast current. Everything and everybody can seem to be going the other way. Messages in the media. Pressure from your kids and their peers. Judgments from *your* peers.

Please remember to focus on the people who share your determination. If you focus on the negative and hear yourself blaming others, or playing "ain't it awful," adjust by talking to the ones who believe as you do. What you focus on, expands. Expand on what you know to be best for you and for your children. Strengthen your connections with spouses, partners, parent support persons, and with your various communities.

IDENTIFYING OVERINDULGENCE

As you read the following stories of overindulgence, identify whether each is a case of over-nurture, soft structure, or too much.

Prom

Trevor's senior prom is a month away. He and his buddies want to rent a hotel suite to which they and their dates can go hang out after the dance. "Everyone does it." The hotel won't rent rooms to them even though they have the money, so he asks Dad to rent the suite for them. Against Dad's better judgment, and at Mom's insistence, he rents the room and pays for it to help Trevor defray some of the prom expenses.

Too Much _____ Over-Nurturing _____ Soft Structure _____

Graduation

The long-awaited adult high school graduation ceremonies began with a flourish. The chairperson welcomed the thirty graduates and their guests, announcing that each graduate could say a few words if they chose. It was apparent the small staff had created a memorable celebration.

As each name was called, the student was individually featured, given a diploma, and applauded.

Victor was a guest invited by a graduate whom he employed in his print shop. He was quite taken aback when, after the fifth graduate had been celebrated, practically one entire row of guests stood up and left. *What's going on?* he thought. *Is the whole family leaving?* A minute later a party of six noisily made their way to the back of the auditorium to rendezvous with the young man who had just been awarded his diploma. Then another group got up to join another graduate in the center aisle. They chatted and moved toward the rear door while the next graduate was being announced. Victor found himself angry and wanting to jump up and shout, "We were here to celebrate your graduation. You should stay and help celebrate ours!"

Too Much _____ Over-Nurturing _____ Soft Structure _____

A Pile of Leaves

Bailey's mom raked the leaves into a neat pile and went to get the leaf sacks. As she returned she let out an "Oh, no!" just as her neighbor approached. Bailey, age seven, just stood there. She had romped through the leaf pile, scattering leaves over half of the neighbor's yard.

"Bailey, what on earth were you thinking? You owe Mrs. Jones an apology and now you must rake up the leaves in her yard."

Mrs. Jones patted Bailey on the shoulder. "Oh, that's okay. I know it was a mistake. I'll do it."

Too Much _____ Over-Nurturing _____ Soft Structure _____

Curfew

In Bergville there is a nine o'clock weekday curfew for children under the age of fourteen. The police don't enforce it.

Too Much _____ Over-Nurturing _____ Soft Structure _____

In Amesville, Garrett's parents are critical of the police for enforcing the nine o'clock weekday curfew for children under the age of fourteen.

Too Much _____ Over-Nurturing _____ Soft Structure _____

You will identify other clutter on the overindulgence shoulder of the parenting highway. Remember that an occasional drift onto the shoulder doesn't hurt, but plowing down that unreliable path regularly ends up hurting the overindulged—and the overindulgers. We can do better than that for our children and ourselves.

A LITTLE LEAVEN
LEAVENETH THE WHOLE LUMP OF DOUGH.
—I Corinthians 5:6

LETTER OF HOPE

Dear readers who are recovering from being overindulged as children,

There is always hope. When the extent and the hazards of overindulgence seem daunting, that is the time to remember hope. Hope helps us feel lighter, stand taller, and bite off the one piece we will do today. Here is what we hope for anyone who was overindulged.

We hope you keep the good things you have experienced and change what you need to change one thing at a time.

We hope you collect enough people who will listen to your stories. People who give equal attention and empathy to *all* the things that happened, the horrific things and the seemingly insignificant things.

We hope you remember not to expect the ones who overindulged you to be part of that empathic group. If their intent was loving, stay with that and deal with the impact yourself.

We hope you persevere in replacing overindulgence with healthy parenting, with respectful interactions—even though that effort may be met with disdain or even hostility. Changing the legacy is worth it. Giving children what they really need is a blessing.

We hope, if the changes are too hard to make, if some old emptiness is holding you back, that you get the help that you need. Counseling, therapy, spiritual guidance, books, classes, whatever it takes, because your needs are important too, and your children's needs are better met by parents whose needs are met.

And last of all, we hope every one of you embraces not only hope, but also joy. We hope you celebrate every positive change you make, every step forward, even every mistake because mistakes are something to learn from. Appreciate the gifts you have been given as well as the ones you are giving.

And remember that every time your impact matches your loving intent, you are making a difference in the world.

Connie, Jean, and David

GLOSSARY

Abandonment: Failure to establish rules and/or failure to monitor rules and enforce compliance.

Abundance: An extra amount that adds color and enjoyment to life, but does not satiate.

Assertive care: Meeting the needs of another who is unable to do so himself. Ordinarily, the caregiver identifies the need and meets it without being asked.

Attachment: The affectional bonds developed between two people, the prototype of which originates in infancy. An attachment relationship is measured by its relative security or insecurity. An attachment relationship is characterized by trustworthiness and reliability.

Blended family: When different families come together and re-configure as one.

Boundaries: As used in this book, the imaginary line between safety and harm; the personal line marking what's acceptable (healthy) from what is invasive or usurping and unhealthy.

Center of attention: When adult attention is continually given to children over the age of three, no matter what the circumstances.

Co-dependent: Over-functioning for others and under-functioning for self.

Consequence: The result or effect of a decision or behavior. May be either positive or negative.

Controlling: Manipulation and direct control exerted to make someone else change. In other words, to direct the choices and behaviors of others.

Developmental stages: Specific questions about self and self in relation to others that arise during growing up. The questions present themselves as tasks particular to certain ages. Parent behaviors can either encourage or discourage a child's accomplishing these tasks (resolving the questions about oneself in the world).

Dysfunctional attitude: Negative self-deprecating attitudes and thoughts that have been associated with low self-esteem, depression, and poor interpersonal functioning.

Enough: The amount that provides for health and growth.

Family adaptability: The amount of flexibility or change in a family system which can range from rigid to chaotic.

Family cohesion: The emotional bonding (e.g., togetherness, boundaries, decision-making, etc.) that family members have toward one another, which can range from disengaged to enmeshed.

Harm (as used in the Test of Four): Hurt, damage, injury.

Identity: The perception one has of oneself, built from decisions about self made over the course of life experiences. Identity formation is a life-long process and a major developmental task in adolescence.

Impact: The effect of an intent or action or set of actions.

Intent: The purpose or resolve to move toward a given goal.

Leader, Effective: The one who makes decisions, makes sure that things get done, and whose directions are most likely to be followed.

Leader, Family: As used in this book, the one whose wishes and decisions guide the family activities.

Leader, Psychological: The powerful one who must always be pleased or placated; the one whose energy sets the direction of family activities.

Leader, Responsible: The one whose title designates him or her as the pre-eminent leader. The responsible leader in the family is the parent.

Locus of control: Attitudes and beliefs associated with personal destiny. If internal, the person believes power resides within. If external, the person believes others or fate control their destiny.

Marshmallow: Term used to describe a parental practice of setting rules and then changing them, with or without pressure, in order to be pleasing to a child.

Material overindulgence: Another way to describe Too Much.

Narcissism: Being excessively centered on one's own needs.

Negotiable rule: A rule that is negotiated based on changing conditions, especially the development of the child (or worker). Negotiation can be initiated by either party, but the person in charge seeks information about proposed changes and on the basis of the quality of the thinking behind the information provided, determines when a nonnegotiable rule is appropriate. When equals negotiate, both should be satisfied with the new rule. When parents negotiate with children, the new rule should meet the parents' need to provide security for the child and is frequently based on some nonnegotiable rule.

Nonnegotiable rule: Expresses a limit or demands a standard with consequences for compliance and noncompliance. Within the boundaries of the rule, there is safety and security. Rules provide predictability and encourage competence and responsibility.

Nurture: All the ways (feeding, clothing, housing, touching, comforting, listening, etc.) that one person meets the care needs of another. Includes affirming the other and encouraging accomplishment of developmental tasks.

Overcorrection (in the Highway metaphor): In the recovery process, swinging hard from one set of unwanted behaviors to another and missing the desired target, the healthy center of the highway.

Over-nurture: Caring for others who are fully capable of caring for themselves, without asking if the help is needed or wanted.

Participants or subjects: Individuals involved in experimental studies.

Permissiveness: Lenient or lax parenting practices.

Power, Personal: The sense that no matter what happens, you will find a way to handle it, even if that means an admission of powerlessness, which is the beginning of handling many problems. The sense that what is wanted can be obtained or attained and what is unwanted can be purged or avoided. Effectiveness.

Recovery: Grieving the loss of relinquished outworn or archaic beliefs or behaviors and replacing them with life-enhancing ones over time.

Recycling: The process of doing developmental tasks, tasks that were primary at an earlier age, in ever more competent or sophisticated ways in order to become more effective in ever-changing life situations.

Relational overindulgence: Another way to describe over-nurture.

Research: The scientific investigation of a subject in order to identify facts and draw new conclusions.

Rule: A limit defined in consideration of protection and safety of one and all. It is the primary tool for teaching responsibility. To be effective, every rule needs to have both a positive and negative consequence.

Scarcity: An amount less than is needed for health and well-being.

Self-control: Regulating the self, including affect regulation, and restraining self when necessary.

Self-efficacy: The sense of feeling capable of dealing effectively with problems as they arise in one's life.

Self-esteem: The condition of believing and feeling and acting as if one is both lovable and capable and of treating others in ways that assume that they are lovable and capable also.

Soft structure: Having lax rules or no rules and failing to allow for the child's skill development. Not expecting another to contribute to the group's success or meet standards. Allowing too much freedom.

Stopped: Being halted by a barrier preventing progress.

Structural overindulgence: Another way to describe soft structure.

Structure: Includes the boundaries which keep humans safe, the skills to do what is necessary to life, and the morals and values on which choices are based.

Support team: The friends, family and co-recovering persons who care about you and care that you succeed in making changes to improve the quality of your life.

Supportive care: Offering to help another, or being asked for help and agreeing to provide it. The terms and conditions of the aid are subject to negotiation. The bulwark of reciprocity in relationships. Only offered when the caregiver is willing to accept "no" as an answer.

Test of Four: Four questions that can be applied to any action or circumstance to determine whether it is or is not a case of overindulgence.

Too Much: Giving things that cost money beyond the level of enough or abundance.

Triangulation: When communication between two people is conducted through a third. Being triangulated means being in service of the relationship of others who are avoiding one another and keeping distance in their relationship.

APPENDIX A

Ages and Stages

STAGE ONE, BEING—FROM BIRTH TO ABOUT SIX MONTHS

T HE first stage is about deciding to be, to live, to thrive, to trust, to call out to have needs met, to expect to have needs met, to be joyful. These decisions are important to nourish and amplify throughout our whole lives.

1. *Job of the child (developmental tasks)*
   * To call for care.
   * To cry or otherwise signal to get needs met.
   * To accept touch.
   * To accept nurture.
   * To bond emotionally, to learn to trust caring and safe adults and self.
   * To decide to live, to be.

2. *Typical behaviors of the child*
   * Cries or fusses to make needs known.
   * Cuddles.
   * Makes lots of sounds.
   * Looks at and responds to faces, especially eyes.
   * Imitates.

3. *Affirmations for being*
   * "I'm glad you are alive."
   * "You belong here."
   * "What you need is important to me."
   * "I'm glad you are you."

❖ "You can grow at your own pace."
❖ "You can feel all of your feelings."
❖ "I love you and I care for you willingly."

4. *Helpful parent behaviors*
   ❖ Affirm the child for working on developmental tasks.
   ❖ Provide loving, consistent care.
   ❖ Respond to infant's needs and feelings with confidence.
   ❖ Think for the baby.
   ❖ Hold and look at baby while feeding.
   ❖ Talk to child and echo child's sounds.
   ❖ Nurture by touching, looking, talking, and singing.
   ❖ Get help when unsure of how to care for baby.
   ❖ Be reliable and trustworthy.
   ❖ Get others to nurture you.

5. *Unhelpful parent behaviors*
   ❖ Feeding before baby signals (overindulgence).
   ❖ Overstimulating infant by providing too many toys that move or make noise (overindulgence).
   ❖ Not responding to the baby's signals.
   ❖ Not touching or holding enough.
   ❖ Rigid, angry, agitated responses.
   ❖ Punishment.
   ❖ Lack of healthy physical environment.
   ❖ Lack of protection, including from older siblings.
   ❖ Criticizing child too much.
   ❖ Continual hovering (overindulgence).

STAGE TWO, DOING—
FROM ABOUT SIX TO ABOUT EIGHTEEN MONTHS

Stage Two—the "doing" stage—is a powerful time when it is important for the child to decide to trust others, to trust that it is safe and wonderful to explore, to trust his senses, to know what she knows, to be creative and active, and to get support while doing all these things.

1. *Job of the child (developmental tasks)*
   ❖ To explore and experience the environment.
   ❖ To develop sensory awareness by using all senses.

❖ To signal needs; to trust others and self.
❖ To continue forming secure attachments with parents.
❖ To get help in times of stress.
❖ To start to learn that there are options and not all problems are easily solved.
❖ To develop initiative.
❖ To continue tasks from Stage One.

2. *Typical behaviors of the child*
   ❖ Tests all senses by exploring the environment.
   ❖ Is curious.
   ❖ Is easily distracted.
   ❖ Wants to explore on own but be able to retrieve caregiver at will.
   ❖ Starts patty-cake and peek-a-boo.
   ❖ Starts using words during middle or latter part of stage.

3. *Affirmations for doing*
   ❖ "You can explore and experiment and I will support and protect you."
   ❖ "You can use all of your senses when you explore."
   ❖ "You can do things as many times as you need to."
   ❖ "You can know what you know."
   ❖ "You can be interested in everything."
   ❖ "I like to watch you initiate and grow and learn."
   ❖ "I love you when you are active and when you are quiet."

4. *Helpful parent behaviors*
   ❖ Affirm child for doing developmental tasks.
   ❖ Continue to offer love.
   ❖ Provide a safe environment.
   ❖ Protect child from harm.
   ❖ Continue to provide food, nurturing touch, and encouragement.
   ❖ Say two yesses for every no.
   ❖ Provide a variety of sensory experiences (massages, music, peek-a-boo and patty-cake, pots and pans, blocks, soft toys, toys that make noise, etc.) for child.
   ❖ Refrain from interrupting child when possible.
   ❖ Refrain from interpreting the child's behavior. "You like looking at yourself in the mirror."

❖ Instead, report the child's behavior. "Judy is looking in the mirror."
❖ Echo sounds child makes.
❖ Talk to child a lot.
❖ Respond when child initiates play.
❖ Take care of own needs.

5. *Unhelpful parent behaviors*
❖ Does not allow child to struggle to reach a toy (overindulgence).
❖ Provides more than a few simple toys at one time (overindulgence).
❖ Fails to provide protection.
❖ Restricts mobility.
❖ Criticizes or shames child for exploring or for everything.
❖ Punishment.
❖ Expects child not to touch "precious" objects.
❖ Expects toilet training.

STAGE THREE, THINKING—FROM ABOUT EIGHTEEN MONTHS TO ABOUT THREE YEARS

In order to separate from parents, children must learn to think and solve problems. Learning to express and handle feelings is also important. These lessons are the focus of Stage Three—the "thinking" stage.

1. *Job of the child (developmental tasks)*
❖ To establish ability to think for self.
❖ To test reality, to push against boundaries and the authority of others.
❖ To learn to think and solve problems with cause and effect thinking.
❖ To start to follow simple safety commands: stop, come here, stay here, go there.
❖ To express anger and other feelings.
❖ To separate from parents without losing their love.
❖ To start to give up beliefs about being the center of the universe.
❖ To learn to do simple chores.
❖ To continue tasks from earlier stages.

2. *Typical behaviors of the child*
   ❖ Begins cause-and-effect thinking.
   ❖ Starts parallel play.
   ❖ Starts to be orderly, even compulsive.
   ❖ Sometimes follows simple commands, sometimes resists.
   ❖ Tests behaviors: "No, I won't, and you can't make me."
   ❖ Some try out the use of tantrums.

3. *Affirmations for thinking*
   ❖ "I'm glad you are starting to think for yourself."
   ❖ "It's okay for you to be angry, and I won't let you hurt yourself or others."
   ❖ "You can say no and push and test limits as much as you need to."
   ❖ "You can learn to think for yourself and I will think for myself."
   ❖ "You can think and feel at the same time."
   ❖ "You can know what you need and ask for help."
   ❖ "You can become separate from me and I will continue to love you."

4. *Helpful parent behaviors*
   ❖ Affirm the child for doing developmental tasks.
   ❖ Continue to offer cuddling, love, safety, and protection.
   ❖ Encourage cause-and-effect thinking.
   ❖ Provide time and space for child to organize thinking.
   ❖ Expect child to think about own feelings and start to think about other's feelings.
   ❖ Celebrate the child's new thinking ability.
   ❖ Help child make transitions from one activity to another.
   ❖ Teach names of things.
   ❖ Provide reasons, how-tos, and other information.
   ❖ Start simple chores.
   ❖ Accept positive and negative expression of feelings.
   ❖ Teach options for expressing feelings instead of hitting or biting.
   ❖ Set reasonable limits and enforce them.
   ❖ Refrain from getting into win/lose battles.
   ❖ Remain constant in face of child's tantrums or outbursts; neither give in nor overpower.

❖ Give simple, clear directions child can follow; encourage and praise achievement.
❖ Teach child basic safety commands, e.g. come, no, go, sit, stay, wait.
❖ Think of and refer to child as a "Terrific Two."
❖ Take care of own needs.

5. *Unhelpful parent behaviors*
❖ Allowing child to be the center of the universe (overindulgence).
❖ Refusing to set limits or expectations (overindulgence).
❖ Not insisting on simple chores (overindulgence).
❖ Refusing to use discipline for not thinking (overindulgence).
❖ Using too many don'ts and not enough dos.
❖ Getting caught in power struggles.
❖ Trying to appear to be a good parent by having a compliant child.
❖ Referring to the child as a "Terrible Two."
❖ Setting expectations too high.
❖ Expecting child to play "with" other children before learning to play "near" others.
❖ Shaming the child.

STAGE FOUR, IDENTITY AND POWER—
FROM ABOUT THREE TO ABOUT SIX YEARS

The tasks of this stage focus on learning and activities that help the child establish an individual identity, learn skills, and figure out role and power relationships with others.

1. *Job of the child (developmental tasks)*
❖ To assert an identity separate from others.
❖ To acquire information about the world, himself, his body, and sex role.
❖ To learn that behaviors have consequences, both positive and negative.
❖ To discover effect on others and place in groups.
❖ To learn to exert power to affect relationships.
❖ To practice socially appropriate behavior.
❖ To separate fantasy from reality.

- ❖ To learn what he has power over and what he does not have power over.
- ❖ To do simple chores.
- ❖ To continue learning earlier developmental tasks.

2. *Typical behaviors of the child*
- ❖ Engages in fantasy play, possibly with imaginary companions.
- ❖ Gathers information: how, why, when, how long, what, where, and so on.
- ❖ Tries on different identity roles by role playing.
- ❖ Starts learning about power relationships by watching, pushing, and setting up power struggles.
- ❖ Practices behaviors for sex role identification.
- ❖ Starts cooperative play.
- ❖ Practices socially appropriate behavior.
- ❖ Begins interest in games and rules.

3. *Affirmations for identity and power*
- ❖ "You can explore who you are and find out who other people are."
- ❖ "You can be powerful and ask for help at the same time."
- ❖ "You can try out different roles and ways of being powerful."
- ❖ "You can learn the results of your behavior."
- ❖ "All of your feelings are okay with me."
- ❖ "You can learn what is pretend and what is real."
- ❖ "I love who you are."

4. *Helpful parent behaviors*
- ❖ Insist the child do regular, simple chores.
- ❖ Affirm child for doing developmental tasks.
- ❖ Continue to offer love, safety, and protection.
- ❖ Be supportive as child continues to explore the world of things, people, ideas, and feelings.
- ❖ Encourage child to enjoy being a boy, or a girl; teach that both sexes are okay.
- ❖ Expect child to express feelings and to connect feelings and thinking.
- ❖ Provide information about child's environment and correct misinformation.
- ❖ Give answers to questions.

❖ Provide appropriate positive or negative consequences for actions.

❖ Use language that is clear about who is responsible for what.

❖ Encourage child's fantasies and separation of fantasy and reality.

❖ Compliment appropriate behavior and interfere with inappropriate behavior.

❖ Respond matter-of-factly and accurately to child's curiosity about the human body, and the differences between boys and girls.

❖ Maintain contact with supportive people who help parent nurture self.

❖ Resolve their own identity problems that surface.

5. *Unhelpful parent behaviors*
   ❖ Does not require chores (overindulgence).
   ❖ Provides so many toys, child has difficulty putting them away (overindulgence).
   ❖ Allows or encourages child to be the center of the universe (overindulgence).
   ❖ Teases.
   ❖ Is inconsistent.
   ❖ Does not expect child to think for self.
   ❖ Not answering questions with accurate information.
   ❖ Ridicules role play or fantasies.
   ❖ Responds to child's fantasies as if real.
   ❖ Uses fantasy to frighten or confuse child.
   ❖ Engages in judgments or arguments over who is right or wrong or who/what is better or worse.

STAGE FIVE, STRUCTURE— FROM ABOUT SIX TO ABOUT TWELVE YEARS

During Stage Five, children learn more about Structure and install their own internal Structures. This includes understanding the need for rules, the freedom that comes from having appropriate rules, and the relevancy of rules. Examining the values on which our rules are based is important. Another major task of this stage is acquiring many kinds of skills.

1. *Job of the child (developmental tasks)*
   - ❖ To learn skills, learn from mistakes, and decide to be adequate.
   - ❖ To learn to listen and look in order to collect information and think.
   - ❖ To gradually become skillful at and responsible for complex household chores.
   - ❖ To practice thinking and doing.
   - ❖ To reason about wants and needs.
   - ❖ To check out family rules and learn about structures outside the family.
   - ❖ To learn the relevancy of rules.
   - ❖ To experience the consequences of breaking rules.
   - ❖ To disagree with others and still be loved.
   - ❖ To test ideas and values and learn value options beyond the family.
   - ❖ To develop internal controls.
   - ❖ To learn what is one's own responsibility and what is others' responsibility.
   - ❖ To learn when to flee, when to flow, and when to stand firm.
   - ❖ To develop the capacity to cooperate.
   - ❖ To test abilities against others.
   - ❖ To identify with one's own sex.
   - ❖ To continue to learn earlier tasks.

2. *Typical behaviors of the child*
   - ❖ Asks questions and gathers information.
   - ❖ Practices and learns skills.
   - ❖ Belongs to same-sex groups or clubs.
   - ❖ Compares, tests, disagrees with, sets, breaks, and experiences consequences of breaking or keeping rules.
   - ❖ Challenges parental values, argues, and hassles.
   - ❖ May be open and affectionate or cantankerous, self-contained or self-centered, or may alternate among these.

3. *Affirmations for structure*
   - ❖ "You can think before you say yes or no and learn from your mistakes."
   - ❖ "You can trust your intuition to help you decide what to do."
   - ❖ "You can find a way of doing things that works for you."
   - ❖ "You can learn the rules that help you live with others."
   - ❖ "You can learn when and how to disagree."

❖ "You can think for yourself and get help instead of staying in distress."

❖ "I love you even when we differ; I love growing with you."

4. *Helpful parent behaviors*
   ❖ Affirm the child for doing developmental tasks.
   ❖ Continue to offer love, safety, and protection.
   ❖ Make an accurate assessment of the safety of the child's world and teach conflict-resolution skills.
   ❖ Affirm children's efforts to learn to do things their own way.
   ❖ Give lots of love and lots of positive response for learning skills.
   ❖ Insist that child does family chores.
   ❖ Insist that child cares for own belongings.
   ❖ Be a reliable source of information about people, the world, and sex.
   ❖ Challenge negative behavior and decisions; encourage cause and effect thinking.
   ❖ Be clear about who is responsible for what.
   ❖ Affirm children's ability to think logically and creatively.
   ❖ Offer problem-solving tools.
   ❖ Discuss with child how and when to flee, flow, or fight.
   ❖ Set and enforce needed nonnegotiable and negotiable rules.
   ❖ Allow children to experience non-hazardous natural consequences for their actions and ways of doing things.
   ❖ Point out that you do continue to care for the child even when the child disagrees with you.
   ❖ Promote the separation of reality from fantasy by encouraging children to report accurately.
   ❖ Be alert to teenage-type behaviors and discourage child from growing up too fast.
   ❖ Be responsible yourself and encourage the child to be responsible for own decisions, thinking, and feeling.
   ❖ Encourage child's skills development by providing in the area of their interest: first, a teacher who is encouraging and enthusiastic, then one who teaches skills and insists on quality performance; still later, probably not until adolescence, one who acts as model and mentor.

5. *Unhelpful parent behaviors*
   ❖ Uneven enforcement of rules (overindulgence).

- ❖ Fail to limit child's time with electronic devices, including television (overindulgence).
- ❖ Insist on perfection.
- ❖ Expect child to learn needed skills without instructions, help, or standards (overindulgence).
- ❖ Fill all of the child's time with lessons, teams, and activities so child lacks the unstructured time to explore interests and learn the relevancy of rules (overindulgence).
- ❖ Buy anything child asks or pressures for (overindulgence).
- ❖ Overindulge child by not insisting on completion of household chores and other ways of being a contributing family member.
- ❖ Unwillingness to allow child to feel miserable for brief times.
- ❖ Rules and values too rigid or lacking.
- ❖ Unwillingness or lack of ability to discuss beliefs and values, to reevaluate rules, and to expect the child to develop skills for personal responsibility.
- ❖ Give in to child's pressure to have things child's way (overindulgence).
- ❖ Allow child to believe her wants are more important than those of other family members (overindulgence).

STAGE SIX, IDENTITY, SEXUALITY, AND SEPARATION— FROM ABOUT THIRTEEN TO ABOUT NINETEEN YEARS

The tasks of this stage focus on identity, separation, sexuality, and increased competence.

1. *Job of the adolescent (developmental tasks)*
    - ❖ To take more steps toward independence.
    - ❖ To achieve a clearer, emotional separation from family.
    - ❖ To emerge gradually, as a separate, independent person with own identity and values within the context of the family.
    - ❖ To be competent and responsible for own needs, feelings, behaviors as one moves out into the world.
    - ❖ To find and support a healthy peer group.
    - ❖ To continue to do family chores.
    - ❖ To integrate sexuality into sense of identity.
    - ❖ To continue to participate in family celebrations and rituals.

❖ To gradually acquire the skill of independent, moral thinking.

2. *Typical behaviors of the adolescent*

Adolescents make some of their identity and separation choices by revisiting or recycling the tasks of earlier stages—being, doing, thinking, identity, power, and structure—with new information and with the sometimes confusing pressures of their emerging sexuality. Therefore, adolescents may act very grown up one moment and immature the next. The ages at which they usually recycle and incorporate these earlier tasks are as follows:

Onset of puberty or about age thirteen, recycling the being and the doing tasks, of infancy and toddlerhood:
❖ Sometimes independent and sometimes wanting to be fed and cared for.
❖ Exploring new areas without necessarily being concerned with standards or finishing.

Age fourteen, recycling tasks of a two-year-old, independent thinking:
❖ Sometimes reasonable and competent with intermittent rebellious outbursts.

Ages fifteen, sixteen, and seventeen, recycling tasks of ages three to five years, and identity and power:
❖ Asking questions, "Why?" and "How come?" Working out new role identity with same sex and opposite sex with both peers and adults. Learning to solve complex problems.

Ages sixteen through nineteen, recycling the tasks of six to twelve years, structure.
❖ Being adult and responsible with sudden short journeys back to earlier rule-testing behaviors.
❖ May also break rules as part of separation from parent.

3. *Affirmations for identity, separation, and sexuality*
❖ "You can know who you are and learn and practice skills for independence."
❖ "You can learn the difference between sex and nurturing and be responsible for your needs, feelings, and behaviors."

❖ "You can develop your own interests, relationships, and causes."
❖ "You can learn to use old skills in new ways."
❖ "You can grow in your maleness or femaleness and still be dependent at times."
❖ "I look forward to knowing you as an adult."
❖ "My love is always with you. I trust you to ask for my support."

4. *Helpful parent behaviors*
❖ Affirm the adolescent for doing developmental tasks.
❖ Continue to offer love, safety, and protection.
❖ Insist adolescent does regular household chores.
❖ Expect adolescent to support the physical, emotional, and social welfare of the family.
❖ Expect adolescent to participate in family rituals and celebrations.
❖ Monitor adolescent's activities and friends.
❖ Accept all of the adolescent's feelings and talk about what it was like when you had emerging sexual feelings.
❖ Confront unacceptable behavior.
❖ Be clear about position on alcohol and drug use and on sexual behaviors.
❖ Identify the ways the adolescent is becoming separate and affirm the ways that are supportive of independence.
❖ Understand and affirm his reworking of tasks from earlier developmental stages.
❖ Celebrate adolescent's growing-up and welcome her to adulthood.
❖ Encourage adolescent's growing independence and accept the identity that the adolescent is forging, urging the adolescent to "be who he is" and to find accommodations with socially acceptable behaviors. This may be different from the parent's expectations or dreams for him.
❖ Support adolescent's contributing to the benefit of the community.
❖ Take community action to make schools and streets safe.

5. *Unhelpful parent behaviors*
❖ Does not insist adolescent does chores and does them for her (overindulgence).
❖ Protect adolescent from uncomfortable consequences of his behavior (overindulgence).

- Not willing to allow adolescent to feel miserable for brief times (overindulgence).
- Unresponsive, uncaring behavior.
- Abuse or withhold loving touch.
- Respond sexually to adolescent's developing sexual maturity.
- Use rigid rules or no rules or unevenly enforced rules or refuse to negotiate rules (overindulgence).
- Neglect to expect thinking and problem-solving behavior (overindulgence).
- Cruelly tease about sexuality, interests, fantasies, dreams, appearance, or friends.
- Fail to confront destructive or self-defeating behaviors— anything from drug abuse to limited friends and interests (overindulgence).
- Attempt to keep adolescent from separating (overindulgence).
- Allow adolescent to be with friends to exclusion of family (overindulgence).
- Allow freedom without accountability (overindulgence).
- Provide money, toys, clothes, activities, vehicles, without effort on adolescent's part (overindulgence).
- Fail to stay in charge of adolescent's recreation and vacation activities (overindulgence).
- Fail to call on outside help if unable to hold adolescent accountable (overindulgence).

YOUNG ADULTS LIVING AT HOME

Parenting does not stop at nineteen or twenty-one or ever. A parent is always a parent. The way that parents offer and accept support changes through the decades, but the love and caring does not end.

For many young adults there is a transition stage of both dependence and independence, when they are not yet financially or perhaps fully emotionally independent adults, so they need to live at home. This stage is made more difficult for the young adults if their parents treat them as children, cook, clean, and do laundry for them, or support them financially with no expectation that they provide for part of their expenses, or if parents demand that young adults rigidly adhere to rules established during their teen years.

It is helpful for parents and young people to remember some things about each other.

❖ The young peole are starting to move into the adult stage, interdependence.

❖ Parents are still expected to set nonnegotiable rules about any area of lifestyle that is crucial to their values and beliefs, and young people must comply as long as they remain at home.

❖ Most other rules can and should be negotiated.

❖ It is usually better to anticipate needs, to set or negotiate rules as well as plan initial labor divisions before the parents and young adult begin their joint living arrangement.

❖ It is usually better not to make any assumptions about who will do what, but to ask about and negotiate all tasks.

❖ It is okay for parents to help their grown children as long as the help does not marshmallow or overindulge the young adult and as long as the parents do not resent it.

❖ It is all right for young adults to live with parents if the young adults pay room and board, share fully in household tasks, and participate with the same consideration and courtesy they would if they were living with some other family.

❖ It is helpful for parents to be aware that there are four ways young people separate from parents.
  • Some leave home and return grown-up.
  • Some stay home and grow up.
  • Some leave and come back several times.
  • Some break family rules so their parents will force them to leave.

The way a young person chooses to leave may be different from the way the parents used. The important issue is not how young people leave, but that they do become separate adults, capable of making their own decisions, and willing to interact with their parents as supportive adults.

❖ It is important for parents to encourage their children to become adults and to treat them as such no matter where they are living.

❖ It is important for young adults to let their parents grow up, to see, experience, and treat their parents as growing people and not to cling to the images they had when they were four or nine or seventeen years old.

❖ It is all right for young adults to parent their parents in areas where the young adults have information that is helpful to their parent.

❖ It is wonderful for both young adults and their parents to realize that these years can be a source of satisfaction and enjoyment while they discover each other as caring adults.

❖ It can be an ideal time for both young adults and parents to do some important growing up again.

STAGE SEVEN, INTERDEPENDENCE—ADULTS

The developmental tasks of adulthood focus on the journey from independence to interdependence, and include regular recycling of earlier tasks in ways that support the specific adult tasks.

1. *Job of the adult*
    ❖ To master skills for work and recreation.
    ❖ To find mentors and to mentor.
    ❖ To grow in love and humor.
    ❖ To offer and accept intimacy.
    ❖ To expand creativity and honor uniqueness.
    ❖ To accept responsibility for self and to care for the next generation and the last.
    ❖ To find support for one's own growth and to support the growth of others.
    ❖ To expand commitments beyond self and family to the community, the world.
    ❖ To balance dependence, independence, and interdependence.
    ❖ To deepen integrity and spirituality.
    ❖ To refine the arts of greeting, leaving, and grieving.

2. *Behaviors of the adult*
    There are many behaviors typical of the long years of the adult stage. The important ones for you right now are the ones you are doing; so list behaviors that are typical for you now:

    _____

    _____

    _____

    _____

    _____

    _____

3. *Affirmations for adults*
   - ❖ "Your needs are important."
   - ❖ "You can be uniquely yourself and honor the uniqueness of others."
   - ❖ "You can be independent and interdependent."
   - ❖ "Through the years you can expand your commitments to your own growth, to your family, your friends, your community, and to all humankind."
   - ❖ "You can build and examine your commitments to your values and causes, your roles, and your tasks."
   - ❖ "You can be responsible for your contributions to each of your commitments."
   - ❖ "You can be creative, competent, productive, and joyful."
   - ❖ "You can trust your inner wisdom."
   - ❖ "You can say your hellos and good-byes to people, roles, dreams, and decisions."
   - ❖ "You can finish each part of your journey and look forward to the next."
   - ❖ "Your love matures and expands."
   - ❖ "You are lovable at every age."

4. *Helpful adult behaviors toward self*
   - ❖ Affirm developmental tasks of all stages.
   - ❖ Regard self with love, objectivity, and forgiveness.
   - ❖ Assess own growing-up experiences and address any deficits if overindulgence occurred.
   - ❖ Celebrate successes, however large or small.
   - ❖ Grow and change.
   - ❖ Make and meet commitments toward family and communities.
   - ❖ Participate in behaviors that support the fulfillment of the affirmations.
   - ❖ Re-evaluate and restate values regularly and improve, if necessary.

5. *Unhelpful adult behaviors toward self*
   - ❖ Refuse to learn what is enough (overindulgence).
   - ❖ Substitute material things for spiritual growth (overindulgence).
   - ❖ Resistance to the changes of aging (overindulgence).
   - ❖ Refuse to learn, grow, and change (overindulgence).

- ❖ Greed. Take at the expense of others (overindulgence).
- ❖ Compete with others, including children, to get emotional needs met (overindulgence).
- ❖ Impose own definition of the world on others (overindulgence).
- ❖ Accept the definition of the world imposed by others.
- ❖ Passivity, addiction, and codependency.

APPENDIX B

Parental Overindulgence Assessment Tool

(For parents of children age two and older)

The majority of the time . . .

1. I give my child all the clothes she/he wants.	☐ Yes ☐ No		
2. I give my child all the toys he/she wants.	☐ Yes ☐ No		
3. I allow my child lots of privileges.	☐ Yes ☐ No		
4. I make sure my child is entertained.	☐ Yes ☐ No		
5. I schedule my child for lots of activities, lessons, and sports.	☐ Yes ☐ No		
6. I give my child more than he/she asks for.	☐ Yes ☐ No		
7. I give my child things that she/he has not asked for.	☐ Yes ☐ No		

The majority of the time . . .

8. I do not make rules for my child.		☐ True ☐ False	
9. I do not enforce the rules I make for my child.		☐ True ☐ False	
10. I do not have my child do chores.		☐ True ☐ False	
11. I give my child lots of freedom.		☐ True ☐ False	
12. I let my child take the lead and dominate family matters.		☐ True ☐ False	
13. I do not expect my child to learn the same skills as other children.		☐ True ☐ False	
14. I do not hold my child to consistent standards.		☐ True ☐ False	

The majority of the time . . .

15. I am involved in everything my child does.			☐ Yes ☐ No
16. I give my child a great deal of attention.			☐ Yes ☐ No

	Too Much	Soft Structure	Over-nurturing
17. I do things for my child that he/she should be doing for him/herself.			❑ Yes ❑ No
18. I do things for my child rather than see her/him in distress.			❑ Yes ❑ No
19. I do things to make my child love me.			❑ Yes ❑ No
20. I hate to see my child be frustrated.			❑ Yes ❑ No
21. I anticipate what my child needs and provide it.			❑ Yes ❑ No
Total number of Yes/False answers	Too Much = ———	Soft Structure = ———	Over-nurturing = ———
Scores	**Too Much** 0–1 Overindulgence unlikely 2–3 Possible overindulgence 4–5 Caution— overindulgence 6–7 Serious overindulgence	**Soft Structure** 0–1 Overindulgence unlikely 2–3 Possible overindulgence 4–5 Caution— overindulgence 6–7 Serious overindulgence	**Over-nurturing** 0–1 Overindulgence unlikely 2–3 Possible overindulgence 4–5 Caution— overindulgence 6–7 Serious overindulgence

APPENDIX C

Household Jobs Participation Chart

The chart lists common household tasks, the percentage of children involved with the task, and the average age of children at different levels of involvement.

Symbols:

H means the child needs help with the task
R means the child needs reminding or supervision
A means the child does a task as needed without reminding or supervision

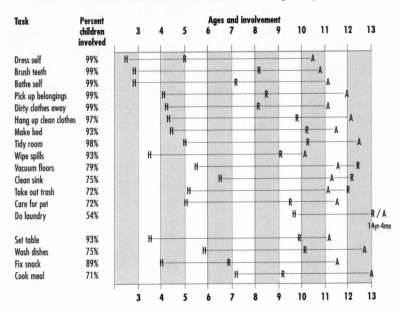

Task	Percent children involved	Ages and involvement (3–13)
Dress self	99%	H · · · · R · · · · · A
Brush teeth	99%	H · · · · · R · · · · A
Bathe self	99%	H · · · · · · R · · · · A
Pick up belongings	99%	H · · · · · R · · · · A
Dirty clothes away	99%	H · · · · · R · · · A
Hang up clean clothes	97%	H · · · · · · R · · A
Make bed	93%	H · · · · · · R · A
Tidy room	98%	H · · · · · · R · · A
Wipe spills	93%	H · · · · · · · R · A
Vacuum floors	79%	H · · · · · · · A · · R
Clean sink	75%	H · · · · · · A · R
Take out trash	72%	H · · · · · · · A · R
Care for pet	72%	H · · · · · · · R · · A
Do laundry	54%	H · · · · · · R / A 14yr-4mo
Set table	93%	H · · · · · · R · A
Wash dishes	75%	H · · · · · · R · · A
Fix snack	89%	H · · · · · R · · · A
Cook meal	71%	H · · · · · · · R · · A

APPENDIX D

The Overindulgence Project

THE Overindulgence Project began in 1996 with the mission of studying the relationship between having been overindulged during childhood and subsequent adult problems and parenting practices. To date, we (myself, Jean Illsley Clarke, Connie Dawson, and our research assistants) have conducted three studies investigating overindulgence involving a combined 1,195 participants (Bredehoft, Mennicke, Potter & Clarke, 1998; Bredehoft, Clarke & Dawson, 2001; Bredehoft, Clarke & Dawson, 2003; Bredehoft, Dawson, Clarke & Morgart 2003). These studies provide the scientific basis for this book. Despite each of our samples' convenient nature, we feel that the results add to the body of knowledge on overindulgence and give us new insights into the parenting problems associated with this issue. A brief summary of the findings from our three studies are presented here.

Conclusions and Summary Findings*

STUDY	CONCLUSIONS AND SUMMARY OF FINDINGS
Study I: *Perceptions Attributed by Adults to Parental Overindulgence During Childhood*	1. Parents are responsible for the majority of overindulgence. 2. The overindulgence was most often related to some issue from the parents' experience (e.g., growing up in poverty, or working all of the time). 3. Overindulgence is complex. In addition to too many things, it involves lack of soft structure and over-nurture. 4. Adults who were overindulged as children grow up with negative personality traits such as: feeling unlovable, needing constant outside affirmation, having a lack of skills, and not knowing how to take care of themselves. 5. Adults who were overindulged as children are more likely to continue the cycle of overindulgence by overindulging their own children. 6. Adults who were overindulged as children are more self-indulgent adults resulting in gaining weight, feeling guilty, lower self-esteem, poor health, and loneliness. **Findings from this study resulted from a researcher-developed inventory based on interviews with adults who were overindulged as children.
Study II: *Relationships Between Childhood Overindulgence, Family Cohesion and Adaptability, Self-Esteem, Self-Efficacy, Self-Righteousness, Satisfaction with Life, Dysfunctional Attitudes, and Life Distress in Late Adolescence and Young Adulthood*	1. Overindulgence is complex. It is related to too many things (e.g., clothes, toys, being entertained), soft structure (e.g., didn't have rules, did not enforce rules), and over-nurture (too much attention). 2. Overindulgence occurs in all family system types (balanced, midrange and extreme). 3. Childhood overindulgence is related to adolescent/young adulthood dysfunctional thinking, feelings of ineffectiveness, and self-righteousness. 4. Childhood overindulgence does not appear to be associated with late adolescent/young adulthood self-esteem, life satisfaction, or life distress. **Findings from this study resulted from the use of the following normed psychological scales with established reliability and validity: Family Adaptability and Cohesion Evaluation Scales; the Rosenberg Self-Esteem Scale; the Dysfunctional Attitude Scale; the Life Distress Inventory; the Self-efficacy Scale; the Self-righteousness Scale; the Satisfaction With Life Scale, and fourteen author-developed likert-style questions on overindulgence.

STUDY	CONCLUSIONS AND SUMMARY OF FINDINGS
Study III: *Relationships Between Childhood Overindulgence, Family Cohesion and Adaptability, Self-Esteem, Dysfunctional Attitudes, and Locus of Control in Parents*	1. Childhood overindulgence is related to self-esteem (adult parent), family adaptability (family of procreation) and dysfunctional attitudes. 2. Childhood overindulgence is related to ineffective parenting beliefs such as: "My child controls my life," "I have little control over my child," and "I am not responsible for my child's behavior." 3. There are three types of overindulgence: material overindulgence (too many things), structural overindulgence (soft structure), and relational overindulgence (over-nurture). **Findings from this study resulted from the use of the following normed psychological scales with established reliability and validity: Family Adaptability and Cohesion Evaluation Scales; the Rosenberg Self-Esteem Scale; the Dysfunctional Attitude Scale; the Parental Locus of Control Scale, and fourteen author-developed likert-style questions on overindulgence.

*For detailed information about these studies point your browser to www.overindulgence.info and click on research.

REFERENCES

Bredehoft, D. J., Mennicke, S. A., Potter, A. M., & Clarked, J. I. (1998). Perceptions attributed by adults to parental overindulgence during chldhood. Journal of Family and Consumer Sciences Education. 16(2), 3–17.

Bredehoft, D. J., Clarke, J. I., & Dawson, C. (2001). Overindulgence, personality, family interaction, and parental locus of control. Papr presented at the Minnesota Council on Family Relations Annual Meeting, Hopkins, Minnesota.

Bredehoft, D. J., Dawson, C., & Morgart, M. J. (2002). Relationships between childhood overindulgence, family cohesion and adaptablility, self-esteem, self-efficacy, self-righteousness, satisfaction with life, dysfunctional attitudes, and life distress in late adolescence and young adulthood. Manuscript submitted for publication.

Bredehoft, D. J., Dawson, C., & Clarke, J. I. (2002). Relationships between chldhood overindulgence, family cohesion and adaptablility, self-esteem, dysfunctional attitudes, and ocus of control in parents. Manuscript submitted for publication.

Introduction: *What Is Overindulgence, Anyway?*

[1] The three studies in the Overindulgence Research Project: Study I, "Perception Attributed by Adults to Parental Overindulgence During Childhood" conducted by David J. Bredehoft, Sheryll A. Mennicke, Alisa M. Potter, and Jean Illsley Clarke, 1998. Study II, "Overindulgence, Personality and Family Interaction Among College Students" conducted by David J. Bredehoft, Jean Illsley Clarke, and Connie Dawson, 2000. Study III, "Overindulgence, Personality and Family Interaction and Parental Locus of Control" conducted by David J. Bredehoft, Jean Illsley Clarke, and Connie Dawson, 2001. See Appendix D for additional material on this project.

Chapter 1: The Truth about "Way Too Nice": *Does Overindulgence Really Make a Difference?*

[1] Study I. Table—Childhood Feelings Resulting from Overindulgence is reproduced with permission of the authors and publisher from: Bredehoft, D. J., Mennicke, S. A., Potter, A. M., and Clarke, J. I. "Perceptions Attributed by Adults to Parental Overindulgence during Childhood." *Journal of Family and Consumer Sciences Education.* 1998, 16(2), 3–17. © 1998 Journal of Family and Consumer Sciences Education.

[2] Summary of Study I respondents.

[3] Indicators of Overindulgence reproduced with permission of the authors. © 2002 David J. Bredehoft, Jean Illsley Clarke, and Connie Dawson.

[4] Study I and II.

[5] *Minneapolis Star Tribune* newspaper report of a bank robbery.

Chapter 2: Yikes! Look At That Spoiled Child: *When the Situation Looks Like Overindulgence but Turns Out Not to Be*

[1] Study I, II, III.

Chapter 3: What's Wrong with That?: *When the Situation Looks Normal but Actually Is Overindulgence*

[1] It may be advisable to find out if Damian has an organic condition (Attention Deficit Disorder, learning disorders, etc.) that is affecting his ability to do schoolwork.

Chapter 4: Have Some More: *The Many Ways of Giving Too Much*

1 *Stuff* was written by some of the participants in Study II.
2 Items 1–5 are reproduced with permission of the authors. © 2002 David J. Bredehoft, Jean Illsley Clarke, and Connie Dawson.

Chapter 5: I Want Something to Play With:
When I Was Growing Up, My Parents Gave Me Lots of Toys

1 Study II.
2 David Walsh, National Institute on Media and the Family (Minneapolis, MN 2003). Regular copies of *Media Wise* are available from (888) 672–5437 or on www.mediafamily.org.
3 Thanks to Rosie Cunningham for sharing her poem.

Chapter 6: I've Got Nothing to Wear:
When I Was Growing Up, I Was Allowed to Have Any Clothes I Wanted

1 Study III. Study II. First two bulleted items are reproduced with permission of the authors from: Wiseman, A. N., & Beck, A. T. *Development and validation of the dysfunctional attitude scale: A preliminary investigation.* Paper presented at the meeting of the American Education Research Association, Toronto, Canada, 1978. © A. N. Wiseman & A. T. Beck, 1978.

Chapter 7: So Much to Do, So Little Time:
When I Was Growing Up, My Parents Over-Scheduled My Time

1 Study I.
2 Brad Steinfield as quoted in Nina Rogozen and Patricia Bailey's article, "Shedding Light on Mental Illness in Children." (North West Health, Winter 2002).
3 David Walsh, National Institute on Media and the Family (Minneapolis, MN 2003). Regular copies of *Media Wise* are available from (888)672–5437 or on www.mediafamily.org.

Chapter 8: How Much Is Enough?: *I Don't Know What Enough Means*

1 Study I.
2 Thanks to Kaara Ettesvold and Ksenia Weisz for sharing this story.
3 Study I percentages do not add to 100 percent because of rounding.
4 Thanks to Sandy Keiser for sharing this toast.

Chapter 9: I Want the Best for You: *What Is Nurture?*

1 Studies I, II, III. Bulleted items are reproduced with permission of the authors. © David J. Bredehoft, Jean Illsley Clarke & Connie Dawson.

Chapter 10: I'll Do it for You: *When I Was Growing Up,*
My Parents Did Things for Me that I Should Have Done for Myself

1 Gopnik, Alison, Meltzoff, Andrew N., and Kuhl, Patricia K. *The Scientist in the Crib: What Early Learning Tells Us About the Mind.* New York: Harper Perennial, 2000.
2 Crary, Elizabeth. *Pick Up Your Socks . . . And Other Skills Growing Children Need!* Seattle: Parenting Press, 1990.
3 Study II.

[4] Pearson, Carol S. *Awakening the Heroes Within.* San Francisco: Harper SanFrancisco, 1991.

[5] Studies I, II.

Chapter 11: Smother Love: *When I Was Growing Up, My Parents Gave Me Too Much Attention*

[1] Study I.

[2] The word *narcissism* is used among mental health professionals to mean a Narcissistic Personality Disorder diagnosis. Lay people usually think of narcissism as describing someone who is self-centered or self-absorbed. Stephanie Donaldson-Pressman and Robert M. Pressman in *The Narcissistic Family* (San Francisco: Jossey-Bass, 1994) define that family as one where "the needs of the parent system took precedence over the needs of the children." They go on to say, "Narcissism implies self-absorption, lack of genuine caring, a certain superficiality, concern with external appearances, shallowness, distancing—an unwillingness to get too close or give too much." The Pressmans suggest when referring to a person that triggers an "All she thinks about is herself" observation, the observer may be "transposing narcissism for solipsism, the view that the self is all that exists, can be known, or has importance."

[3] Study III.

Chapter 12: The Little Prince and Princess: *When I Was Growing Up, I Was Allowed Lots of Privileges*

[1] Center for a New American Dream reported in *The Christian Science Monitor*, August 7, 2002.

Chapter 13: A World of Entertainment: *When I Was Growing Up, My Parents Made Sure that I Was Entertained*

[1] Study II. Bulleted items from the *Rosenberg Self-Esteem Scale* reproduced with permission of the Morris Rosenberg Foundation from: www.bsos. umd.edu/socy/Rosenberg.html. © Morris Rosenberg Foundation, 2003.

Chapter 14: The Nurture Highway: *The Roadway of Parenting*

[1] Thanks to Jim Jump from Kalamazoo, Michigan, for the metaphor of nurture as a highway.

[2] Study I.

[3] Study I.

Chapter 15: Soft Structure: *A Blueprint for Insecurity*

[1] From: Porter County Juvenile Probation Home Page, *Overindulgence danger,* from John Rosemond's *Guide to Parenting.*

[2] Studies II, III.

Chapter 16: Who Was Your Slave Last Week?: *When I Was Growing Up, My Parents Did Not Expect Me to Do Chores*

[1] Study I.

[2] Study II. First two bulleted items are reproduced with permission of the authors from: Wiseman, A. N., and Beck, A. T. "Development and Validation of the Dysfunctional Attitude Scale: A Preliminary Investigation." Paper presented at the meeting of the American Education

Research Association, Toronto, Canada, 1978. © A. N. Wiseman and A. T. Beck, 1978.

3 Rossman, Dr. Marty. "Involving children in household tasks: Is it worth the effort?" *ResearchWORKs*, U. of MN, College of Education and Human Development, 2002.

4 *Seattle Post-Intelligencer*, June 18, 2002, "Parent Nagging the Norm for Many Kids," by Martha Irvine, Associated Press.

5 This is especially so if the child has reason to be distrustful of a parent's ability to be in charge in a good and safe way. Terry M. Levy and Michael Orlans, *Attachment, Trauma, and Healing,* Child Welfare League of America Press, 1998.

6 Cline, Foster, M.D. and Jim Fay. *Parenting with Love and Logic: Teaching Children Responsiblity.* Colorado Springs: Pinion Press, 1990.

Chapter 17: You Don't Need to Do That: When I Was Growing Up, I Was Not Expected to Learn the Same Skills as Other Children

1 By Dean E. Murphy, *Los Angeles Times* as published in the *Seattle Times*, Oct. 4, 1999.

2 Study I.

3 Study II. Bulleted items are reproduced with permission of the authors from: Wiseman, A. N., and Beck, A. T. "Development and Validation of the Dysfunctional Attitude Scale: A Preliminary Investigation". Paper presented at the meeting of the American Education Research Association, Toronto, Canada, 1978. © A. N. Wiseman and A. T. Beck, 1978.

Chapter 18: No More Rules!: When I Was Growing Up, My Parents Didn't Have Rules or Make Me Follow Them

1 Study II. Items are reproduced with permission of the authors from: Wiseman, A. N., and Beck, A. T. "Development and Validation of the Dysfunctional Attitude Scale: A Preliminary Investigation." Paper presented at the meeting of the American Education Research Association, Toronto, Canada, 1978. © A. N. Wiseman and A. T. Beck, 1978.

2 Study III.

3 In a personal communication, Aug. 13, 2001.

4 *What's New in Research: Parental disapproval helps prevent smoking.* Brown University Child and Adolescent Behavior Letter, January 2002.

5 *Bottom Line Newsletter*, Box 735, Springfield, NJ 07081.

Chapter 19: Do As You Like: When I Was Growing Up, My Parents Gave Me Too Much Freedom

1 *The Christian Science Monitor*, Sept. 4, 2001, in a college version of "Stop and smell the roses" by Mark Clayton.

2 Third bulleted item is reproduced with permission of the authors from: Wiseman, A. N., and Beck, A. T. "Development and Validation of the Dysfunctional Attitude Scale: A Preliminary Investigation." Paper presented at the meeting of the American Education Research Association, Toronto, Canada, 1978. © A. N. Wiseman and A. T. Beck, 1978.

3 Diana Baumrind, "Rejoinder to Lewis's Reinterpretation of Parental Firm Control Effects: Are Authoritative Families Really Harmonious?" *Psychological Bulletin,* 94, 132–142, 1983); Diana Baumrind, "Parenting Styles and Adolescent Development." In J. Brooks-Gunn, R. Lerner, and

A. C. Petersen (Eds.), The Encyclopedia of Adolescence, pp. 758–772. New York: Garland, 1991.

Chapter 22: Take Me to Your Leader: *When I Was Growing Up, My Parents Allowed Me to Take the Lead or Dominate the Family*

[1] Erickson, Martha Farrell. "Creating a Culture for Healthy Marriage." *American Experiment Quarterly,* Summer 2001; Vol. 4, No. 2.

Chapter 23: I'll Never Do That!: *How Having Been Overindulged Affects Parenting*

[1] Study III.

[2] Study III. Bulleted items are reproduced with permission of the authors from: Campis, L. K., Lyman, R. D., and Prentice-Dunn, S. "The Parental Locus of Control Scale: Development and Validation." *Journal of Clinical Child Psychology,* 1986, 15(3), 260–267. © L. K. Campis, R. D. Lyman, and S. Prentice-Dunn 1986.

[3] Study III. Bulleted items are reproduced with permission of the authors from: Campis, L. K., Lyman, R. D., and Prentice-Dunn, S. "The Parental Locus of Control Scale: Development and Validation." *Journal of Clinical Child Psychology,* 1986, 15(3), 260–267. © L. K. Campis, R. D. Lyman, and S. Prentice-Dunn 1986.

[4] Study III. Bulleted items are reproduced with permission of the authors from: Campis, L. K., Lyman, R. D., and Prentice-Dunn, S. "The Parental Locus of Control Scale: Development and Validation." *Journal of Clinical Child Psychology,* 1986, 15(3), 260–267. © L. K. Campis, R. D. Lyman, and S. Prentice-Dunn 1986.

[5] Items reproduced with permission of the authors from: Campis, L. K., Lyman, R. D., and Prentice-Dunn, S. "The Parental Locus of Control Scale: Development and Validation." *Journal of Clinical Child Psychology,* 1986, 15(3), 260–267. © L. K. Campis, R. D. Lyman, and S. Prentice-Dunn 1986.

Chapter 25: Hazards on the Road: *Outside Pressures to Overindulge*

[1] "Navy students learn hard lesson in honor," *Minneapolis Star Tribune,* April 3, 1994.

RECOMMENDED READING

Ashner, Laurie and Mitch Meyerson. *When Is Enough, Enough?: What You Can Do If You Never Feel Satisfied*. Center City: Hazelden, 1996.

Baylor, Byrd. *The Table Where Rich People Sit*. New York: Aladdin Paperbacks, 1994.

Bianco, Margery Williams. *The Velveteen Rabbit*. Camelot, reissue 1996.

Berne, Eric. *The Structure and Dynamics of Organizations and Groups*. New York: Grove Press, 1963.

Bloom, Benjamin S. (Ed.). *Developing Talent in Young People*. New York: Ballantine Books, 1985.

Bosch, Carl W. *Bully on the Bus*. Seattle: Parenting Press, 1988.

Chapman, Gary and Ross Campbell. *The Five Love Languages of Children*. Chicago: Northfield Publishing, 1997.

Childs-Gowell, Elaine. *Good Grief Rituals*. New York: Station Hill Press, 1992.

Clarke, Jean Illsley. *Connections: The Threads That Strengthen Families*. Center City: Hazelden, 1999.

———. *Time-In: When Time-Out Doesn't Work*. Seattle: Parenting Press, 1999.

———. *Self-Esteem: A Family Affair*. Center City: Hazelden, 1978.

Clarke, Jean Illsley and Connie Dawson. *Growing Up Again, Parenting Ourselves, Parenting Our Children* (second edition). Center City: Hazelden, 1998.

Cline, Foster, M.D., and Jim Fay. *Parenting with Love and Logic*. Colorado Springs: Pinon Press, 1990.

Coles, Robert. *Privileged Ones: The Well-Off and Rich in America* (Children of Crisis, Vol. 5). Boston: Little, Brown & Co., 1980.

Crary, Elizabeth. *Pick Up Your Socks*. Seattle: Parenting Press, 1990.

Curran, Dolores. *Tired of Arguing With Your Kids: Wisdom from Parents Who Have Been There*. Minneapolis: Family Information Services, 1999.

DeGaetano, Gloria and Kathleen Bander. *Screen Smarts: A Family Guide to Media Literacy*. New York: Houghton Mifflin Co., 1996.

Doherty, William J., Ph.D. *The Intentional Family: How to Build Family Ties in Our Modern World*. Reading: Addison-Wesley Publishing Co., 1997.

————. *Take Back Your Kids: Confident Parenting in Turbulent Times.* Notre Dame: Sorin Books, 2000.

Elkind, David. *The Hurried Child: Growing Up Too Fast Too Soon.* Reading: Addison-Wesley Publishing Co., 1981.

Estess, Patricia Schiff. *Kids, Money and Values.* Cincinnati: Betterway Books, 1994.

Gallo, Jon and Eileen. *Silver Spoon Kids.* Chicago: Contemporary Books, 2002.

Giannetti, Charlene C. and Margaret Sagarese. *Cliques: 8 Steps to Help Your Child Survive the Social Jungle.* New York: Broadway Books, 2001.

Goldin, Barbara Diamond. *Just Enough Is Plenty: A Hanukkah Tale.* New York: Viking Kestrel, 1988.

Goleman, Daniel. *Emotional Intelligence.* New York: Bantam Books, 1997.

Gopnik, Alison, Andrew N. Meltzoff, and Patricia K. Kuhl. *The Scientist in the Crib: Minds, Brains, and How Children Learn.* New York: William Morrow and Company, Inc., 1999.

Gossen, Diane Chelsom. *Restitution: Restructuring School Discipline.* Chapel Hill: New View Publications, revised 1996.

Gottman, John, Ph.D. *Raising an Emotionally Intelligent Child.* New York: Fireside Books, 1997.

Gray, Deborah. *Attachment in Adoption.* Indianapolis: Perspectives Press, 2002.

Hammerseng, Kathryn M. *Telling Isn't Tattling.* Seattle: Parenting Press, 1995.

Heath, Harriet, Ph.D. *Using Your Values to Raise Your Child to Be an Adult You Admire.* Seattle: Parenting Press, 2000.

Jones, Elizabeth, and Gretchen Reynolds. *The Play's the Thing: Teachers' Roles in Children's Play.* New York: Teachers College Press, 1992.

Kanyer, Laurie, M.A. *25 Things To Do When Grandpa Passes Away, Mom and Dad Get Divorced, or the Dog Dies.* Seattle: Parenting Press, 2003.

Kiyosaki, Robert T. and Sharon L. Lechter. *Rich Dad, Poor Dad: What the Rich Teach Their Kids About Money That the Poor and Middle-Class Do Not.* Paradise Valley: TechPress, 1998.

McDonell, Nick. *Twelve.* New York: Grove Press, 2002.

O'Neill, Jessie H. *The Golden Ghetto, the Psychology of Affluence.* Center City: Hazelden, 1997.

Pert, Candace B., Ph.D. *Molecules of Emotion: The Science Behind Mind-Body Medicine.* New York: Simon & Schuster, 1997.

Pollock, David C. and Ruth E. Van Reken, *Third Culture Kids.* Nicholas Brealey Intercultural Press, Inc., 2001.

Simons, Laurie. *Taking "No" for an Answer.* Seattle: Parenting Press, 2000.

Sprinkle, Patricia H. *Children Who Do Too Little: Why Your Kids Need to Work Around the House (and how to get them to do it).* Zondervan Publishing House, 1996.

Ury, William. *The Third Side.* New York: Penguin Books, 2000.

Walsh, David, Ph.D. *Dr. Dave's Cyberhood.* New York: Fireside Books, 2001.

ACKNOWLEDGMENTS

MANY, many people have contributed to this book. We thank all of you who have been willing research subjects, offered your stories, encouraged us, and nudged and sometimes doggedly pushed us to complete this project. Many of you contributed anonymously. If you helped us in any way, please feel deeply appreciated, even if your name is not listed.

For very special support we thank: A. Myrth Ogilvie, Gloria Wallace, Ada Alden, Sandy Keiser, and especially Judi Klingsick for putting us in touch with our agent.

For encouragement, support, and general cheering-on in many ways we thank: Phyllis and Bob Porter, Trudi Newton, Rosemary Napper, Susannah Temple, Marty Rossman, Rose Allen, Susan Legender Clarke, Dennis Thoennes, Betty Cooke, Deane Gradous, Joyce McFarland, Sue Murray, Marsha Meyers and the Peninsula Girls, Mary Paananen and the 33rd Avenue Support Team, Jean Scott, the staff of the Attachment Center Northwest, Kate Calhoun, Pam McElmeel, the Sparkle Sisters, Pat Daunt, Ginty Furmage, Ev Goodall, Betsy Crary, Maggie Lawrence, Susan Hoch, Carl Schoenbeck, President Robert Holst, and Connie Strohschein.

We are indebted to the following people who read the manuscript and gave us valuable feedback: Dick Lundy, Kelly Donaldson, Joan Comeau, Beverly Cuevas, Suzanne Rogers, Wendy Bertony, Gill Samuel, Kris Jacobson, Melinda Creed, Kristin Croteau, Marilyn Sackariason, Susan Courtney, Nancy Gonzalez, Todd Nichols of the Family Attachment Center of Minnesota, Melissa Wendorf, Tish Poserina, Ulla Kuleoea, Marion Mowrooz, Kaye Centers, Susan Farmer, Sue Johnson, Diane Wagenhals, Claire Williams, Steve Morgan, Barbara Schoenbeck, Michael Walcheski, and Marylyn Reineck.

We are grateful to the following people for offering us the stories in this book. Only the names have been changed: Kay Lagerquist, Paula Pugh, Shirley Nyberg, Susan Makepeace, Kathleen Anderson, Fanita English, Drew Lenore Betz, Jane Legwald, Leanne M. Sponsel, Bruce Kidd, Kathy Morris, Sissy Hessler, Carol Carper, Mary Ann Walters, Valerie Redman, Robin Brooks, Maren Noyes, Rosie Cunningham, Karen Bradley, Beth McComb, Eileen Piersa, Kaara Ettesvold, and Carole Gesme.

Research assistants Kimberly Clary, Jessa Walters, Heather Dyslin, and Megan Morgart, gave invaluable help in collecting the research data and assisting with the overindulgence project.

Technical and computer support was supplied by Eric LaMott, Mark Schuler, Jason Moran, and Reagan Hicks.

From Connie Dawson

I appreciate my family's pushing me to change and acknowledging the changes I've made. My gratitude to Tom, Mary Claire, Charles and their mates and to grandchildren Anya, David, Elly, Sean, Tom, Emma, Tina, Lily Beth, and to Aneta Engelbrecht Goodridge.

From Jean Illsley Clarke

The members of my family have contributed more than they know. Great thanks to Dick, Marc, Jennifer, Wade, and Amy Clarke, Gary Rowland, and especially grandchildren Gressa, Freya, Disa, Adelaide, Katherine, and Alex.

From David Bredehoft

Thanks to all of my family for taking an interest in this project and giving me loving support along the journey: Elsie Bredehoft, Mark Bredehoft, Bev Watson, Jennifer Bredehoft, John Bredehoft, Linda Bredehoft, Michael and Joey Bredehoft, Barbara Tanner, Linda Bethane, Gene Shepherd, Opal Shepherd, Debbie Shepherd, Geoff Gregg, Tyler and Jake Gregg, and Rachel, Chuck and Anne Gregg. And most important, a very special thank you to my wife Adena Shepherd Bredehoft for her understanding and love.

Most especially we thank our agent Scott Edelstein for believing in our book and finding a home for it, to our editor Sue McCloskey for her vision and encouragement, and to Athalie Terry for the daily support that made this book happen.

INDEX

There will be two leader guides to use with this book:

Connie Dawson's guide, *Deciding How Much Is Enough: Recovering from Overindulgence*, is a six session psychoeducational model for use by facilitators of groups for adults who experienced overindulgence as children.

Jean Illsley Clarke's guide, *Parents Explore How Much Is Enough,* is a six session teaching model for parent educators who wish to help parents make full use of *How Much Is Enough?*

For more information, contact Connie Dawson and Jean Illsley Clarke, c/o Marlowe & Company, 245 W 17th Street, 11th Floor, New York, NY 10011-5300, (212)981-9919.